PEACE OPERATIONS AFTER 11 SEPTEMBER 2001

THE CASS SERIES ON PEACEKEEPING
ISSN 1367-9880
General Editor: Michael Pugh

This series examines all aspects of peacekeeping, from the political, operational and legal dimensions to the developmental and humanitarian issues that must be dealt with by all those involved with peacekeeping in the world today.

1. *The UN, Peace and Force*
    edited by Michael Pugh
2. *Mediating in Cyprus: The Cypriot Communities and the United Nations*
    by Oliver P. Richmond
3. *Peacekeeping and the UN Agencies*
    edited by Jim Whitman
4. *Peacekeeping and Public Information: Caught in the Crossfire*
    by Ingrid A. Lehmann
5. *Beyond the Emergency: Development within UN Missions*
    edited by Jeremy Ginifer
6. *The Evolution of US Peacekeeping Policy Under Clinton: A Fairweather Friend?*
    by Michael G. MacKinnon
7. *Peacebuilding and Police Reform*
    edited by Tor Tanke Holm and Espen Barth Eide
8. *Peacekeeping and Conflict Resolution*
    edited by Oliver Ramsbotham and Tom Woodhouse
9. *Managing Armed Conflicts in the 21st Century*
    edited by Adekeye Adebajo and Chandra Lekha Sriram
10. *Women and International Peacekeeping*
    edited by Louise Olsson and Torunn L. Tryggestad
11. *Recovering from Civil Conflict: Reconciliation, Peace and Development*
    edited by Edward Newman and Albrecht Schnabel
12. *Mitigating Conflict: The Role of NGOs*
    edited by Henry F. Carey and Oliver P. Richmond
13. *Ireland and International Peacekeeping Operations 1960–2000: A Study of Irish Motivation*
    by Katsumi Ishizuka
14. *Peace Operations After 11 September 2001*
    edited by Thierry Tardy

This book is edited by Thierry Tardy,
with the logistical and intellectual support of
The Geneva Centre for Security Policy

CENTRE DE POLITIQUE DE SECURITE - GENEVE
GENEVA CENTRE FOR SECURITY POLICY

PEACE OPERATIONS AFTER 11 SEPTEMBER 2001

Editor Thierry Tardy

Routledge
Taylor & Francis Group

LONDON AND NEW YORK

First Published in 2004 in Great Britain by
Routledge
2 Park Square, Milton Park,
Abingdon, Oxon, OX14 4RN
605 Third Avenue, New York, NY 10017

*Routledge is an imprint of the Taylor & Francis Group, an
informa business*

British Library Cataloguing in Publication Data

Peace operations after 11 September 2001. – (The Cass
  series on peacekeeping; 14)
  1. Peace-building 2. Peacekeeping forces 3. Intervention
  (International law) 4. War on Terrorism, 2001–   5. September
  11 Terrorist Attacks, 2001 – influence
  I. Tardy, Thierry
  327.1'7

Library of Congress Cataloging-in-Publication Data

Peace operations after 11 September 2001/edited by Thierry Tardy.
  p. cm. – (The Cass series on peacekeeping, ISSN 1367-9880; 14)
  Includes bibliographical references and index.
  ISBN 0-7146-5647-X (cloth)
  1. Peacekeeping forces. 2. Peace-building. 3. Terrorism. I. Title: Peace operations after
eleven September 2001. II. Tardy, Thierry. III. Series.

JZ6374.P36 2003
341.5'84–dc22

                                                                                2003055856

Typeset in 11/13pt Ehrhardt by Vitaset, Paddock Wood, Kent

ISBN13: 978-0-7146-5647-2 (hbk)
ISBN13: 978-0-415-40864-6 (pbk)

Contents

Contributors   vii
Foreword by Fred Tanner   xi
Acknowledgements   xiii
Abbreviations   xv

Introduction   Thierry Tardy   1

The Response of State Actors

1. UN Peace Operations in Light of the Events
    of 11 September 2001   Thierry Tardy   13

2. US Policy Toward Peace Operations   Eric P. Schwartz   39

3. NATO's Shifting Priorities: From Peace
    Support Operations to Counter-Terrorism   Dick A. Leurdijk   58

4. The European Union, Peace Operations
    and Terrorism   Jolyon Howorth   80

Inside Peace Operations

5. Peace Operations and Governance:
    Lessons Learned and Perspectives   Winrich Kühne   101

6. UNMIBH: Combating Organized Crime
    and Terrorism Through Law Enforcement
    Capacity Building   Jacques Paul Klein   125

7. NGOs and Peace Operations in the
    post-11 September Context   Nicholas Stockton   139

8. Opposing Insurgents, During and Beyond
   Peace Operations   John Mackinlay 159

9. Conclusion: Change, Continuity and   Donald C. F. Daniel 179
   Conceptions of World Order   and Michael Pugh

   Select Bibliography   190
   Abstracts   197
   Index   201

Contributors

Donald C. F. Daniel is a professor in the Strategic Studies Program in the Edmund E. Walsh School of Foreign Service of Georgetown University. He has previously been a Special Advisor to the Chairman of the US Government's National Intelligence Council and held the Milton E. Miles Chair of International Relations at the US Naval War College. He has also been a research associate at the International Institute for Strategic Studies and a research analyst in UNIDIR's Disarmament and Conflict Resolution Project.

Jolyon Howorth is Jean Monnet professor of European Politics and professor of French Civilization at the University of Bath (UK). Recent publications include 'European Integration and Defence: the Ultimate Challenge?' (*Chaillot Paper*, Paris: WEU-Institute for Security Studies, 2000); *Defending Europe: The EU, NATO and the Quest for European Autonomy* (co-edited, Palgrave, 2003); and *NATO and European Security* (edited, Palgrave, 2003). In 2002–04, he was a Visiting Professor of Political Science at Yale University.

Jacques Paul Klein was the Special Representative of the Secretary-General and Co-ordinator of the United Nations Operations in Bosnia and Herzegovina. Prior to this post, he was the Principal Deputy High Representative, Office of the High Representative in Bosnia and Herzegovina; and the UN Transitional Administrator for Eastern Slavonia, Baranja and Western Sirmium (UNTAES). He is a distinguished career member of the Senior Foreign Service of the US Department of State and a decorated retired Major General of the US Air Force.

Winrich Kühne is Director of the recently founded Zentrum für Internationale Friedenseinsätze (ZIF) (Centre for International Peace Operations) in Berlin. Prior to this post he was Deputy Director of the Stiftung

Wissenschaft und Politik (SWP), an independent research body and political consultant to the German parliament and administration. He is also visiting professor at the Johns Hopkins University, SAIS Bologna Centre (Italy), and member of the informal 'International Advisory Group' to the UN's Lessons-Learned Unit (Department for Peacekeeping Operations).

Dick A. Leurdijk is a UN expert and senior research fellow, lecturer, policy advisor and political commentator at the Netherlands Institute of International Relations 'Clingendael' in The Hague. He has published on a wide-range of UN-related issues, including peace support operations, the relationship between the UN and NATO in former Yugoslavia and Kosovo, and the 'war on terrorism'.

John Mackinlay left the British Army in 1991 to become a research academic at Brown University, Rhode Island, followed by teaching appointments at the Marshall Center in Garmisch, the UK Joint Services Staff College and King's College London, where he currently researches and teaches in War Studies.

Michael Pugh is Reader in International Relations and Director of the International Studies Centre, University of Plymouth, UK. He is the editor of *International Peacekeeping*, and has published widely on peacekeeping, peacebuilding and humanitarianism. His most recent works are: *The UN and Regional Security: Europe and Beyond*, co-edited with Waheguru Pal Singh Sidhu (Rienner, 2003); and *War Economies in their Regional Context: The Challenges for Transformation*, with Neil Cooper and Jonathan Goodhand (Rienner, 2003).

Eric P. Schwartz was a senior fellow at the United States Institute of Peace in Washington at the time of his authorship, as well as a Visiting Lecturer of Public and International Affairs at Princeton University. Between 1993 and 2001, he served at the US National Security Council (NSC). He finished his tenure at the NSC as Special Assistant to the President and Senior Director for Multilateral and Humanitarian Affairs, where his responsibilities included US policy toward United Nations peacekeeping. He has also worked for the Foreign Affairs Committee of the US Congress and for the human rights organization Asia Watch (now Human Rights Watch/Asia).

Nicholas Stockton is currently an independent international aid consultant. He has spent over 25 years working for development and humanitarian organizations, 17 of which were resident in Africa. He spent several years as

Oxfam GB's Emergencies Director before becoming Deputy International Director, a post he left in 2002. He now resides in Corsica.

Fred Tanner is the Deputy Director and Head of Academic Affairs of the Geneva Centre for Security Policy. He is also the Honorary Chairman of the Inter-University Steering Committee on Security Studies of Bosnia and Herzegovina and the Co-Chair of the 'PfP Consortium Working Group on Curricula Development'. His current research deals with conflict resolution, peacekeeping and Mediterranean security. He is the author of numerous publications and articles, including *From Versailles to Baghdad* (United Nations, 1993), *The EU as a Security Actor in the Mediterranean* (Zürich: ETH, 2001), *Refugee Manipulation* (co-editor, Brookings, 2003).

Thierry Tardy is a Faculty Member at the Geneva Centre for Security Policy. He is Doctor of Political Science (International Relations) and holds an M.A. in International Studies from the University of Birmingham (UK). He was formerly a researcher at the Foundation for Strategic Research (Paris) and Lecturer at the *Institut d'Etudes politiques* (Paris) and at the War College. He published *La France et la gestion des conflits yougoslaves (1991– 1995). Enjeux et leçons d'une opération de maintien de la paix de l'ONU* (Brussels: Bruylant, 1999).

Foreword

This publication reflects the ongoing efforts of the Geneva Centre for Security Policy (GCSP) to encourage – in addition to its international training and networking activities – research and publication projects that are conducted by its faculty members in collaboration with partner institutions and international experts. The book aims at examining how much the terrorist attacks on 11 September 2001 and the aftermath shaped policy agendas of states, international and regional organizations, and NGOs in their commitment to peace operations. The principle setting for the examination of this topic was an international workshop at the GCSP bringing together scholars and practitioners working on issue-areas related to peace operations and international action in complex emergencies and state-building. The findings of this collective endeavour were presented to the 5th International Security Forum in Zürich in the autumn of 2002.

This book appears at a timely moment when peace operations are undergoing an accelerated and fundamental transformation. The 11 September, and its aftermath in the war against the Taliban and the increasingly complex task of state-building in post-war Iraq, epitomizes the challenges to today's peace operations. The unexpected appearance of international terrorism as an intervening variable to peace operations compelled the authors to take a fresh look at peacekeeping in a very broad perspective that includes intervention, state-building and governance promotion.

The relationship between terrorism and peace operations is delicate and possibly overrated. However, its examination brings to the fore the rapidly emerging challenge to the classic principles of the peacekeeping doctrine: that the anti-terrorist dimensions of peace operations are partial, interventionist, and sometimes lack legitimacy.

The terrorist conundrum brings out an underlying malaise of multinational peace operations: the differing and sometimes incompatible policy agendas of contributing states. Terrorism is a political issue and will thus require politically sensitive policies that may not be commensurate with the anti-terrorist templates of some troop contributors or donor states. This dilemma is reinforced by the dominant role of the United States in the global fight against terrorism, and its simultaneous reluctance to engage in peace operations.

This publication shows that the surge of terrorism is as much an obstacle to reconstruction and nation-building as corruption, spoilers and the impunity of war criminals. It jeopardizes the difficult work of transitional administrations and fuels tensions in civil-military relations. It represents a great challenge to policy planners to tackle such diverse problems with a coherent political-military strategy.

On behalf of the entire faculty of the Geneva Centre for Security Policy, we would like to extend our thanks and appreciation to our colleague Thierry Tardy who acted as editor and author for this publication. He assured that the authors lived up to the high standards expected from such a publication. We hope that this book will make an important contribution to the topic of peace operations in a post-11 September environment both to the policy making and academic communities.

Fred Tanner
Geneva Centre for Security Policy

Acknowledgements

This volume is the result of a collective effort of the Geneva Centre for Security Policy (GCSP), its Faculty, and its Support Staff. The starting point was a GCSP-organized seminar, held in Geneva in April 2002 on the theme 'Peace Operations in Light of the Events of 11 September 2001'. The GCSP and myself would like to thank Nicole Pinter-Krainer for the organization of this meeting.

The editing process of the book greatly benefited from the rigorous work of Joanna Schemm and Emily Munro, who efficiently palliated my hesitant English. I am grateful to them for their indispensable cooperation. I would also like to thank Rolf Schwarz for his assistance in research, and Alexandra Novosseloff for her comments on my chapter.

This book would not have come about without the logistical assistance and intellectual input from the GCSP, and in particular I acknowledge the help and support of Pal Dunay, Jan Hyllander, Neil MacFarlane, Mike Pope and Fred Tanner. I am also grateful to Michael Pugh who has been instrumental in the realization of this project. Finally, I express my gratitude to all the contributors to this book for their participation in this collective effort.

Thierry Tardy
Geneva Centre for Security Policy
January 2003

Abbreviations

CENCOM	Central Command (US)
CFSP	Common Foreign and Security Policy
CIVPOL	International Civilian Police
CJCMTF	Coalition Joint Civil–Military Task Force
CSCE	Conference on Security and Cooperation in Europe
CTC	Counter-Terrorism Committee (UN)
DCI	Defence Capabilities Initiative (NATO)
DDR	disarmament, demobilization and reintegration
DFID	Department for International Development (UK)
DPA	Department of Political Affairs (UN)
DPKO	Department of Peacekeeping Operations (UN)
DRC	Democratic Republic of Congo
ECAP	European Capability Action Plan
ECOMOG	Economic Community of the Western African States Military Observer Group
ECPS	Executive Committee on Peace and Security (UN)
ESDP	European Security and Defence Policy
EU	European Union
EUPM	European Union Police Mission (Bosnia and Herzegovina)
FRY	Federal Republic of Yugoslavia
FYROM	former Yugoslav Republic of Macedonia
GAC	General Affairs Council (EU)
GFAP	General Framework Agreement for Peace
GCSP	Geneva Centre for Security Policy
ICC	International Criminal Court
ICRC	International Committee of the Red Cross
IFOR	Implementation Force in Bosnia and Herzegovina
IFRC	International Federation of Red Cross and Red Crescent Societies
IMTF	Integrated Mission Task Force

INTERFET	International Force in East Timor
IPTF	International Police Task Force (UN)
ISAF	International Security Assistance Force (Afghanistan)
JHA	Justice and Home Affairs (EU)
KFOR	Kosovo Force (NATO)
MISAB	Inter-African Monitoring Force
MNF	Multinational Force
MONUC	UN Mission in Congo (Democratic Republic)
MSF	*Médecins sans Frontières*
NAC	North Atlantic Council
NATO	North Atlantic Treaty Organization
NGO	non-governmental organization
NRC	NATO–Russia Council
OECD	Organization for Economic Cooperation and Development
OHR	Office of the High Representative (Bosnia and Herzegovina)
OSCE	Organization for Security and Cooperation in Europe
PSC	Political and Security Committee (EU)
RRF	Rapid Reaction Force (EU)
RUF	Revolutionary United Front
SFOR	Stabilization Force in Bosnia and Herzegovina (NATO)
SRSG	Special Representative of the Secretary-General (UN)
STOP	Special Trafficking Operations Programme
UNAMA	UN Assistance Mission in Afghanistan
UNAMIL	UN Assistance Mission in Liberia
UNAMIR	UN Assistance Mission in Rwanda
UNAMSIL	UN Assistance Mission in Sierra Leone
UNAVEM	UN Assistance Mission in Angola
UNDP	UN Development Programme
UNEF	UN Emergency Force
UNFICYP	UN Force in Cyprus
UNHCR	UN High Commissioner for Refugees
UNICEF	UN Children's Fund
UNITA	National Union for Total Independence of Angola
UNITAF	Unified Task Force (Somalia)
UNMEE	UN Mission in Ethiopia and Eritrea
UNMIBH	UN Mission in Bosnia and Herzegovina
UNMIH	UN Mission in Haiti
UNMIK	UN Mission in Kosovo
UNMISET	UN Mission of Support in East Timor
UNOMIL	UN Observer Mission in Liberia

UNOMOZ	UN Operation in Mozambique
UNOMSIL	UN Observer Mission in Sierra Leone
UNOSAL	UN Operation in El Salvador
UNOSOM	UN Operation in Somalia
UNPROFOR	UN Protection Force
UNTAC	UN Transitional Authority in Cambodia
UNTAES	UN Transitional Administration in Eastern Slavonia
UNTAET	UN Transitional Administration in East Timor
UNTAG	UN Transitional Assistance Group
UNTSO	UN Truce Supervision Organization
WEU	Western European Union
WMD	weapons of mass destruction

Introduction

Thierry Tardy

Since the first blue helmet peacekeeping operation, created in 1956 to help defuse the Israel–Egypt conflict in the context of the Suez crisis, peace operations have always reflected the state and the evolution of the international system. Such was the case when the paralysis of the United Nations (UN) during the cold war led to the ad hoc mechanism of consent-based and non-intrusive peacekeeping that is now called 'traditional'. This was also the case in the 1990s, when the fundamental changes within the international system had direct consequences for the nature of 'peacekeeping'. The end of the east–west confrontation, the quasi-disappearance of inter-state conflicts, the erosion of state sovereignty and the corresponding evolution of the practice of intervention, and of course the revival of liberal thinking in general and of the UN in particular, were all reflected in the quantitative as well as the qualitative evolution of peace operations.

Peace operations nowadays occupy a crucial place within the evolving international security system, as major tools of crisis management, and as one of the main activities of the operational dimension of institutions such as the UN, NATO, the Organization for Security and Cooperation in Europe (OSCE), and to a lesser extent the European Union (EU). Peace operations have shaped in numerous ways defence and security policies of many western states, and many non-state actors are involved in them and contribute to their evolution. Peace operations are as criticized and debated as they are indispensable but imperfect responses to conflicts.

Peace operations are appoached in this book as a broad concept, covering military and civilian activities led by state- and non-state-actors in a host state (or two), and aimed at dealing with a crisis or with the consequences of a crisis, at different possible stages (before, during and after a crisis). Most importantly, peace operations are short of war, the principle of impartiality being theoretically indissociable from peace operations. The central and primary objective of any peace operation is the promotion of peace, not the defeat of one of the parties involved.

Those operations are however not easy to grasp. Peace operations have always been extremely difficult to define, and this is even more the case with the 'new' peace operations of the post-cold war era. Strictly speaking, 'peace-keeping' refers to 'traditional peacekeeping', the deployment of neutral military forces between two armed factions to supervise a ceasefire in a non-coercive and consent-based way. Traditional peacekeeping has not disappeared with the end of the cold war.[1] But the word 'peacekeeping' has also been (and is still) used as a generic term.[2] Yet peacekeeping operations, generally referring to military dimensions, have been generally subsumed by peace operations.

More broadly, peace operations are supposed to embrace the whole gamut of the new activities performed by states, international organizations and other actors when dealing collectively with a conflict. Peace operations is a UN term; the Brahimi Report on Peace Operations talks about 'UN peace operations [that] entail three principal activities: conflict prevention and peacemaking; peacekeeping; and peace-building'.[3] NATO uses the term 'Peace Support Operations' or 'Crisis Response Operations', while the European Union prefers the broader expression 'Conflict Prevention and Crisis Management'. States have developed different and sometimes diverging views on peace operations, both theoretically and practically. The Nordic approach to peace operations is not necessarily the same as the US approach, which may differ from the Nigerian or the Russian approach. Even within the European Union, the debates over the 'Petersberg Tasks'[4] have shown how difficult it is to have common views about what peace operations are.

Peace operations are also difficult to grasp because they entail many different activities that are fundamentally different in nature, and that involve different actors, all having their own approach to the concept, their own agenda, and their own motives. One of the major characteristics of modern peace operations is their multidimensional, multifaceted, multi-functional nature; it is also one of the major sources of confusion. If peace operations encompass the deployment of a military force to supervise a ceasefire line but also the establishment of a judiciary system in a post-conflict environment; if they can be legally consent-based or coercive, or both (within the same operation); if they can take place before, during or after a conflict with, in each case, different military and civilian implications; if they simultaneously refer to the activities of the UN in East Timor and of the Commonwealth of Independent States (CIS) in Georgia; if they can be peace-enforcement or humanitarian assistance; if all these activities belong to peace operations, then needless to say that this generic term is much too large to be precisely defined and therefore conceptually coherent. Legal and political typologies do exist, as the distinction between first, second, third, and even fourth generation peace operations, but they very much reflect the heterogeneity of the concept.[5]

By the same token, in its military dimension, the concept of peace operations is blurred partly because of the difficulty of locating these operations on the 'intervention spectrum' at the state level. First, though peace operations are often referred to as *interventions*, some of them, to the extent that they are half hearted measures, may express a will *not* to intervene in a particular conflict. Second, states face a paradox in that while peace operations have become for many of them a major activity of the armed forces, one can also observe a general reluctance of (western) states to see peace operations as a full category of military operations, and to draw the consequences of such a choice. This consideration leads us back to our preliminary remark about peace operations being the mirror of evolutions of the international system. The shift from a system where security was mostly a military related issue that was dealt with at the state level to a system where a 'multifaceted conception of security' has entailed (or should entail) a 'multifaceted approach to security',[6] has had direct repercussions on the broad field of peace operations. The military is not anymore the only actor in peace operations, nor is the state. Peace operations reflect the nature of the evolution of security needs and of the ways to tackle security issues.

The idea behind this book comes from the nature of peace operations being directly influenced by the state of the international system on the one hand, and the events of 11 September 2001 on the other, analysing the way the latter may impact on the environment of the former. The book explores the possible consequences of the events of 11 September 2001, and of the 'fight against terrorism', on the way peace operations are perceived and conducted, and on the way that states, international organizations, and non-state actors will consider these operations.

The attacks on the United States on 11 September 2001 may be seen as a defining moment in world politics. There is little doubt that these events will not influence international relations to the same extent that the end of the cold war did, but they will unquestionably (and symbolically) remain a key event in the evolution of the international system. Yet the attacks of 11 September 2001 are more a demonstration of evolutions that had been going on for years than an unexpected event that would mark the beginning of a new era. These events are a symbolic, tragic and extremely violent expression of phenomena that had characterized the international system for years, although not with such extreme brutality. As written soon after the attacks, this act of terror was 'an event with which [the] world had long been pregnant, and there had been many urgent and well-informed warnings of its imminent delivery'.[7]

The events of 11 September nonetheless constitute a defining moment in world politics in the sense that they have had and will have major consequences on the reality of international security. They mark a clear intrusion of a highly dangerous non-state actor on the inter-state arena, forcing states to dramatically reconsider their understanding of their own security, as well as the means of achieving it. They also constitute a new and decisive blow to the already shattered distinction between internal and external security, and between military and civilian security. The mere fact that the United States, the sole superpower, was the target of the attacks, is liable to imply some significant changes in international politics, because of the meaning of the attacks, and because of the multifaceted response that has followed.

As far as the response to the events of 11 September is concerned, several aspects have to be taken into account. Straight after the attacks, states and international organizations have considered different policy options aimed at fighting existing terrorist groups through a series of legal, political, and military means, in Afghanistan, and in other places. Those measures have included short-term and long-term actions, of an operational and normative nature, but the great majority of them have been about the 'suppression' of terrorist acts, rather than about their prevention. In parallel, some longer-term options were examined, aimed at addressing the causes of terrorism, though with some reluctance for fear of being seen as bringing some justification to the scourge of terrorism.

At the inter-state level, all security institutions have been involved in the process with differing capabilities and levels of conviction. For different reasons, the UN, NATO, the OSCE and the European Union have initially perceived the events of 11 September as a direct challenge to their very existence, and embarked upon policies supposedly aimed at suppressing the threat of terrorism and/or at addressing its causes: the UN with its normative role, its action in Afghanistan, the creation of the Counter-Terrorism Committee (CTC) and the financial dimension of the fight against terrorism;[8] NATO with its clear evolution to embrace anti-terrorism activities,[9] after its absence in the immediate response to the 11 September attacks, in spite of the invocation of the article 5 of the Washington Treaty; the OSCE with the 'Bucharest Plan of Action for Combating Terrorism',[10] and later the 'OSCE Charter on Preventing and Combating Terrorism';[11] and the EU with its 'Plan of Action'[12] and related efforts, mainly falling within the third pillar ('Justice and Home Affairs') of the EU structure.

Beyond the necessity to respond to a threat to their member states, these institutions were driven by the need to assert their relevance in the changing environment, and possibly to display some comparative advantages, at different levels of the fight against terrorism. The liberal approach put the stress on the need for states to cooperate, through international institutions among other channels, as there was no way the transnational threat of terrorism could be addressed nationally, or by a restricted number of countries. Such a necessity was particularly underlined by the UN and its Secretary-General, but also through Security Council resolutions. The urgent necessity to approach the international system, more than ever, as a multi-centric system, where non-state actors have an increasing role, often to the detriment of states, was also emphasized.

Simultaneously, the relevance of international organizations in general, and security institutions in particular, to the overall fight against terrorism, appeared to be put into question, especially insofar as the 'suppression' of terrorism is concerned. The EU is a particular case in this respect, mainly due to the imbrication of its third pillar activities with national policies. But the fact is that the events of 11 September and the fight against terrorism are characterized by the domination of realist perspectives, to the detriment of the role of international organizations. The 'war on terrorism' is arguably shaped by the notion of self-help, the domination of the United States and its unilateral approaches to the use of force, the necessity for the United States to 'demonstrate its power',[13] and the short-term analysis of national interests and state survival. As Paul Wilkinson wrote in 2000, although 'the realist paradigm is all too clearly inherently incapable of contending with new transnational threats to human rights and security posed by international terrorism', and if, 'ideally all countries should cooperate fully to ensure that those involved in terrorist crimes are brought to justice, ... in practice, the anarchic nature of the international system and the fact that there are states that use, sponsor, support and sympathize with specific terrorist groups are basic reasons why terrorism is likely to remain the most ubiquitous form of political violence well into the future'.[14]

Conceptually as well as practically, one major obstacle to a significant role for international organizations in the fight against terrorism is that this fight takes place in an environment largely dominated by states. The role of security institutions has been rhetorically praised, but in practice, the response has to be primarily state-led, at least on the short run. Similarly, security institutions have not been able to shape states behaviour, or even to convincingly orient the debate on terrorism. They have not played a significant role in 'fixing the meanings', that is, 'establish[ing] the parameters, the very boundaries, of acceptable action'.[15] Finally, any analysis on the consequences of the events of 11 September and the response to be given should take into consideration the extreme difficulties of defining terrorism, and therefore the notion of the fight against it. This has a particular importance when looking at the causes of terrorism, which is intimately linked to the understanding of the phenomenon.

It is against this highly sensitive context that the question of the link between the events of 11 September and peace operations must be posed. Such a link is not obvious, and in any case it is a matter of controversy. As a terrorist act, or an act of aggression against a state, the events of 11 September have little to do with the concept of peace operations. As a demonstration of the evolution of the international system, with the growing role – in this case destructive – of non-state actors, the 11 September attacks illustrate, as peace operations do in a different context, the widening of the security agenda, as well as the persistence of instability and the need to deal with it one way or the other, but through a wide range of means, military and non-military, in a preventive as well as in a curative way. As an attack on the United States, the events of 11 September will have a major impact on the definition of US foreign and defence policies.[16] If the 'war against terrorism' becomes the 'organizing principle of US foreign policy',[17] US perceptions of the virtues of international institutions, the US policy vis-à-vis multi-lateral efforts to manage crises that do not constitute direct threats to the US national interest, and therefore US views of peace operations, are likely to be significantly affected. The American domination of the overall response to the events of 11 September may also have consequences on policies and capacities of other actors, international organizations, but also non-governmental organizations (NGOs), that are dependent upon public aid, and that will face 'powerful forces of incorporation and instrumentalisation'. Similarly, as the expression of a threat to states that may become targets of other attacks, the 11 September events have had consequences on the definition of security policies, on the hierarchy of priorities, and on the resources to be allocated to different activities, among which are peace operations. Such consequences should also be observed at the level of security institutions – the main actors of peace operations – which will have to adapt to the new environment.

These different elements mean that the 'international' environment of peace operations, that is, the roles and capacities of the actors involved in them (states, international organizations, NGOs) are likely to be modified, while the 'local' environment of peace operations, i.e. the need to manage crises through external interventions, has remained largely unchanged. Consequently, peace operations might be affected by the events of 11 September 2001 as they are generally affected by major international events.

Furthermore, a link between the 11 September events and peace operations may be made as peace operations are sometimes deployed in environments where terrorism has been prevalent or is likely to emerge. Two issues are to be considered here. First, some components within peace operations can be tasked to fight groups that are directly involved in terrorist activities or connected with terrorist groups. This has been the case for peace operations in Bosnia and Herzegovina, Kosovo, and Afghanistan. This first element refers to the 'suppression' of terrorism. Second, peace operations operate in environments that may be seen as intrinsically fertile grounds for the emergence of terrorist groups. Such is the case with 'failed states', where peace operations are often deployed, and mandated to tackle certain forms of instability that may lead to the emergence of violent movements. In a longer-term approach, peace operations could therefore be involved, voluntarily or by coincidence, in activities also aimed at addressing the ill-defined 'root causes of terrorism'. Peace operations could then be seen as possible 'contributors' to the overall fight against terrorism, both in short-term and in long-term policies, though probably in a limited way.

These links and their implications are to be taken into account by international institutions, such as the UN, NATO or the EU. The fields of prevention and peacebuilding, the latter including the rule of law and governance issues, are particularly concerned. At the UN, the link between peace operations and the issue of terrorism is implicitly made,[18] although not formally. Yet, such a recognition has not yet been reflected in policy. NATO is in a different situation, as its post-11 September evolution tends to emphasize the need to suppress terrorism rather than to tackle its roots in a longer-term approach. But its involvement in peace operations in the Balkans, where organized crime may be connected with terrorist groups, puts NATO in a new situation that directly links peace operations with the issue of terrorism. As far as the EU is concerned, the events of 11 September forced the organization to re-assess its security and defence policy (ESDP), it is not clear however to what extent the EU will take heed of the terrorism issue in defining its nascent policy in the field of peace operations.

At the level of states, the perceptions about peace operations may theoretically change if peace operations appear to be seen as instruments to address the root causes of terrorism, and not 'only' the root causes, or the consequences, of conflicts. Participation in peace operations would then become, in some cases, a 'strategic necessity',[19] which is rarely the case at the present time; a role for peace operations in partly addressing the issue of terrorism may create new incentives to contribute. The idea here is less to see whether peace operations could be created to fight terrorism than to see to what extent, once they are deployed, they could address, in one way or another, the issue of terrorism. But to push the reasoning further, it is not possible to exclude situations where the deployment of international forces in a particular state – in a peace operation – is made even more necessary by the fact that the state in question is directly concerned by the issue of terrorism (as a host state). Unless the 'terrorism issue' is, on the contrary, a disincentive to get involved for states reluctant to have to deal with so sensitive an issue.

An evolution of the mandate of peace operations to include tasks related to the fight against terrorism is not to be excluded. But then the question of the risks that such an evolution would entail will have to be raised, especially insofar as the compatibility of this evolution with the nature of peace operations is concerned (and particularly their impartial characteristic).

This book is a collection of essays that combines academic thinking and practitioners' views. It comprises two parts. The first part deals with the response of state actors to the events of 11 September, analyzing the direct and indirect impact of those events on the broad spectrum of peace operations. The roles of international organizations, such as the UN (Thierry Tardy), NATO (Dick Leurdijk) and the EU (Jolyon Howorth) are addressed, as well as the particular case of the US policy (Eric Schwartz). In the second part, authors look at peace operations through particular angles. The evolution of peace operations prior to 11 September and the main lessons learned are analyzed (Winrich Kühne). The case of the UN role in Bosnia and Herzegovina is then tackled (Jacques Klein), as well as the impact of the 11 September events on the role of NGOs, in peace operations and beyond (Nicholas Stockton). A prospective approach to the evolution of peace operations taken in a very broad sense is finally proposed (John Mackinlay). Concluding remarks are offered by Don Daniel and Michael Pugh, in a co-written chapter.

NOTES

1. The UN Protection Force (UNPROFOR) that was deployed in Croatia between 1992 and 1995, or more recently the UN Mission in Ethiopia and Eritrea (UNMEE), are very similar to 'traditional peacekeeping'.
2. At the UN for example, with the Department of Peace-Keeping Operations or the Special Committee on Peace-Keeping Operations, or in the literature (as in the journal *International Peacekeeping*).
3. 'Report of the Panel on United Nations Peace Operations', A/55/305, S/2000/809, 21 Aug. 2000, para. 10.
4. The 'Petersberg Tasks' designate the crisis management operations that the EU is supposed to run.
5. See Ramesh Thakur and Albrecht Schnabel, 'Cascading Generations of Peacekeeping:

Across the Mogadishu Line to Kosovo and Timor', in Thakur and Schnabel (eds), *UN Peacekeeping Operations. Ad Hoc Missions, Permanent Engagement*, Tokyo: United Nations University Press, 2001. Also see Winrich Kühne's chapter in this book.

6. Kenneth Bush and Fuat Keyman, 'Identity-Based Conflict: Rethinking Security in a Post-cold war World', *Global Governance*, Vol. 3, No. 3, 1997, p. 312.

7. Owen Harries, 'An End to Nonsense', *The National Interest*, No. 65-S, 2001, p. 117.

8. On the role of the UN in fighting terrorism, see Thomas Weiss and Jane Boulden (eds), *The UN and Terrorism: Before and After September 11th*, Bloomington, IN: Indiana University Press, 2004.

9. See in particular 'Prague Summit Declaration', North Atlantic Council, Nov. 2002.

10. 'Bucharest Plan of Action for Combating Terrorism', OSCE Ministerial Council, Bucharest, Dec. 2001.

11. 'OSCE Charter on Preventing and Combating Terrorism', Porto Ministerial Council, 7 Dec. 2002.

12. 'Plan of Action of the Extraordinary European Council Meeting', 21 Sept. 2001.

13. See Charles Krauthammer, transcript of the symposium 'After September 11: A Conversation', *The National Interest*, No. 65-S, 2001, pp. 68–9.

14. Paul Wilkinson, 'International Cooperation against Terrorism', in Wilkinson (ed.), *Terrorism Versus Democracy. The Liberal State Response*, London: Frank Cass, 2000, pp. 200–1.

15. Michael Barnett and Martha Finnemore, 'The Politics, Power, and Pathologies of International Organizations', *International Organization*, Vol. 53, No. 4, Autumn 1999, p. 711.

16. For a neo-conservative approach, see Krauthammer, 'After September 11: A Conversation', sections on 'Foreign Policy' and 'Defense Policy'; 'One Year On: Power, Purpose and Strategy in American Foreign Policy', *The National Interest*, No. 69, Autumn 2002; Robert Kagan, 'Strategic Dissonance', in 'One Year After: A Grand Strategy for the West', *Survival*, Vol. 44, No. 4, Winter 2002–03.

17. Krauthammer, 'After September 11', p. 67.

18. See Jean-Marie Guéhenno, 'Opérations de maintien de la paix: la nouvelle donne', *Le Monde*, 18 Dec. 2002; 'Report of the Policy Working Group on the UN and Terrorism (Annex)', United Nations, S/2002/875, 6 Aug. 2002.

19. See *A Force for Peace and Security. US and Allied Commanders' Views of the Military's Role in Peace Operations and the Impact on Terrorism of States in Conflict*, Washington DC: Peace Through Law Education Fund, 2002.

Part I:
The Response of State Actors

UN Peace Operations in Light of the Events of 11 September 2001

Thierry Tardy

The fundamental evolutions that UN peace operations faced during the 1990s were to a large extent a consequence of the end of the cold war. This defining moment in the life of the international system led to a revitalized United Nations, which was directly reflected in the field of peacekeeping. Peacekeeping operations became more and more numerous, and above all embraced new and quite challenging activities. The era of 'traditional peacekeeping' seemed to come to an end, to be replaced by the ill-defined 'multidimensional peacekeeping', which in reality was much broader than mere peacekeeping.

More generally, throughout the 1990s peace operations were reflections of some of the evolutions of the international system itself. The difficulty in identifying security interests, and therefore security policies, the growing contest of state primacy (with eroding state sovereignty and the increasing weight of non-state actors), the evolving role of international institutions (true actors of the system or simply tools used by the states), and the barely contested American domination were all factors that have had a direct impact on the way UN peace operations were defined and conducted.

This said, insofar as they constitute another defining moment of international life,[1] the events of 11 September may as well have had some impact on peace operations, at a time when the whole field of peace operations is being reconsidered. This chapter aims to present and analyze the possible consequences of the events of 11 September on the way UN peace operations are created and conducted, and on the way that states see the role of the UN in this field. Briefly presented, the argument is that the events of 11 September have had no fundamental and observable consequences on the UN's role in maintaining peace and security in general, and on peace operations in particular. The fight against terrorism might imply some modifications in the mandates and practices of peace operations; the two fields of conflict prevention and peacebuilding could be affected in particular, but the overall approach should not be dramatically altered.

To address this issue, the chapter will look first at the role of the UN before the events of 11 September. It will then examine what the UN response to the attacks has been. Finally, it will assess the extent to which those events have modified or can influence peace operations policies on the longer term.

THE UN ROLE BEFORE 11 SEPTEMBER 2001

A 'marginalized' UN role in peace operations

The 1990s have undoubtedly been the richest period in the life of UN peace operations. These have been thoroughly studied and extensively criticized.[2] To summarize, one can distinguish two main periods of activity in UN peace operations, with the Dayton Peace Agreement in Bosnia and Herzegovina in November 1995 constituting a symbolic turning point.

In the early 1990s, the revitalized UN was the uncontested central actor in peace operations at the legal, political and operational levels. No other organization was in a position to compete with the UN, and states had not really begun to consider the possibility of conducting peacekeeping outside of the UN framework. From Cambodia to Somalia, El Salvador to Bosnia and Herzegovina, UN peace operations were ambitious, multifunctional and above all considered as appropriate responses to the so-called new conflicts. This period of euphoria, marked at the theoretical level by the release of *An Agenda for Peace* in June 1992,[3] did not last very long. By 1993, the many difficulties encountered by the operations in Somalia and Bosnia led to a reappraisal of UN capability. The credibility of the UN started to erode, and the organization progressively lost its centrality.

In the United States as well as in Europe, governments grew sceptical about the UN's ability to manage crises, while 'regional organizations', if one includes NATO, and to a certain extent the Western European Union (WEU), the Organization for Security and Cooperation in Europe (OSCE) and later the European Union, acquired some competence, and therefore comparative advantages, at the expense of the UN. In parallel, states got involved in peacekeeping activities in coalitions, outside of the UN framework at the operational level, but in missions legally sanctioned by the Security Council. The UN was discredited and held responsible for the failures of state policies in Somalia and Bosnia and Herzegovina. Consequently, the second part of the 1990s – at least until 1999 – was characterized by the UN being set aside as a peacekeeping actor. The UN kept its legal role, but was marginalized in its political and operational capacity, especially insofar as complex and coercive activities were concerned.[4] The implementation of the Dayton Peace Agreement in Bosnia and Herzegovina illustrates the shift, as NATO and the OSCE were substantially involved, and the UN confined to a small observation mission, in no respect comparable to its role in the early 1990s. In parallel, the number of personnel deployed within UN peace operations substantially decreased, with fewer than 15,000 troops being deployed at the end of 1998, compared with some 76,612 in August 1994.[5]

The year 1999 then marked a new evolution in the life of the UN, with three series of disparate events. First, the UN, as a legal authority, was by-passed by NATO and its member states in Operation Allied Force in Kosovo, adding to the UN's marginalization. Second, and in spite of being discredited, the Organization made a kind of come back, with the creation and conduct of three ambitious operations: in Kosovo (UNMIK in June), East Timor (UNTAET in October) and Sierra Leone (UNAMSIL in October), giving the UN a new role in different configurations. And third, the UN Secretariat and its Secretary-General Kofi Annan displayed a fair degree of self-criticism, with the release of the reports on the fall of Srebrenica and on the genocide in Rwanda.[6]

To summarize, the role of the UN in the second half of the 1990s, and on the eve of 11 September 2001, can be encapsulated by the three following points:

- The UN went through a period of discredit, and was no longer considered as the central actor in the field of crisis management, especially by western states (see table 1 and 2 in the appendix on page 33). It was consequently relatively marginalized, in favour of regional institutions (in Europe) or coalitions of states.[7]

- The UN tried to focus its activities on conflict prevention on the one hand, and on peacebuilding on the other, at the expense of peacekeeping activities *per se* at least until 1999. The UN has therefore been increasingly involved in consent-based activities.[8]

- In spite of this trend, the UN created and conducted three important operations from 1999 onwards, and in August 2001 deployed about 47,000 military personnel and civilian police in 15 operations, demonstrating that the UN's role in peacekeeping was far from insignificant, both in terms of personnel being deployed and in terms of mandate, especially in Africa.

The Brahimi Report on peace operations

It is in this mixed context that the 'Report of the Panel on UN Peace Operations', known as the Brahimi Report, was released in August 2000.[9]

This simultaneously recognized the limited capacity of the UN and advocated a restored central role. To achieve this objective, the emphasis was placed on three key elements: the reform of the organization, and especially the Secretariat and its Department of Peacekeeping Operations (DPKO); the necessity to have better defined operations and clear mandates, with the means to implement them (robust force, rapid deployment capabilities, and so on); and the necessity to get stronger political commitment from the states, especially western states.[10]

At these different levels, in spite of the repeated official support coming from the states, and despite the ongoing restructuring of the DPKO, on the eve of 11 September 2001 the full implementation of the Brahimi Report was still a sensitive issue.[11] Beyond the practical and financial aspects of the implementation of the Report, thinking about it in the context of the lasting discredit of the UN, and the general reluctance of western states to get involved in peace operations, leads us to question the link between the efficacy of the 'tool' (UN/Secretariat), and the will of the states to use it. In other words, to what extent would western states be willing to participate in UN peace operations (in Africa for example) when/if the UN is better equipped? What is the link between the efficacy of the structure and the political will of states to act through it? The answer to these questions probably lies in the nature of the operations contemplated. Western states might want to resort to a reformed UN more than they do today if the organization were dealing with non-coercive/civilian activities. But they would avoid the UN anyway if peace operations were complex, multi-dimensional, and contained a militarily coercive dimension. Despite reform of the institution, the tendency to set the UN aside is likely to endure when it comes to politically and militarily risky crisis management.

It is against this background that the events of 11 September have to be examined. Here, a distinction has to be drawn between the UN role in dealing with the events of 11 September and with the 'Afghan crisis' on the one hand, and what such events and roles tell us about UN peace operations for the longer run on the other.

THE UN RESPONSE TO THE 11 SEPTEMBER ATTACKS AND TO THE 'AFGHAN CRISIS'

The immediate response

The different decisions and actions taken by the 'international community' immediately after the attacks of 11 September do not directly relate to peace operations, but they are informative about the place of the UN in the international system. Three issues need to be considered which reveal both a relatively important role for the UN as well as its limits as a security actor primarily aimed at maintaining international peace and security. First was the adoption of resolution 1368 by the Security Council; second the adoption of resolution 1373; and third the immediate US posture towards the UN.[12]

The unanimity behind resolution 1368
The UN Security Council, and also the General Assembly,[13] displayed an uncontested unity following the 11 September attacks, though this can hardly be considered an achievement of the organization given the nature of the attacks. The adoption of resolution 1368 on 12 September 2001 instantly involved the Security Council in its legal and political capacity.[14] It was adopted unanimously, with the concurring votes of China and Russia. The text unsurprisingly recognized the 'inherent right of individual or collective self-defence' for the United States, and may therefore be considered as the legal ground for Operation Enduring Freedom, unless the right of self-defence is the legal basis in itself, without the need for a specific resolution.

The right to respond is theoretically 'strictly limited in time',[15] until, under article 51 of the Charter, the Security Council 'has taken measures necessary to maintain international peace and security'. In resolution 1368 the Council expressed 'its readiness to take all necessary steps to respond to the terrorist attacks'. Yet, it was in no position to go much further at this stage, and therefore arguably did not play its role of guarantor of international peace and security. A related issue is the question of the length of time that the United States can enjoy the inherent right to self-defence: Until when can the United States invoke this right? What is the benchmark beyond which a (new) Security Council resolution will be considered necessary to legalize a US military action? In the same vein, the fact that the attacks were presumably perpetrated by a non-state actor and led to a 'war' against the state identified as playing host to the terrorist group raises the question of the UN's legal and political ability to address non-state threats.[16] More specifically, it raises the issue of whether terrorist attacks are considered as an 'armed attack' against a state, or as 'threats to international peace'.[17]

Such a debate did not take place in the first months following the attacks. In fact no real legal debate was held – contrary to what happened during and after the Kosovo crisis and Operation Allied Force. It was as if a broad consensus could be assumed to back the American position,[18] with the noticeable exception of the status of the prisoners held in Guantanamo Bay, the way they would be treated and judged.

In this context, resolution 1368 was certainly welcomed, but it can hardly be interpreted as a step that gave the UN a particular role. And as far as the 'war' on terrorism was concerned, the resolution was more pertinent for states participating in the coalition along with the United States than for the United States itself. Finally, the western media paid much more attention to the adoption, on the same day, by the North Atlantic Council, of a Statement mentioning the possible invocation of article 5 of the Washington treaty,[19] than to the UN resolution.

The ambition of resolution 1373

The second important measure taken by the Security Council a few weeks after the attacks was the adoption of resolution 1373 on 28 September 2001, containing a series of measures to fight terrorism mainly by suppressing its financing, and establishing the Counter-Terrorism Committee (CTC) to monitor implementation of the resolution. The CTC has been chaired by the British ambassador to the UN, Jeremy Greenstock, and is meant to remain under the close political control of the P-5. In spite of difficulties in its implementation, it is undoubtedly the most important text in terms of giving the UN a role in the international response to the events of 11 September. It is also a resolution that US officials regularly quote as a key text in the global fight against terrorism.[20]

The immediate US posture towards the UN

The third issue is the way the Bush Administration referred to the UN in the weeks following 11 September (see Eric Schwartz's chapter in this volume). The extent to which US officials paid attention to the UN in the immediate response to the attacks is a matter of controversy. One could argue that the will to bring together a broad coalition to fight terrorism led the United States to rely on the UN for 'validation, legitimacy and political support'.[21] Some measures taken towards the UN in the immediate aftermath of the attacks may be interpreted as a demonstration of goodwill;[22] as well as the creation of the CTC and the recurrent references to resolution 1373. And, as expected, Bush's address to the UN General Assembly in November 2001, contended that the 'struggle [against terrorism] is a defining moment for the United Nations itself. The world needs its principled leadership. [...] The United Nations depends, above all, on its moral authority, and that authority must be preserved.'[23]

However, the nature of the situation, combined with the usual attitude of the Republicans towards the UN, led to a general neglect of the organization by the Bush Administration. References to the UN have been extremely rare in the US official discourse, especially when the audience has been primarily American and when military issues have been raised.[24] US officials made it very clear that the United States did not need any authorization from the UN to intervene in Afghanistan, since it was acting in 'accordance with [its] inherent right of individual and collective self-defense'.[25] In the first weeks following the attacks, the UN did not really appear to be an issue for the United States, and was only considered as such through its diplomatic talks on Afghanistan and in a post-conflict, 'nation-building' role. During those first weeks, the UN was less important than the need to build a coalition. A multilateral approach did not give the UN a central role in this particular case.[26]

The terrorist attacks of 11 September were attacks to the vital interests of the United States, and thus created a situation that by its very nature, has not been conducive to a significant role for international institutions. In the United States as well as elsewhere, the response to terrorism has been a state response.[27] Furthermore, it is difficult to see in what ways the UN could have been more involved, given the UN capacity and its very limited role in dealing with terrorist issues prior to 11 September; and the context of an aggression against the sole superpower. In this highly sensitive and politicized context, one could even argue that the UN was involved as much as it could possibly have been. But in this defining moment, what is likely to be retained is the very limited role of an organization that is not tailored to address such issues, and could hardly be seen as a possible option in fighting terrorism.

The UN in Afghanistan: the only security organization involved

Soon after the immediate response to the 11 September attacks, the UN became more involved in the management of the Afghan crisis, despite the numerous constraints of the situation. The UN was involved at two different levels:[28] through its humanitarian agencies, coordinated by an 'Afghan Task Force', headed by the United Nations Regional Humanitarian Coordinator, to assure the relief of the Afghan population; and at the political and diplomatic level, through the Secretary-General's Special Envoy, Lakhdar Brahimi, appointed on 3 October 2001 and the 'UN Talks on Afghanistan', which led to the Bonn Agreement on 5 December 2001.[29]

With this engagement (including the actions of the CTC) the UN was the only international organization actively involved in the management of the crisis. If we set aside the action of international financial institutions, no other institution could claim to have played a role in this matter. In this context however, the UN (here the Secretariat) has consistently ruled out the two most ambitious options that were discussed at various times in October and November, that is, a UN-led peacekeeping force to help implement a peace agreement, and UN involvement in a 'transitional administration', that might be established following the restoration of a 'negative' peace in Afghanistan.

A UN-led peacekeeping force

On 10 October 2001, former King of Afghanistan, Mohammad Zaher Shah, addressed a letter to the UN Secretary-General 'conveying his concerns about a power vacuum if the Taliban were to collapse and asking for the deployment of a United Nations force'.[30] More generally, the idea that a possible power vacuum had to be dealt with by some kind of security force in Afghanistan was rapidly accepted by both the United States, the allies, and the local forces, and a debate was held on the nature and composition of such a force.

However, in a press briefing held at UN Headquarters in mid-October, Lakhdar Brahimi 'cautioned the Security Council not to "rush" into Afghanistan with a peacekeeping force that lacks the political and financial support required to succeed', and stressed that 'the Council should set achievable and realistic goals'. Referring to the Balkan operations of the early 1990s, Brahimi concluded that there 'were ten years of experience between the Balkans and now. I hope we have learned something from that experience.'[31] On 13 November 2001, Brahimi presented three options to the Security Council: an all-Afghan security force; a multinational force (MNF); and a UN peacekeeping force. He then dismissed the idea of a UN-led force, arguing that: 'This is not a role for "Blue Helmets".'[32] Such a stance was consistent with one of the leitmotifs of the Brahimi Report, according to which the UN should not embark on an operation unless it had a good chance for success: 'that requests for United Nations implementation of ceasefires or peace agreements need to meet certain minimum conditions before the Council commits United Nations-led forces to implement such accords'. Conditions included 'operationally achievable' tasks, 'with local responsibility for supporting them specified', 'robust rules of engagement' enabling peacekeepers to defend themselves 'against those who renege on their commitments to a peace accord or otherwise seek to undermine it by violence', and, most importantly, 'solid commitments from member states for the forces'.[33] Moreover, the Brahimi Report confirmed the reservations about UN involvement in operations that would imply enforcement measures explicitly falling within Chapter VII. Such conditions and concerns, combined with the limits of UN capacity explain Brahimi's reluctance to create a peace operation for Afghanistan. Within the Secretariat, a UN-led operation was never seriously considered, as none of the possible contributors seemed to be satisfied that it should be UN-led.

For other, but no less solid, reasons the option of an all-Afghan security force was also dismissed as a short-term option, and the Security Council eventually opted for a UN-mandated force (International Security Assistance Force – ISAF).[34] The concept was laid down in Annex I of the Bonn Agreement.[35] It was consistent with the 'sub-contracting model' that has been followed since the mid-1990s, and by which the UN Security Council legally creates an operation, but delegates its implementation to either a regional organization or a coalition of states.

The UN avoidance of a 'transitional administration'

As mentioned above, an important trend in UN crisis management in the last five or six years has been a shift to consent-based activities, and above all to post-conflict peacebuilding. The coordination of civilian activities in a post-conflict environment is an area for which the UN may claim to have some comparative advantages, and has developed a savoir-faire, as shown in Namibia and Cambodia in the early 1990s, and in Kosovo and East Timor more recently. A division of labour is even sometimes promoted, by which states (gathered in a coalition of the willing or in a regional organization) would deal with the coercive aspects of an operation – especially during a conflict – and the UN would then intervene to assist in the implementation of a peace plan. This division of labour can be seen in the case of Kosovo and East Timor, where the UN has been involved once an agreement was reached and after a military operation led in very different environments – by a regional organization in the case of Kosovo (NATO-led operation 'Allied Force'), and by a coalition of states in the case of East Timor (Australian-led operation INTERFET).

Many different options in post-conflict situations can be contemplated by the UN. One of the most ambitious and challenging is what the Brahimi Report called the 'transitional civil administration'. The Report dedicated only a few lines to the 'Challenges of transitional civil administration',[36] in which the panellists were rather dismissive about such activities, even wondering whether 'the UN should be in this business at all, and if so whether it should be considered an element of peace operations or should be managed by some other structure'.[37] However, the idea that the UN could be involved in a transitional administration in Afghanistan was put forward by the United States in October 2001, although with some ambiguities as to whether the UN should be 'in charge' or only supervise the process.[38] President Bush talked about the UN taking over 'the so-called "nation-building" … after our military mission is complete'.[39] The necessity for the UN to play a 'leading role' in shaping a post-Taliban Afghanistan was repeatedly mentioned, with the clear objective to fill the political vacuum in

Kabul after the collapse of the Taliban regime.[40] The idea would match the principle of division of labour, here between the United States, that would be in charge of eliminating bin Laden and the Al Qaeda network in a war-type operation, and the UN in charge of filling the political vacuum in Kabul in a peace operation.

Once again, the UN Secretariat did not display a strong enthusiasm for being involved in what was perceived as favourable ground for mission creep, and in contradiction with the recommendations of the Brahimi Report. Brahimi was well aware that one of the challenges in Afghanistan would be 'the creation of good governance', but without denying the role of the UN in post-conflict rehabilitation,[41] he repeated that it was the Afghans themselves who could 'help constitute a transitional administration, which would be far more credible, acceptable and legitimate in the eyes of the population, than a transitional administration run by the UN'.[42] The US Administration went along with this, and on 14 November 2001, the Security Council adopted a resolution which, while endorsing the approach of the Secretary-General's Special Representative, expressed its 'strong support for the efforts of the Afghan people to establish a new and transitional administration leading to the formation of a government', and affirmed that 'the UN should play a central role in supporting' such efforts.[43] In practice, this meant that the UN would not be in charge of the administration.

If one considers what the UN did and did not do during the first three to four months following the September attacks, one can conclude that the UN role was consistent with what it was before 11 September, in the sense that the UN dealt with the civilian/political aspects of the response of the 'international community', but not with any aspect that could be seen as too ambitious or too risky for the convalescent Organization. To summarize, the UN was involved through a range of different types of action:

• adoption by the Security Council of several resolutions, among which resolution 1368, 1373, and 1386 (that created the ISAF);
• creation of the Counter-Terrorism Committee; conduct of the 'UN talks on Afghanistan'; and later creation of the UN Assistance Mission in Afghanistan (UNAMA); and
• coordination of humanitarian activities.

Moreover, it is difficult to identify any UN action in dealing with the crisis that was a direct result of 11 September, in the sense that UN deeds or abstentions were confirmations of the situation that prevailed prior to 11 September rather than examples of a new approach to international security in general, and peace operations in particular. Consequently one can argue that the events of 11 September have had no tangible consequences on the way the UN has defined its own role, or on the way states see such a role. And the UN as a whole has been rather complacent about its role. Neither Kofi Annan, Lakhdar Brahimi nor member states convincingly insisted on giving the UN a different role. There has been a broad consensus on the level of the UN involvement, in line with the spirit of the Brahimi Report, but also with some concerns about the American agenda, by which 'everything is defined in terms of terrorism'.[44]

THE LONG-TERM CONSEQUENCES FOR PEACE OPERATIONS

We have seen that the UN response to the 11 September attacks was not fundamentally different from its previous role; the management of the Afghan case illustrates this continuity. Bearing this in mind, one needs to have a look at the long-term implications – insofar as we can tell – for UN peace operations. Two aspects need to be considered in this respect: the political will of states to support UN peace operations and the implementation of the Brahimi Report; and the very nature of peace operations and practices within existing ones.

Political will and the Brahimi Report: the priority shift

As argued previously, one of the major shortcomings of peace operations lies in the lack of political support from states, especially western states. Insofar as the events of 11 September have had a major impact on the way states define their security policies, and threats to their own security, one should look at the possible consequences of such reappraisals on peace operations. Are peace operations likely to be more, or less, politically supported in the aftermath of the events of 11 September? By the same token, will states be more, or less, inclined to back the implementation of the Brahimi Report than prior to 11 September?

The first element to take into account is that for many states, one of the consequences of 11 September has been a shift of priorities in defence and security policies. This is especially true for the United States, but for European states too. Countries such as India or Pakistan, that are important troop contributors to UN operations, may also be affected. This means that the financial and human resources to be allocated to UN peace operations are unlikely to increase at a time when 'fighting terrorism' becomes, at least theoretically, a more urgent necessity. A priori, what was not a priority before 11 September is unlikely to become one when efforts are to be reoriented. This priority shift would logically affect the political will of states to back UN operations, as long as there is no obvious positive link between the terrorist threat and the UN's role in peace operations. None of the reservations of western states vis-à-vis UN operations have been positively altered after 11 September. As a matter of fact, their low participation in UN peace operations prior to 11 September has not been modified since (see Table 2 in Appendix).

By the same token, the implementation of the Brahimi Report is likely to suffer the same kind of limitation. UN reform is not less needed, but the incentives to invest in the field of peacekeeping – through the UN – may be more difficult to identify in the new context. The decreasing attention paid to the implementation of the Brahimi Report in western administrations is revealing of the post-11 September mindset. At the level of the UN Secretariat, the priority shift should not however be as important as at state level. The implementation of the Brahimi Report falls to the Vice-Secretary-General, and is dealt with independently from countering terrorism (be it at CTC level, within Vienna-based institutions,[45] or in other bodies).[46] The reports issued by the Special Committee on Peacekeeping Operations as well as the report of the Secretary-General on the implementation of the Brahimi Report (issued after 11 September) do not address the issue of the consequences of 11 September on peace operations, and therefore implicitly assume the absence of a link between the two elements.[47] The only mention is in the Secretary-General's report of December 2001, where it is said that the proposal (made in the Brahimi Report) for a small support secretariat to service the Executive Committee on Peace and Security (ECPS) was even more relevant after 11 September, since the ECPS was strongly solicited.[48] By the same token, the Afghan crisis led to the creation of an Integrated Mission Task Force (IMTF), as recommended in the Brahimi Report.[49] However, this measure is less a consequence of 11 September than the implementation of one of the recommendations of the Brahimi Report, which could have occurred anyway in another operation.

Finally, political support for UN operations and implementation of the Brahimi Report remain highly dependent upon the US position (see Eric Schwartz's chapter in this volume). More than any other state, the United States is concerned about the priority shift and the need to allocate resources to the fight against terrorism, but it is also one of the only countries that is ready to increase overall resources. Yet, the combination of US reluctance to participate in UN peace operations, traditional Republican disquiet about the UN, and the political and military priorities implied by 11 September, are unlikely to lead to a renewed effort to support UN peacekeeping. As clearly stated by the US Ambassador to the UN, John Negroponte, in a speech titled 'The UN Agenda in the Wake of September 11': 'our over-arching priority at the UN now and for the foreseeable future must be the war against global terrorism. Global terrorism cuts across too many US interests not to be the first and last subject addressed each and every day'.[50] This does not leave much space for UN peace operations that are not seen as being directly related to the 'war'.

Furthermore, whenever peace operations are contemplated, there are not many situations in which the UN would appear as the most appropriate option for the United States. The US tendency to adopt 'multilateralism à la carte' – called 'selective multilateralism' by the State Department[51] – also finds applications in peace operations, where the UN seems to offer no obvious comparative advantage. The United States will continue to back some UN operations, and to play a role in the training of African contingents, but their own participation remains as improbable as before. Another element is that US forces deployed abroad – in peace operations among others – are possible targets for terrorist acts. This implies careful consideration of all foreign deployment and limiting as much as possible deployments that are not seen as absolutely necessary. Of course, all these considerations are even more acute in a post-Iraq war context.

Such issues raise the question of the role of the UN in the aftermath of 11 September, where multilateral tools are not necessarily dismissed by the United States, but where the UN has only a restricted role to play. The post-11 September environment is not conducive to increased US support of the UN in general and peace operations in particular.

Peace operations and terrorism: the uneasy indirect link

The two issues of 'peace operations' and the 'fight against terrorism' are a priori two separate themes that are not spontaneously connected. Peace operations take the form of a deployment of military and civilian components to help solve a particular conflict or to address the consequences of a conflict in an impartial way. The fight against terrorism, insofar as it can be defined, embraces many different activities in many different places, to fight and dismantle terrorist groups, and theoretically to address the causes of terrorism.

Moreover, whereas peace operations have gone through a 40-year history, the fight against terrorism is a new approach to international action and cooperation. The UN has no experience in it. Theoretically and practically, those two types of activities appear to be fundamentally different. Their purpose, their means and their contexts are different. More broadly, there seems to be no direct link between the essence of peace operations and the security issues raised by the response to terrorism, in the sense that the *problématique* of peace operations, as well as the need for international crisis management, remains unchanged. As argued before, peace operations might suffer from the new environment as resources and political commitment may be affected, but situations that led to the establishment of peace operations in Kosovo, Sierra Leone, East Timor, the Democratic Republic of Congo, Ethiopia and Eritrea, will continue to exist, with similar needs for external interventions, and few common features with the questions raised by terrorism.

However, peace operations do have an indirect link with terrorism in the sense that they are sometimes deployed in environments that may be favourable grounds for the development of terrorist groups. Some peace operations are established in 'failed states', and 'failed states' constitute such fertile grounds, as well as possible havens for terrorist groups. Peace operations may be linked indirectly therefore to the issue of terrorism. More specifically, the two themes are linked implicitly through the common root causes of terrorism and conflict, the latter being addressed by both conflict prevention and peacebuilding. Following the 1972 episode of the Palestinian group's attempt to take Israeli athletes hostage during the Munich Olympic Games, the UN General Assembly adopted several resolutions that referred to 'the underlying causes of those forms of terrorism and acts of violence which lie in misery, frustration, grievance and despair'.[52] Since then, the General Assembly has regularly adopted resolutions on 'Measures to prevent international terrorism', reasserting the importance of considering the context as well as the causes of terrorist acts. Along similar lines, the Secretary-General's report on 'Prevention of armed conflict', issued in June 2001, states that 'one of the principal aims of preventive action should be to address the deep-rooted socio-economic, cultural, environmental, institutional and other structural causes that often underlie the immediate political symptoms of conflicts'.[53] In the same vein, in a declaration on peacebuilding, the Security Council reaffirmed that the 'quest for peace requires a comprehensive, concerted and determined approach that addresses the root causes of conflicts, including their economic and social dimensions'. Peacebuilding is to play a particular role here, in 'fostering sustainable institutions and processes in areas such as sustainable development, the eradication of poverty and inequalities'.[54]

The two fields of conflict prevention and peacebuilding are two of the three elements of peace operations defined in the Brahimi Report that have been emphasized as giving the UN a role.[55] More than in peacekeeping (the third component of peace operations), the future of the UN appears to lie in peacebuilding and in conflict prevention. Insofar as conflict prevention is concerned, a follow-on to the Secretary-General's report of June 2001, asserts that: 'the menace of terrorism and weapons of mass destruction has ... heightened the need for far-reaching cooperation in the international community in its move towards a culture of prevention.'[56] The link between the root causes of conflict and the root causes of terrorism is further established in the Report of the Policy Working Group on the UN and Terrorism:

> Operational prevention is relevant because any measures that alleviate crises and prevent armed conflicts from developing or expanding could lower the likelihood that terrorist acts related to such conflicts would occur.
>
> [And if structural prevention] assist[s] societies to resolve conflict peacefully within the rule of law, grievances that might have been expressed through terrorist acts are more likely to be addressed through political, legal and social means.[57]

The concept of prevention thus acquires a new dimension that is relevant to the fight against terrorism.

Peacebuilding activities are also concerned, partly because they aim at creating a 'sustainable peace in which terrorism will have less cause to breed and grow',[58] partly because there are some similarities between policies aimed at restoring law and order in war-torn societies and anti-terrorism policies. As stated in the Peace Through Law Education Fund report on the US military role in peace operations:

> The rule of law issue is problem number one not only because it is our exit strategy, ... but also because its absence in war-torn states provides an environment for terrorist and organized crime to thrive. In the post-September 11 world, it cries even louder for a solution.[59]

The same report even establishes a link between 'skills gained in peace operations' and 'skills needed in the multi-dimensional war against terrorism', arguing that:

> Participating in coalitions, fighting organized crime, hunting down terrorist cells, disarming the populace, exposing corruption, collecting intelligence, apprehending and bringing war-criminals to trial, supporting a professional police force and judicial system, running detention centers, and cooperating with the United Nations and other international institutions and non-

governmental organizations, are just some of the non-traditional skills that will be in high demand in the twenty-first century military.[60]

Theoretically, this new approach would also lead to a reappraisal of cost/benefit calculations made by states in their policies vis-à-vis peace operations. These ones would be considered differently if they are seen as playing some role in the overall fight against terrorism. They would gain some strategic importance from this new role. The above-mentioned report establishes a strong link between the events of 11 September and the participation in peace operations: 'Before September 11, participation in multilateral peace operations was in our interests for reasons of regional stability, but now, participation is in our direct national security interests.'[61] In the same logic, the Under-Secretary-General for Peacekeeping Operations, Jean-Marie Guéhenno, argues that:

> Until 11 September 2001, the interest for areas of crisis, where states are failing from the inside, was primary a humanitarian concern: we were thinking about the populations of those countries, that are always the first victims; we did not realize that this humanitarian concern is also a security imperative, and that stabilization of these areas by peacekeeping operations is a strategic necessity.[62]

With these factors in mind, the link between terrorism and peace operations seems to acquire some relevance. The Bosnian case provides a good example, where UN and NATO forces have had to counteract groups linked with terrorism (see Jacques Klein's and Dick Leurdijk's chapters in this volume). To what extent then could and should peace operations participate in the overall fight against terrorism? Can they be considered as possible tools to tackle terrorism, beyond the theoretical link that may be established between the two issues?

The unlikely contribution of peace operations to the fight against terrorism

An assessment of the contribution that peace operations could bring to the fight against terrorism would first require a precise definition of the notion of 'fight against terrorism'. The political sensitivity of the issue of terrorism and of its definition have led to difficulties in identifying what fighting it may imply. Short-term activities aimed at dismantling terrorist groups would have to be distinguished from long-term activities aimed at addressing the 'root causes of terrorism'. Normative issues would also have to be separated from operational issues. As for peace operations, a distinction should be made between the consequences of terrorism as a threat to the way these operations are conducted, and the contribution that they may bring to the response.

Within UN peace operations, terrorism as a threat is certainly a factor that will have to be taken into account. A sub-module on terrorism has been added to the 'Security Awareness' module as part of the 'Standardized Generic Training Modules' provided by the DPKO. In the same vein, the DPKO has worked on the possible consequences of the use of weapons of mass destruction in places where UN troops are deployed (in the Middle East in particular), without being necessarily targets of an attack themselves. But those legitimate concerns will not change the very nature of the operations.

In regard to a longer-term approach, the link between terrorism and peace operations has remained a controversial and sensitive issue within the UN Secretariat. In both the DPKO and the Department of Political Affairs (DPA), the idea that 'failed states' may favour the emergence of terrorist groups is broadly accepted, and so is the link, even if indirect, between peace operations and the possible consequences of state collapse. But neither these two departments nor states have yet really considered the implications of such a link. Reports issued by the Secretary-General on UN peace operations since 11 September do not reflect major changes in UN practice, and hardly mention the issue of terrorism.[63]

Within the DPKO, peace operations are not seen as 'likely to be a direct response to terrorism', but certainly as possible 'instruments to help address a root cause and enabling environment'.[64] There might also be the sentiment that peace operations are all the more important as they help stabilize and keep under control failing states in the post-11 September world. In this respect, any link being made between peace operations and the root causes of terrorism could hopefully help to get a renewed interest in peace operations from western states.[65] Yet, terrorism is not particularly discussed within the DPKO; it has not changed the daily work of a department still in charge of 15 operations in which terrorism has not become a matter of priority. And as for peace operations being seen as 'strategic necessities' by states, such a move has not yet occurred, with no tangible prospects of change.

Within the DPA (in charge of conflict prevention and peacebuilding, which also has responsibility for the Policy Working Group on the UN and Terrorism, and serves as the secretariat of the CTC), the issue of terrorism is also of a peculiar nature. There is clearly a sense within the DPA that terrorism has its roots in situations that both prevention and peacebuilding should be addressing. But the difficulties in defining terrorism – including the distinction between terrorism and liberation movements – as well as the need to avoid doing anything that could be seen (especially by the United States and Israel) as a justification for terrorism, leads the DPA to handle the whole issue with great care. In practice, the two departments are also confronted by a loss of momentum. More than a year after the 2001 attacks, the attention paid to terrorism has faded, after a period when almost everything that the UN did had to be linked to the fight against terrorism.

Beyond these institutional elements, peace operations, especially when they are UN-led, follow a logic that is not easily squared with anti-terrorism. The primary purpose of UN peace operations, as it has been defined and re-defined since the 1990s, makes it difficult to envisage a strong role for peace operations in anti-terrorism, especially as implied by the expression 'war on terror'. The concept of impartiality, which is an underlying concept of peace operations, would be difficult to maintain in an operation also mandated to fight terrorist cells. Besides, the UN's ability to embrace such ambitious tasks is doubtful; the tendency is for the UN to be restricted to consent-based and non-coercive activities, which do not include the 'war' that counter-terrorism seems to entail. A critique of peace operations in Bosnia and Herzegovina and in Somalia was the deleterious mix of non-coercive and coercive activities, that is, the confusion about what UN forces were supposed to do, and along what principles. Including counter-terrorism as a dimension of peace operations would profoundly change their nature, which cannot be done without a rigorous and systematic assessment of the possible consequences.

As far as longer-term policies are concerned, peacebuilding activities might pay more attention to the underlying causes of terrorism, especially when operations are deployed in countries that are particularly of concern. But such activities should not fundamentally differ from those that currently belong to peacebuilding, nor are operations likely to be created primarily for the purpose of addressing the 'root causes' of terrorism. Here is raised the controversial issue of the 'root causes of terrorism' and their relevance to the particular case of Al Qaeda. This explains some of the reservations expressed within the UN itself, and questions the pertinence of analysis about the common root causes of conflict and terrorism, and about links between the identified root causes of terrorism and the particular motivations of the Al Qaeda network.

Furthermore, US dominance of counter-terrorism affects perceptions about such a policy. On the one hand, if the idea that failed states are breeding grounds for terrorism has any merit, then the United States might be willing to be more involved in activities aimed at helping weak states to become stronger (see Eric Schwartz's chapter). This may be channelled through development aid, as stated in President Bush's speech on global development on 14 March 2002,[66] through different kinds of assistance programmes, and also, in particular cases, through peace operations.[67] The Peace Through Law Education Fund report is explicit – and quite optimistic – about the 'strategic necessity' for the United States to participate in UN operations. But given the general US approach towards peace operations, it would be somehow paradoxical to see those operations gaining such an importance. Furthermore, not only has such a necessity not yet been integrated into US policy, or any other country's reasoning, the issue of fighting terrorism is also not perceived with the same priority by all states and by all possible contributors to peace operations. The US position and discourse might lead to an official consensus, by which 'international terrorism is a global threat that has to be fought by all and by all means', but the threat assessment and effective commitment of other states and international organizations will vary. And within the UN, the US agenda where 'everything is defined in terms of terrorism'[68] also causes reservations, especially as the US emphasizes short-term and operational activities rather than long-term programmes dealing with root causes. Finally, the 'use' of peace operations as possible actors of the fight against terrorism would lead to a deleterious selectivity, in contradiction with the very concept of peace operations. Operations would be more easily contemplated in places where terrorism has been an issue, or is likely to be, and less easily considered in 'terrorist-free' places (see Nicholas Stockton's chapter), with all the inherent risks of operations diverted from their primary purpose by states with mixed motives. But for many states, would the argument rather be, on the contrary, that the 'terrorism issue' is a disincentive to get involved, for fear of being involved in a too risky operation? While such developments cannot be a priori excluded, they would hardly correspond to what the UN has been trying to do in the field of peace operations in the last years.

From this it follows that despite the theoretical links between peace operations and counter-terrorism, the former can hardly be seen as instruments in the latter. At best, as suggested in the Policy Working Group on the UN and Terrorism, 'while the prevention and resolution of armed conflict should not primarily be conceived of as anti-terrorist activities, they can assist such activities by narrowing the space in which terrorists operate'.[69] Anti-terrorist activities should not be primary concerns in UN peace operations, but when such operations are deployed in countries where 'terrorism has been prevalent', the UN should be mindful of including measures to 'ensure that the mandates ... are sensitive to terrorism-related issues, providing, for instance, that civilian police officers received appropriate training on measures to identify and counter terrorist groups'.[70] In any case, the contribution of UN peace operations to counter-terrorism should be limited and confined to cases of particular sensitivity. Yet, in such cases, the UN is unlikely to play a key operational role, and other channels could be preferred.

CONCLUSION

The events of 11 September will shape aspects of international relations in years to come. However they should not fundamentally alter the nature of UN peace operations and the trend to marginalization of the UN since the mid-1990s. The UN's role in responding to the 11 September attacks was not defined by the nature of the attacks and could have been observed in other circumstances. In accordance with its approach to crisis management prior to 11 September, the UN dealt only with consent-based activities and refused to be involved in more ambitious and ill-defined mandates in Afghanistan. In the same vein, ongoing UN peace operations have not been significantly affected, nor state's policies vis-à-vis the whole *problématique* of UN peace operations.

In the longer term, it is likely that the events of 11 September will not have dramatic consequences on peace operations either, partly because these operations are, by nature, different from what counter-terrorism may imply. Prevention and peacebuilding might be directly concerned with the problem, especially in areas where the issue of terrorism has been prevalent, but in ways that are difficult to identify for the time being.

Beyond these observations, the whole issue of the role of the UN in a globalized and multicentric world will have to be addressed. Insofar as the current crisis will lead to a reappraisal of key concepts ruling the international system, and of the role of different actors, one could argue that there should be no alternative to a reinforced UN as a key legal and political actor. The events of 11 September do not make the UN less relevant. They were perpetrated a few minutes before the Peace Bell rang announcing the opening of the 56th session of the General Assembly. The UN as such was not a target, but the events of 11 September signalled in part a contest between the established international system, which the UN partly represents, and societies dominated and disadvantaged by it. One might argue, thus, for a UN more open to the disempowered in the international system,[71] and a UN better equipped to respond to the often destructive challenges posed in the post-cold war era. A more potent UN role in dealing with international peace and security is also a way to address the root causes of conflict, and the root causes of terrorism.

APPENDIX

TABLE 1

THE ROLE OF THE UN IN AND OUTSIDE OF EUROPE

| | *UN Role* | | | *Role of other Regional Organizations* | *Ability of Regional Powers to support the action of International / Regional Organizations or to take their place* |
	Legal Role	*Political Role*	*Operational Role*		
In Europe	Central but might be challenged	Marginal	Weak to very Weak	Strong	Yes
Outside of Europe	Central but might be challenged	Central	Central	Weak in Africa Non existent in Asia	Weak

TABLE 2

THE 'WEST' AND UN PEACE OPERATIONS (PARTICIPATION)

	NATO + EU + Japan + Australia + New Zealand	*Total*	*Percentage*
September 2000	10,705	37,888	28%
August 2001	10,365	47,151	22%
September 2002	8,867	44,359	20%

Source: Monthly Summary of Military and Civilian Police Contributions to United Nations Operations, UN website.

NOTES

1. See 'After September 11: A Conversation' (especially sections on 'Foreign Policy' and 'Defense Policy'), and Owen Harries, 'An End to Nonsense', *The National Interest*, No. 65-S, 2001; 'One Year After: A Grand Strategy for the West?', an exchange with Robert Kagan, Christoph Bertram and François Heisbourg, *Survival*, Vol. 44, No. 4, Winter 2002–03; François Heisbourg (ed.), *Hyperterrorisme: la nouvelle guerre*, Paris: Odile Jacob, Oct. 2001.
2. See Mats Berdal, 'Whither UN Peacekeeping. An Analysis of the Changing Military Requirements of UN Peacekeeping with Proposals for its Enhancement', *Adelphi Paper*,

No. 281, 1993; William Durch (ed.), *The Evolution of UN Peacekeeping*, New York: St Martin's Press, 1993; Steven Ratner, *The New United Nations Peacekeeping: Building Peace in Lands of Conflict after the Cold War*, London: Macmillan, 1995; Olara Otunnu and Michael Doyle (eds), *Peacemaking and Peacekeeping for the New Century*, Lanham: Rowman and Littlefield, 1996; Michael Pugh (ed.), *The UN, Peace and Force*, London: Frank Cass, 1997; Ramesh Thakur and Albrecht Schnabel (eds), *United Nations Peacekeeping Operations. Ad hoc Missions, Permanent Engagement*, Tokyo: United Nations University Press, 2001.

3. *An Agenda for Peace. Preventive Diplomacy, Peacemaking and Peacekeeping*, Report of the Secretary-General, United Nations, S/24111, 17 June 1992.

4. For a counter-argument, see Peter Viggo Jakobsen, 'Overload, Not Marginalization, Threatens UN Peacekeeping', *Security Dialogue*, Vol. 31, No. 2, 2000.

5. 'Summary of Contributions to Peacekeeping Operations by Countries', New York: United Nations, Aug. 1994 and Dec. 1998.

6. 'The Fall of Srebrenica', Report of the Secretary-General in application of Resolution 53/35 of the General Assembly, A/54/549, 15 Nov. 1999. *Report of the Independent Inquiry into the Actions of the United Nations during the 1994 Genocide in Rwanda*, 15 Dec. 1999. Also see 'Statement of the UN Secretary-General on Receiving the Report', 16 Dec. 1999.

7. See Thierry Tardy, *The UN in Europe: Towards a Subsidiary Role*, Research Document no. 17, Paris: Fondation pour la recherche stratégique, Oct. 2000.

8. See Mats Berdal, 'United Nations Peace Operations: The Brahimi Report in Context', in Kurt Spillmann, Thomas Bernauer, Gabriel Jürg and Andreas Wenger (eds), *Peace Support Operations: Lessons Learned and Future Perspectives*, Bern: Peter Lang, 2001.

9. 'Report of the Panel on UN Peace Operations', UN Doc., A/55/305, 21 Aug. 2000.

10. The Brahimi Report notes that 77 per cent of the troops in formed military units deployed in UN peacekeeping as of June 2000, were contributed by developing countries. 'Report of the Panel on UN Peace Operations' (para. 103).

11. See 'Implementation of the Recommendations of the Special Committee on PKO and the Panel on UN Peace Operations', Report of the Secretary-General, A/56/732, 21 Dec. 2001; 'Comprehensive Review of the Whole Question of Peacekeeping Operations in all their Aspects', Report of the Special Committee on Peacekeeping Operations, 56th session, March 2002. See also, Winrich Kühne, *The Brahimi Report: Overcoming the North-South Divide*, 6th International Workshop, Berlin, 29–30 June 2001; Berdal, 'United Nations Peace Operations'; Thierry Tardy, *La réforme de l'ONU et les suites du rapport Brahimi. Eléments de réflexion pour une position francaise*, Paris: Fondation pour la Recherche stratégique, Dec. 2000 (unpublished).

12. On the role of the UN in fighting terrorism, see Thomas Weiss and Jane Boulden (eds), *The United Nations and Terrorism: Before and After September 11th*, Bloomington, IN: Indiana University Press, 2004; Jeffrey Laurenti (ed.), *Combating Terrorism: Does the UN Matter ... and How?*, New York: A Policy Report of the UN Association of the USA, 2002.

13. See 'Remarkable Unity in Wake of 11 September Terrorist Attack must be used to Reinforce Multilateral Disarmament Regime, First Committee Told', First Committee, GA/DIS/3198, 56th General Assembly, 8 Oct. 2001.

14. Resolution 1368 was drafted by the French delegation (France was president of the Security Council in September). The same day, the UN General Assembly adopted a resolution that condemned the 'heinous acts of terrorism' in similar terms

(A/RES/56/1, 12 Sept. 2001).
15. By contrast, in 'UN: The End of Collective Action', *Le Monde Diplomatique*, Nov. 2001, Monique Chemillier-Gendreau argues that 'the Security Council has abandoned any idea of collective action in the name of the UN'.
16. See Nico Schrijver, 'Responding to International Terrorism: Moving the Frontiers of International Law for "Enduring Freedom"?', *Netherlands International Law Review*, Vol. XLVIII, No. 3, 2001; and Adam Roberts, 'Counter-terrorism, Armed Force and the Law of War', *Survival*, Vol. 44, No. 1, Spring 2002.
17. See Nico Schrijver, 'The September 11 Terrorist Attacks and International Law Responses', in Weiss and Boulden (eds), *The United Nations and Terrorism*.
18. The American Ambassador to the UN stated the day after the beginning of Operation Enduring Freedom: 'we and others who have been involved in this military action continue to enjoy ... a clear understanding that we are acting in our inherent right of self-defense.' Remarks by Ambassador John Negroponte, US Permanent Representative to the UN at the Security Council, 8 Oct. 2001.
19. See Statement by the North Atlantic Council, 12 Sept. 2001, PR/CP(2001)124.
20. See for example Radio Address by the President to the Nation, 10 Nov. 2001; Secretary of State Colin Powell, Statement to the UN Security Council, 12 Nov. 2001; and Message of the President to the Senate of the United States, 12 Nov. 2002.
21. 'The State of US–UN Relations', report of a conference of The Stanley Foundation, New York, 25–26 Apr. 2002, p. 1.
22. Such as the decision to pay a second instalment of arrears. On the US 'goodwill', see *A Force for Peace and Security. US and Allied Commanders' Views of the Military's Role in Peace Operations and the Impact on Terrorism of States in Conflict*, Peace Through Law Education Fund, Washington DC, 2002, pp. 58–61. In Laurenti, *Combating Terrorism*, William Luers goes as far as to say that 'the UN overnight became a vital partner of the US in the struggle against terrorism' ('Foreword', p. 3).
23. Bush's Address to the UN General Assembly, 10 Nov. 2001.
24. See in particular Bush's Address to a Joint Session of Congress and the American People, Washington, 20 Sept. 2001; and Presidential Address to the Nation, Washington, 7 Oct. 2001. In early 2002, Bush did not mention the UN in his State of the Union Address, Washington DC, 29 Jan. 2002.
25. 'Letter dated 7 October 2001 from the Permanent Representative of the USA to the UN addressed to the President of the Security Council', UN doc., S/2001/946, 7 Oct. 2001. This makes no reference to resolution 1368, and only invokes the 'inherent right of self-defense'. See also Nicholas Kralev, 'US Can Strike without UN Nod', *The Washington Times*, 27 Sept. 2001.
26. For opposing views of US policy see: Steven Miller, 'The End of Unilateralism or Unilateralism Redux?', *The Washington Quarterly*, Vol. 25, No. 1, Winter 2002, pp. 15–29; and Stephen Walt, 'Beyond bin Laden. Reshaping US Foreign Policy', *International Security*, Vol. 26, No. 3, Winter 2001/02, pp. 56–78. Both ignore the role of the UN. See also Joseph Nye, 'The Battle between Unilateralists and Multilateralists', *The Paradox of American Power. Why the World's only Superpower can't go it Alone*, Oxford: Oxford University Press, 2002.
27. See Edward Luck, 'The United States, Counter-Terrorism, and the Prospects for a Multilateral Alternative', in Weiss and Boulden, *The United Nations and Terrorism*.
28. See interview of Danilo Turk, UN Assistant Secretary-General for Political Affairs, *Xinhua*, 16 Oct. 2001.

29. See 'Bonn Agreement', Letter dated 5 December 2001 from the Secretary-General addressed to the President of the Security Council, UN doc., S/2001/1154, 5 Dec. 2001.
30. See 'The Situation in Afghanistan and its Implications for International Peace and Security', Report of the Secretary-General, UN doc., A/56/681–S/2001/1157, 6 Dec. 2001, para. 37.
31. Lakhdar Brahimi, Press Briefing, New York: UN, 17 Oct. 2001; also see Colum Lynch, 'Envoy Urges UN not to Send Peacekeepers', *The Washington Post*, 17 Oct. 2001.
32. Brahimi, Briefing to the Security Council, 13 Nov. 2001.
33. Brahimi Report, pp. 10–11.
34. UN Security Council res. 1386, 20 Dec. 2001.
35. See 'Bonn Agreement', Letter dated 5 December 2001 from the Secretary-General addressed to the President of the Security Council, S/2001/1154, Annex I ('International Security Force'), 5 Dec. 2001.
36. Brahimi Report, paras 76–83.
37. Ibid., para. 78.
38. On 18 October 2001, Richard Haass, US Secretary of State Personal Representative for Afghanistan, met with UN Secretary-General Kofi Annan and his Special Representative Lakhdar Brahimi, for talks on the post-Taliban government in Afghanistan.
39. President Bush Press Conference, Washington DC, 11 Oct. 2001.
40. See Secretary of State Colin Powell, Press Briefing, 16 Oct. 2001. Also see 'United Nations Comes to the Rescue', *The Times*, 26 Oct. 2001.
41. UN Press Release, 18 Oct. 2001.
42. See Brahimi, Briefing to the Security Council, 13 Nov. 2001. See also 'Lakhdar Brahimi revient d'Asie centrale avec de l'optimisme et des propositions', *Le Monde*, 9 Nov. 2001.
43. UN Security Council res. 1378, 14 Nov. 2001.
44. 'The State of US–UN Relations', p. 6.
45. These institutions are the Office for Drug Control and Crime Prevention (ODCCP, renamed Office on Drugs and Crime as of 1 October 2002), the Centre for International Crime Prevention (CICP) and its Terrorism Prevention Branch, and the UN Commission on Crime Prevention and Criminal Justice (CCPCJ).
46. See Jean-Marie Guéhenno, 'Opérations de maintien de la paix: la nouvelle donne', *Le Monde*, 18 Dec. 2002.
47. See 'Implementation of the recommendations of the Special Committee on PKO and the Panel on UN Peace Operations', Report of the Secretary-General, UN doc., A/56/732, 21 Dec. 2001; 'Comprehensive Review of the whole question of Peacekeeping Operations in all their aspects', Report of the Special Committee on Peacekeeping Operations, 56th session, March 2002.
48. Ibid., p. 14.
49. In his briefing to the Security Council (13 Nov. 2001), Brahimi said that 'The complexity of the issues and multiplicity of actors engaged in responding to the Afghanistan crisis necessitate that a fully coordinated and integrated approach be pursued within the UN system ... The IMTF functions in close association with the Special Representative and serves as the primary vehicle for the formulation of internal UN policy, as well as for contingency planning for an expanded UN role and presence in Afghanistan.' However, according to critics: 'The UN Integrated Mission Task Force (IMTF) for Afghanistan in New York is not a control mechanism; it is a clearinghouse. It filters information up to decision-makers and filters conformity of policy downward. It is a sounding board with relatively unrestricted participation. It is not an integrated planning entity with

common operational direction. As such, it does not appear to be distinct from previous UN Task Forces'. Jarat Chopra, Jim McCallum and Alexander Thier, 'Planning Considerations for International Involvement in Post-Taliban Afghanistan', *The Brown Journal of World Affairs*, Vol. VIII, Issue 2, Winter 2002, pp. 51–2. According to Department of Political Affairs (DPA) personnel in interviews with the author (April 2002), in spite of some limits the IMTF was an irreplaceable locus for defining the UN policy in Afghanistan.

50. John Negroponte, 'The UN Agenda in the Wake of September 11', lecture delivered at the Institute for the Study of Diplomacy, Georgetown University, 27 Feb. 2002.

51. See Claire Tréan, 'Les Américains soupçonnés de pratiquer l'ONU "à la carte"', *Le Monde*, 9 Nov. 2001. For Colin Powell, 'Nobody's calling us unilateral anymore. That's kind of gone away for the time being; we're so multilateral it keeps me up 24 hours a day checking on everybody.' Quoted in Patrick Tyler, 'Russia and US Optimistic on Defense Issues', *The New York Times*, 19 Oct. 2001. See also, Joseph Nye, 'Unilateralists and Multilateralists', p. 154.

52. See in particular UN General Assembly res. 3034 (XXVII) of 18 December 1972. See also Rama Mani, 'Attacking the Roots: Peacebuilding and Sustainable Development', in Weiss and Boulden, *The United Nations and Terrorism*.

53. 'Prevention of armed conflict', Report of the Secretary-General, UN doc., A/55/985, 7 June 2001, p. 2.

54. 'Peacebuilding: towards a comprehensive approach', Statement by the President of the Security Council, UN doc., S/PRST/2001/5, 20 Feb. 2001.

55. Whether conflict prevention belongs to peace operations can be contested, as in most cases it does not imply a formal UN deployment but is restricted to diplomatic initiatives.

56. 'Prevention of armed conflict: views of organs, organizations and bodies of the UN system', Report of the Secretary-General, UN doc., A/57/588, 5 Nov. 2002, para. 6.

57. 'Report of the Policy Working Group on the UN and Terrorism (Annex)', UN doc., S/2002/875, 6 Aug. 2002, p. 13.

58. *Challenges of Peace Operations: Into the 21st Century – Concluding Report 1997–2002*, Stockholm: The Challenges Project, Elanders Gotab, 2002, p. 30.

59. *A Force for Peace and Security*, p. 34.

60. Ibid., p. 9. The report also stresses that the United States learns from working with Muslim countries in peace operations, which now participate in the 'war' against Al Qaeda (p. 80).

61. *A Force for Peace and Security*, p. 67.

62. Jean-Marie Guéhenno, 'L'ONU, l'UE, l'OTAN et les autres acteurs régionaux: partenaires pour la paix?', speech at the joint International Peace Academy/EU Institute for Security Studies Conference, Paris, 11 Oct. 2002 (translation by the author).

63. See 'Report of the Secretary-General on the United Nations Disengagement Observer Force (for the period 18 May 2002 through 5 December 2002)', S/2002/1328, 4 Dec. 2002; 'Report of the Secretary-General on the United Nations Interim Administration Mission in Kosovo', S/2002/62, 15 Jan. 2002, and S/2002/679, 19 June 2002; 'Report of the Secretary-General on the United Nations Transitional Administration in East Timor', S/2002/80, 17 Jan. 2002; 'Twelfth and Thirteenth Reports of the Secretary-General on the United Nations Mission in Sierra Leone', S/2001/1195, 13 Dec. 2001, and S/2002/267, 14 March 2002; 'Progress Report of the Secretary-General on Ethiopia and Eritrea', S/2001/1194, 13 Dec. 2001.

64. Correspondence with DPKO personnel, July 2002.

65. See Guéhenno, 'Opérations de maintien de la paix', and 'L'ONU, l'UE, l'OTAN'.
66. President Bush's Speech on Global Development, Inter-American Development Bank, Washington DC, 14 Mar. 2002.
67. The very same day as Bush's Speech on Global Development, the Deputy Assistant Secretary of State for International Organization Affairs, William Wood, was arguing before the House of Representatives that while 'our two overriding foreign policy objectives are now to win the war on terror and to protect American citizens … one of the ways we can do both is through our continued active participation in and support for the United Nations and other international organizations'. Statement by William Wood before the Subcommittee on Commerce, Justice, State and the Judiciary, Committee on Appropriations, House of Representatives, 14 Mar. 2002.
68. See 'The State of US–UN Relations', p. 6.
69. 'Report of the Policy Working Group on the UN and Terrorism', p. 12.
70. Ibid., p. 13.
71. The Under-Secretary-General for Disarmament Affairs, Jayantha Dhanapala, stated that the UN 'would also have to confront more acutely than ever the stark reality of having to focus its attention on both State- and non-State actors'. See 'Remarkable Unity in Wake of 11 September Terrorist Attack must be used to reinforce multilateral disarmament regime, First Committee Told', First Committee, GA/DIS/3198, 56th General Assembly, 8 Oct. 2001.

————◄◦►————

TWO

US Policy Toward Peace Operations

Eric P. Schwartz

The tragic events of 11 September 2001 heightened the prominence of a long-standing Washington policy debate about the importance of peace operations to US foreign policy. In the summer of 2002, this issue was being considered in the context of Afghanistan. In that country, Bush Administration officials had to contend with two challenges related to peace operations that are crucial to the overall effort to root out Al Qaeda influence in the region and to establish a stable and effective government in Kabul. The first challenge is ensuring a secure environment during a political transition in Afghanistan. The second is determining how best to support the post-crisis reconstruction and political development effort. Moreover, in the post-11 September world, stability and development issues have taken on greater relevance in places like Bosnia and Herzegovina, Kosovo, Sierra Leone and the Congo, where fragile peace processes may be susceptible to forces of illegality and terrorism. The US Congress has also engaged the debate, with many members urging a greater degree of US involvement in peace stabilization than the Bush Administration has been willing to envision. Finally, by mid-2002, these issues had become the focus of active study by a range of high-profile Washington-based 'think tanks', including the Henry L. Stimson Centre, the Centre for Strategic and International Affairs, and the US Institute of Peace, among others.

The key question is whether this flurry of debate on issues relating to peace stabilization has had any demonstrable impact on US policy. An examination of that question (which, as of mid-2002, can only yield preliminary conclusions) requires a review of several distinct, yet related, issues. These include US willingness to deploy American soldiers to participate in or otherwise support peace operations, as well as US diplomatic and financial support for peacekeeping when carried out by the militaries of countries other than the United States. An assessment also requires an evaluation of the post-11 September posture of US officials on the issue of post-conflict peacebuilding – or what some in the United States call 'nation-building'. If, as a result of 11 September, US officials believe that promoting the development of viable political and economic institutions in weak or failing states is an important US policy objective, then that conclusion may inform overall US perspectives on the value of peacekeeping. It may also inform policy on support for the non-military, civilian institutions (relating, for example, to the administration of justice and transitional economic assistance) that have proven so important in contemporary peace operations.

The emphasis of much, though not all, of what follows relates to US military support and involvement in peace operations. That has been a major focus of policy debate in Washington in recent years. Moreover, the profound security requirements of contemporary peace operations make the discussion of military support particularly important.

THE CONTEXT: AMBIVALENT MULTILATERALISM

No matter which political party holds the Presidency in the United States, political leaders in both the executive branch and the Congress are likely to exhibit some degree of scepticism about the value of US support and involvement in peace operations. This scepticism coexists – often uneasily – with a general awareness among US officials that American leadership and/or participation in peace operations can be essential for the achievement of important foreign policy objectives. As described briefly below, the resulting US ambivalence is a product of history, philosophy and conceptions of national interest.

In recent years, reluctance has been reflected most notably by the US Congress in its posture toward UN controlled (i.e. blue-helmeted) operations.[1] In 1995, for example, Congress, disregarding the UN formula for peacekeeping assessments then in effect, mandated that the United States would contribute no more than 25 per cent to the cost of assessed UN peacekeeping operations – unilaterally lowering the US share from over 30 per cent. In addition, during much of the 1990s, Congress failed to appropriate funds necessary even to meet the 25 per cent requirement, resulting in a substantial accrual of arrears. Finally, even after the Congress had appropriated annual peacekeeping funds, powerful legislators regularly requested that the Administration withhold actual delivery of payments to the UN pending further congressional review. While the US executive branch is not legally required to comply with such requests, executive-legislative comity (and the desire to avoid future legislative restrictions on funding) resulted in Administration deference to congressional sentiment.

US reluctance is not limited to the issue of financial support, but has also included reservations about US military participation in UN controlled peacekeeping operations. As a practical matter, this has now evolved into a policy presumption against such participation of US troops (other than as military observers). As of early 2002, there were 15 UN peace operations around the world, deploying nearly 50,000 military personnel and civilian police. While the United States accounted for 741 of the international civilian police (CIVPOL) deployed in UN operations world wide, there were only 33 US soldiers deployed as part of UN operations, and 32 of them were military observers.

The US experience in Somalia, discussed in the section on Clinton Administration policy below, has certainly been a major contributor to its reluctance to contribute soldiers to blue-helmeted peace operations. But American reservations about UN peacekeeping, and multilateral institutions in general, are based on cultural, philosophical and geopolitical factors that go beyond the Somalia experience. Both American elites and the American public are much more jealous guardians of sovereignty than their European counterparts, and are far less prepared to enter multilateral arrangements (whether on peacekeeping operations, the International Criminal Court or the Kyoto Protocol) that impose automatic obligations or transfer decision-making from national-level institutions. In Congress, this reluctance has been accentuated by the view among some that UN mandated missions – from the Congo to Sierra Leone to East Timor (prior to September 1999) – have been over-ambitious, ineffective and/or otherwise misguided. Of course, congressional reluctance to support UN peace operations may also reflect a simple disinclination to spend tax dollars to address chaos and political turmoil in locations that are of modest strategic interest (or perceived interest) to the United States.

This is not to say that officials have been completely unprepared to deploy US troops in support of peace operations. In recent years, many thousands of US soldiers have been deployed to the Balkans and, in lesser numbers, to places like East Timor and Sinai. But such deployments have generally been characterized by two related elements. First, the deployments have, to a great extent, been justified in terms of traditional US national security requirements. In the case of the aforementioned examples, those requirements included stability in regions of great importance to the United States, as well as the imperatives of alliance management. While factors such as humanitarianism and 'international good citizenship' have played a role in most deployments (and, in fact, may have been necessary factors in US deployments to the Balkans and East Timor), they may not have been sufficient in and of themselves.

Second, when the US Government has been prepared to deploy the US military in peace operations, soldiers have generally been deployed as 'green helmets', where their command and control arrangements, as well as rules of engagement, are not subject to UN dictates. When contemplating substantial involvement, senior US officials certainly prefer operating under national command and control arrangements. More importantly, in the cases of the Balkans and East Timor, in particular, the security requirements that compelled US involvement went far beyond the practical capabilities of a UN mandated force.

Even green-helmeted US deployments, however, are undertaken reluctantly, and are subject to considerable domestic political debate. In the Balkans, for example, the key issues have been whether US (as opposed to European) interests justified the commitments of US forces, and whether European governments should be assuming even greater responsibilities for peace stabilization.

Beyond historical, philosophical and geopolitical factors that are debated among civilians, the US military, as an institution, has expressed a general reluctance toward participation in peace support operations for a variety of reasons. First, US military officials believe that US military forces should be held in reserve for the highest priority, war-fighting and conventional defence missions, and are concerned about the impact of peace support deployments on overall military readiness. This problem is compounded by what is seen as the intractable nature of many political conflicts, and the resulting requirements for deployments of indefinite duration. US military officials argue that, under such circumstances, soldiers are inevitably pressed into long-term public security and law enforcement missions for which they are ill-suited. Second, US officials note that, with some 250,000 overseas deployments in critical regions around the globe, US troops are already making unique contributions to international peace and security. If peace-keeping must be a role for the world's capable militaries, it is argued that the demands of burden-sharing suggest that others should take the lead in this area.

Even when the US military is prepared to consider involvement in peace operations, there remains a reluctance to consider deployment of ground troops. In addition to the factors described above, this reluctance may be attributable to two additional considerations. First, ground troop deployments in peace operations arguably do not make best use of America's comparative advantages – which, in addition to war fighting, are in the areas of transport, logistics, planning and intelligence. Second, US troops on the ground can become especially attractive targets for 'spoilers' – who well understand that undermining the will of the United States can go a long way toward compromising the will of the international community.

Before considering how these factors are currently evolving, it is worth reviewing their impact on policies of both the Clinton and Bush Administrations prior to the terrorist attacks of 11 September. This is because the range of views in each Administration has set much of the context for the current debates on peace operations underway in Washington.

THE CLINTON ADMINISTRATION

Over the course of the Clinton Administration, US policy on peace operations evolved, and varied, considerably. The Administration entered office with a commitment to 'assertive multilateralism', described by then-US ambassador to the United Nations, Madeleine Albright, as an effort to exercise 'both multilateral engagement and US leadership within collective bodies'.[2] The Administration initially envisaged a substantially enhanced role for peacekeeping within US foreign policy, including stepped-up activity by the Department of Defence and the US military.[3] The Administration elevated the stature of the peacekeeping function within the Department of Defence and drew up plans for the use of Department of Defence funds in support of certain UN mandated peace operations (which, in terms of US contributions, had traditionally been funded solely by the Department of State).

As is well known, however, the ambitious approach supported by the Clinton Administration was scaled back considerably, as a result of resistance within the Department of Defence and Congress. The attitudes of officials in both institutions were significantly affected by the 3 October 1993 deaths of American soldiers during the US military action designed to capture Somali warlord Mohamed Farid Aideed. The United States had acted in support of UNOSOM II, which had a broad mandate to assist in recreating Somali state institutions. Members of Congress argued that the mandate was too ambitious and, in any case, that the United States should not have expanded its own efforts beyond provision of humanitarian relief.

In May 1994, the Administration issued Presidential Decision Directive 25 (PDD 25), on Reforming Multilateral Peace Operations, which established criteria for US support and participation in peacekeeping.[4] Critics contended that the criteria were used to limit US support for peacekeeping post-Somalia, thereby fostering more restrictive policies in this area. Critics also argued that this more restrictive approach helped to deter an effective US response to the 1994 genocide in Rwanda.[5]

There is much truth to this criticism. It would be a mistake, however, to conclude that the Clinton Administration abandoned peacekeeping as an important tool of foreign policy after the Somalia experience. For one thing, PDD 25 committed the United States to active and systematic engagement with the UN in enhancing peacekeeping capabilities. It helped to promote improvements in the operations of the Department of Peacekeeping Operations, by asking tough questions and encouraging the development of more robust and focused planning. In addition, the criteria established by PDD 25 for US support and involvement in peacekeeping missions, which made reference to US national interests, availability of funding and other common sense factors, were, in fact, quite flexible. The presence of gross violations of human rights and humanitarian disasters were explicitly included as factors relevant to a US decision to support peace operations. In other words, the PDD did not, by its terms, dictate the outcome of any policy discussion on the wisdom of US involvement. It established guidelines to inform decision-making, but left to decision-makers the key responsibility of weighing the importance of the various factors in determining the appropriate US government response.

It is also worth noting that the Clinton Administration built on PDD 25, with Presidential Decision Directives relating to the organization of the government for responding to complex humanitarian emergencies, and to US policy on civilian police and administration of justice in the context of peace operations.[6] Each of these PDDs reflected a degree of engagement and commitment to multilateral peace operations.

More significantly, in Haiti, Bosnia and Herzegovina, and Kosovo, Clinton Administration-led military actions came with a clear expectation of a large-scale peace stabilization role for US forces in the follow-on peace stabilization operations. At the highest level within the Administration, action was informed by a strong belief in the connection between political turmoil, regional instability and US national security interests. It was also motivated by a commitment to promote humanitarian objectives when doing so could be accomplished at an acceptable cost and with modest risk to US soldiers.

THE BUSH ADMINISTRATION'S APPROACH PRIOR TO 11 SEPTEMBER

In his presidential campaign and during his first months in office, George W. Bush indicated clearly that he had little regard for the involvement of the US military in operations other than war. He was profoundly sceptical about the value of US military involvement in peace stabilization or, as he and others termed it, 'nation-building'. He and his advisors clearly believed that the Clinton Administration had lacked a strategic focus for US overseas deployments, and that a number of peace operation deployments (including the commitment of resources and the risks to US soldiers) were not merited in terms of the national security interests at stake.

The initial orientation of the Administration came as no surprise to those who had followed the foreign policy debates during the 2000 presidential campaign. In October 2000, at the second presidential debate, in Winston-Salem, North Carolina, candidate Bush mentioned deployments to Somalia and Haiti, and went on to say: 'I don't think our troops ought to be used for what's called nation-building. I think our troops ought to be used to fight and win war.'[7] At an event sponsored by ABC News in January 2000, he went further, betraying very limited sympathies for humanitarian action by the military:

> I think the President of the United States must clearly delineate what's in our national strategic interests. Europe is in our national strategic interest, the Far East is in our national strategic interest, our neighbourhood is in our national strategic interest, as is the Middle East. But beyond that ... the United States is going to have to work with ... organizations like the United Nations to encourage them to stop genocide. We should not ... send our troops to stop ethnic cleansing and genocide in nations outside our strategic interest. I don't like genocide and I don't like ethnic cleansing, but the President must set clear parameters as to where troops ought to be used and when they ought to be used.[8]

Finally, at a February 2000 rally in Kansas City, the candidate fore-shadowed his future Administration's position on the division of labour in Afghanistan between the US military and its allies, when he said: 'I'm going to clearly say to our friends if there's a conflict in your area, you can put the troops on the ground to be the peacekeepers, America will be the peacemaker.'[9]

Shortly after the Administration took office, Secretary of Defence Rumsfeld made clear his intention to cut back on overseas peacekeeping efforts. He told the *Washington Post* that deployments in the Balkans were straining the US military, adding: 'I darn well intend to do something about it.' He further noted that US soldiers did not enter the armed forces to 'be policemen in Bosnia', arguing that '[t]he military job was done there three or four years ago'.[10] Secretary Rumsfeld also took aim at deployments in the Sinai, reportedly pressing for withdrawal of US forces. In both cases, his positions did not prevail, but he made clear his intention to persevere.

It is worth noting that the Defence Department's position on US military involvement in peacekeeping did not translate into high-level hostility within the Administration toward the UN or its role in peacekeeping. In fact, the new Administration took a number of early actions to demonstrate its desire for a productive relationship with the UN. Shortly after assuming office, Secretary of State Colin Powell travelled to New York to meet with the Secretary-General, and not long thereafter, President Bush hosted the Secretary-General in Washington, whose re-election the President endorsed.

Other officials within the Administration also demonstrated an early desire for a positive US relationship with the UN. Testifying before Congress in May 2001, then Assistant Secretary of State David Welch said that 'the Bush Administration wants to clean the slate of the US–UN relationship ... such as by clearing $582 million in arrears and lifting the cap on peacekeeping payments.'[11] Welch's statement reflected endorsement by the new Administration of the deal reached in the closing days of the Clinton Administration on a new regime for UN regular and peacekeeping assessments.[12]

Notwithstanding these efforts, in the months preceding 11 September, the Administration did not secure legislation by Congress that would have permitted the $582 million payment to the UN. Nor did Congress act to lift the cap on peacekeeping assessments. Thus, while the Administration had indicated its desire to see each of these obstacles overcome, there were reasonable questions about the priority it had accorded to general support for UN peace stabilization efforts even when those efforts did not involve US troops. Additionally, the Administration seemed in no hurry to follow up aggressively on other non-military peace stabilization initiatives begun during the Clinton Administration, such as those reflected in PDD 71 relating to international civilian police and administration of justice.

THE IMPACT OF 11 SEPTEMBER: DO FAILED STATES NOW MATTER?

In the aftermath of 11 September and the military intervention in Afghanistan, proponents of active US involvement in international peace stabilization efforts and post-conflict peacebuilding have argued that Afghanistan's emergence as an area of vital US interests taught two compelling lessons. First, US national security can be dramatically affected by political turmoil and state failure in places that seem remote and irrelevant. And second, in many such locales, the United States ignores the challenge of serious engagement, and of nation-building, at its peril.[13]

In fact, advocates for engagement have argued that Afghanistan is the case in point. Between the years following the Soviet withdrawal and 11 September, none of the leaders of the world's major powers were clamouring to help Afghans create viable economic and political institutions. As far as the West was concerned, Afghanistan was a place of strategic irrelevance. On the other hand, there is now broad recognition that the political chaos into which Afghanistan descended after 1989 created a fertile environment for the emergence of the Taliban, and that an effective peace stabilization and international reconstruction effort will be a key element of a preventive strategy to ensure against the recurrence of a terrorist threat from Afghanistan.

A critical question is to what degree does the Bush Administration accept this assessment. Does the Administration believe that nation-building in societies plagued by political violence and state failure can be part of a strategy of prevention?

Indeed, as of mid-2002, there were some signs that President Bush and his Administration had been receptive to this proposition. Remarking to the Inter-American Development Bank on 14 March 2002, just prior to the international 'Financing for Development' conference in Monterrey, Mexico, the President proposed a major increase in US development assistance over a three-year period ending in 2006. On 19 March 2002, Administration officials indicated that this proposal would seek ultimately to increase annual US development assistance by $5 billion, or 50 per cent. In his 14 March 2002 announcement, the President drew an explicit link between underdevelopment, state failure and terrorism, and emphasized the importance of assistance efforts to address these issues:

> This growing divide between wealth and poverty, between opportunity and misery, is both a challenge to our compassion and a source of instability. We must confront it. We must include every African, every Asian, every Latin American, every Muslim, in an expanding circle of development. ...
>
> Poverty doesn't cause terrorism. Being poor doesn't make you a murderer. Most of the plotters of 11 September were raised in comfort. Yet, persistent poverty and oppression can lead to hopelessness and despair. And when governments fail to meet the most basic needs of their people, these failed states can become havens for terror.
>
> In Afghanistan, persistent poverty and war and chaos created conditions that allowed a terrorist regime to seize power. And in many other states around the world, poverty prevents governments from controlling their borders, policing their territory, and enforcing their laws. Development provides the resources to build hope and prosperity, and security.[14]

In the spring of 2002, the details of the Administration's new aid proposal were still being developed. Nonetheless, by his statement, the President recognized a link between state failure, poverty and political instability on the one hand, and US national security interests on the other. His comments essentially reflected a rhetorical acknowledgement that failed states do indeed matter. But did this acknowledgement translate into a different Administration approach toward peacekeeping in particular, and stabilization activities in general?

US INVOLVEMENT IN PEACE STABILIZATION IN AFGHANISTAN

For those eager to see some modification of US perspectives on peace operations after 11 September, Afghanistan offered very limited encouragement as of the spring of 2002. To be sure, the Bush Administration declared the importance of peace stabilization in Afghanistan, and even said it was willing to provide military support to the peacekeepers. In a press conference with interim Afghan leader Hamid Karzai in January 2002, President Bush said: 'We are committing help to the ISAF [the International Security Assistance Force]; in the form of logistical help, in the form of ... a kind of bailout if the troops get into trouble. We ... stand ready to help; in the form of intelligence.'[15]

The President's comments were echoed by Defence Secretary Rumsfeld, who said that the United States has – 'folks at Kandahar, folks at Bagram, we have folks in Kabul. We are helping the ISAF by providing intelligence, logistic and quick reaction force. We have Special Forces people embedded in most of the major Afghan units around the country.'[16] Furthermore, the *Washington Post* reported on 20 March 2002 that the United States was prepared to assist Turkish troops as they took command of the ISAF, through provision of military logistics (including transport and communications), as well as intelligence.[17] US Special Forces were to engage in training an Afghan security force, and the President's 2002 supplemental budget request contained proposed funds for the government of Turkey, as well as for training and salaries of Afghan soldiers, and for expenses of the Afghan Interim Administration and the office of the UN Special Representative.

All these elements signalled substantial US engagement. At the same time, there was little indication that the US military was playing (or would play) a significant role in the day-to-day activities of the peace stabilization force. US officials made clear that their priority would continue to be war fighting, with others taking responsibility for peacekeeping. Moreover, in the initial months of the ISAF deployment the Bush Administration resisted proposals to expand the ISAF beyond Kabul. On 28 March 2002, Secretary Rumsfeld said that '[f]oreign forces in another country are, as we all know, an anomaly'. The Secretary reportedly cited Bosnia as an example of a place where peacekeepers 'can allow circumstances to grow and develop around them in an anomalous way ... [so] that there's a fear that withdrawal could conceivably create an instability, or at least an uncertainty'.[18]

In Washington, Administration officials argued that a meaningful expansion of the ISAF was simply not feasible – that the requirements could outstrip the availability of capable troops.[19] Moreover, they contended that a modest expansion with less than high-quality troops would put the ISAF at risk without demonstrably enhancing security. They did acknowledge that training would not likely have an impact for many months, and that security outside Kabul would be a critical issue in the intervening period.

With these concerns in mind, some US officials discussed deployment of small numbers of US troops to areas outside of Kabul to discourage conflict among warlords,[20] and perhaps to play a role in mediation among them.[21] One inference was that these troops might be among (or perhaps added to) the Special Forces 'embedded in Afghan units' to which Secretary Rumsfeld had alluded.[22] However, given the Pentagon's reluctance to consider US participation in the ISAF, it was unlikely that the liaison mission that some US officials envisaged for US forces would play a broad and systemic role in maintaining public security outside of Kabul.

By May 2002, the United States position on security in Afghanistan had become the subject of serious debate in Washington. At that time, the UN Security Council approved a six-month extension of the ISAF, but did not authorize an expansion beyond Kabul and surrounding areas.[23] Increasingly, members of the US Congress questioned the Administration's approach, with the Chairman of the Senate Foreign Relations Committee, Joseph Biden, urging ISAF expansion.[24] At the same time, the ranking Democrat on the International Relations Committee in the House of Representatives, Tom Lantos, offered a legislative amendment to require President Bush to provide a plan to the Congress explaining how his Administration intended to address the security situation in Afghanistan. It was significant that Henry Hyde, the Republican Chairman of the Committee, supported the amendment, which was included in an Afghanistan aid bill.[25]

POST-11 SEPTEMBER MILITARY INVOLVEMENT IN PEACE OPERATIONS BEYOND AFGHANISTAN

Advocates of greater US engagement in peace operations contend that the events in Afghanistan justify deployments in other regions at risk of instability. In Bosnia and Kosovo, for example, fragile political institutions remain threatened by both transnational crime and international terrorism. Many argue that the intensive involvement of the international community in the

Balkans has been critical in combating these threats directly, and in beginning to build accountable local institutions to do the job in the future. Moreover, the presence of credible forces has helped to ensure an environment of stability in which a political development process, of sorts, can take place.

At least one senior US military official on the ground, General H. Steven Blum, serving as commander of the US forces at Eagle Base in Tuzla in March 2002, asserted the importance of the US military role on the ground. Speaking of the presence of US troops, he said, '[I]f we leave, this place will implode. ... Bosnia would be an even more dangerous place for Europe and for us, because it would be a haven for terrorists.'[26]

At the same time, even after the events of 11 September, there were few indications of alteration of the Pentagon's desire to hasten withdrawal of US troops from the Balkans. In a December 2001 speech to the North Atlantic Council, Secretary Rumsfeld reaffirmed this perspective, when he attributed the continuing NATO requirements to a civilian implementation effort that had lagged behind, and emphasized the need to 'work together to fashion a new, restructured and smaller force in Bosnia over the period ahead – and to see that stability is preserved by assuring that a replacement capacity is ready to take its place. I suggest we commit to do so by no later than 2002.'[27]

This is not to suggest that the United States would move unilaterally, especially in the context of operations that are deemed important by allies. In fact, US officials went to great lengths to assure allies that the United States would act in concert with them on Balkan issues. But the Rumsfeld statement did underscore the Bush Administration's scepticism about a long-term role for military forces, in general, and the US military, in particular, in peace stabilization operations. Of course, the Rumsfeld statement may also have reflected the general desire to enhance combat readiness in the post-11 September environment.

It is certainly conceivable, indeed likely, that the United States will provide specified support for peace operations when officials believe those operations promote US national security, or when US involvement is deemed very important to allies. Not only has this been the case in the Balkans; but it was also true in East Timor, where the government of Australia made clear the importance it attached to tangible US support for the INTERFET deployment.[28] But it is also worth noting that each of those operations were initiated by a Clinton Administration far more inclined to see value in US military involvement in peace operations. And no matter what the philosophical inclinations of senior civilian officials, such military support will come in the context of the general scepticism that prevails in the Pentagon.

When it is provided, US military involvement is unlikely to come in the form of blue-helmeted soldiers, but rather as green-helmeted deployments. As discussed above, this enables the US military to avoid issues relating to operational control of US forces, and allows the military to more easily dictate the terms of participation. In fact, by June 2002, there was considerable potential that the de facto presumption against US involvement in blue-helmeted peace operations was about to be enshrined in official policy, given the advent of the International Criminal Court (ICC) – an institution the Bush Administration has defined as a potential threat to US interests.[29]

The Bush Administration argued that US soldiers participating in UN missions should not be subjected to ICC investigations for actions taken in the context of those missions. During a UN Security Council debate on a resolution authorizing a post-independence, UN follow-on mission in East Timor, US officials sought a provision to exempt UN personnel (including American blue-helmets) in East Timor from the jurisdiction of the ICC.[30] At the time, the United States had only three UN military observers in East Timor, but with the impending entry into force of the ICC Treaty in July 2002,[31] US officials felt it important to establish the principle that US personnel not be vulnerable to action by the ICC.[32] The US position did not prevail in the Council, and, as of May 2002, US officials suggested that the absence of such a safeguard against ICC prosecution could mean the end of (the already very limited) US military participation in UN mandated operations.

Even if the Bush Administration were to establish a policy against US military participation in UN mandated peace operations, this restriction is not likely to be extended to US green-helmeted deployments in support of peace operations, especially as such deployments in recent years have often reflected important national security interests. Officials would be loath to accept what they perceive as ICC-imposed restraints on US freedom of action. On the other hand, because it increases the perceived risks of US involvement, the ICC factor will create another obstacle to US involvement in green-helmeted operations (and another policy hurdle for US proponents of engagement to overcome in internal policy deliberations).

FINANCIAL AND DIPLOMATIC SUPPORT

The issue of US financial and diplomatic support for peacekeeping (including payment of UN peacekeeping assessments) is distinct from the question of US military involvement in peace operations. On the issue of such support, a post-11 September assessment reveals some apparent modifications in approach. These modifications may well have reflected an appreciation among Bush Administration officials that greater support for multilateral institutions can enhance the prospects that other governments will embrace US policy objectives. But here again, modifications in approach do not translate into unambiguous enthusiasm for peacekeeping.

After the events of September, and in the lead-up to the President's address to the UN General Assembly in November 2001, the Administration was able to secure congressional support for payment of $582 million in US arrears. In addition, as of late March 2002, the Department of State reported that there were no congressional 'holds' on peacekeeping payments to the UN, and US officials expressed optimism that the Congress would lift the statutory 25 per cent cap on US contributions. This news – and the heightened level of Administration activity it seemed to reflect – demonstrated recognition by senior officials of the importance of enhancing the relationship with the UN and member states at a time when the United States was seeking support for common efforts against terrorism. It also reflected the fact that senior officials within the Bush Administration – and especially within the Department of State – did not share the hostility toward UN peacekeeping operations that has come from congressional members of the President's party. The progress achieved by the Administration with the Congress might also have been attributable to the ability of a Republican President to persuade Republican members of Congress to support (or at least not actively oppose) the UN.

At the same time, the high-level political support for funding UN activities did not seem to be reflected throughout the Administration and, in particular, at the working level where many important decisions about funding were made. In its budget for the 2003 fiscal year (1 October 2002– 1 October 2003), the Bush Administration proposed cutting assessed peacekeeping contributions from about $844 million to about $725 million, and cutting discretionary funding for non-assessed peace operations from $135 million to $108 million. As part of these latter cuts, the Administration planned reductions in US support for bilateral training of African peacekeepers. At a time when instability in many parts of the continent had encouraged illegality and political turmoil, it was fair to ask whether these numbers should have been increased rather than reduced.[33]

An analysis prepared by the Washington-based Henry L. Stimson Centre provided a useful critique of the Administration's calculations.[34] The proposed budget would have been adequate only if funding requirements for nearly all of the then-current 15 UN peacekeeping operations were reduced. The proposal also assumed no unanticipated costs (such as a larger UN role in Afghanistan), and did not provide funds to support implementation of further UN institutional reforms that would be funded by assessed contributions.[35]

Similarly, as of May 2002, the Administration had given little indication of an intention to raise the profile or the priority of efforts to develop US capacity to support the non-military dimensions of peacekeeping. To be sure, working level officials indicated that the Administration continued to pursue capacity-building objectives of PDD 71 (on civilian police and administration of justice).[36] Nearly two years into the Administration, however, there still had been no high-level, formal endorsement of the PDD, or a significant policy statement or initiative outlining a strategy in this area.

CONCLUSION

The events of 11 September 2001 and their aftermath do appear to have promoted some alteration in US perspectives on issues relating to peace stabilization. First, the Bush Administration more clearly recognized that 'failed states' do matter – that US engagement in reconstruction and development is more than a humanitarian imperative, but can also have important implications for regional security and stability. Second, as compared to its pre-11 September posture, the Administration provided enhanced support for UN peacekeeping activities, though the funding commitment reflected in proposals for 2003 was not robust. Finally, at least in the case of Afghanistan, the Administration acknowledged, though somewhat grudgingly, a modest US support role in peace stabilization.

On the other hand, as of mid-2002, it was difficult to argue that the fundamental perspective of the Administration on the US military's role in peace stabilization had shifted after the events of 11 September. That view consisted of a general resistance to any significant and long-term responsibilities for US ground (or even support) troops in peace operations, a general belief that the military is ill-suited to play a role in ensuring public security, and, as a result, a general desire to secure early military withdrawal when troops have been thrust into a peace support role. The US military seemed to reaffirm these perspectives in May 2002, with a preliminary decision to close the US Army's Peacekeeping Institute.[37] Officials indicated that its functions – which had included training and the development of doctrine on peace operations – would be assumed by other US Army entities, but the signal sent by the Army's action (and the acceptance of such action by senior political leadership) demonstrated the general orientation of the Bush Administration on these issues.

Similarly, and as mentioned directly above, there was no discernible expansion of efforts to develop US or UN capacities to engage effectively in the non-military dimensions of peace operations.

As of mid-2002, the key question was whether this general approach by the Administration was sustainable over time. For example, at a point when a severely burdened British military was asked by the United States to deploy combat troops in addition to troops for peace stabilization, was it reasonable – diplomatically or operationally – for US troops to eschew any such role? Moreover, as a general matter, does this reluctance (and resulting non-involvement) deprive the international community of signals of political resolve that can be critical for the success of operations of geopolitical significance? Finally, given the likelihood that imperatives of alliance management and national security will require some US peacekeeping deployments, does prudence not require that the military be more engaged in planning and training with friendly governments on peace stabilization issues?

In the midst of the Washington debate on these very issues, a report by the Washington-based Peace Through Law Education Fund suggested some answers to these questions.[38] The report describes the views of veteran commanders from the United States and its allies who have acted in a range of operations, from the Persian Gulf to East Timor. According to the report, these leaders generally believe, *inter alia*, that military engagement in peace operations will be a key factor in the war against terrorism, that the United States must be a player on the ground, that peace operations enhance the professional qualifications of soldiers, and that the military must take the lead in establishing law and order in the early phases of a peace operation.

The report represented a very useful contribution to the broader discussion about the direction of US national security policy in the aftermath of 11 September. And while the report's perspectives appeared at variance to the Administration's posture in mid-2002, the discussion within Washington policy circles about the importance of peace operations – and their connection to other post-11 September challenges – will continue. The debate is a welcome one, as these are critically important issues that have profound implications for peace and security both overseas and at home.

NOTES

1. UN ('blue-helmeted') operations are under the operational control of a UN commander, and are funded by assessed contributions of UN member states. 'Green-helmeted' operations involve troops under the command and control of national (or regional authorities) and are not funded through UN assessments. In recent years, green-helmeted operations have generally been authorized or otherwise sanctioned by the UN Security Council.

2. See Ivo H. Daalder, 'Knowing When to Say No: The Development of US Policy for Peacekeeping', in William J. Durch (ed.), *UN Peacekeeping, American Politics, and the Uncivil Wars of the 1990s,* New York: St. Martin's Press, 1996, pp. 35–67.

3. Ibid., pp. 41–2.

4. A summary of PDD 25 accessed at http://clinton2.nara.gov/WH/EOP/NSC/html/documents/NSCDoc1.html.

5. See, for example, Samantha Power, 'Bystanders to Genocide', *The Atlantic Monthly,* Vol. 288, No. 2, Sept. 2001, pp. 84–108.

6. These were designated as PDD 56 (Managing Complex Contingency Operations, 1997) and PDDL 71 (Strengthening Criminal Justice Systems in Support of Peace Operations and Other Complex Contingencies, 2000).

7. Second Presidential Debate, 11 Oct. 2000, accessed at http://www.foreignpolicy2000.org/library/.

8. ABC News-sponsored Roundtable on Confederate Flag and Iowa Caucuses, 23 Jan. 2000, accessed at http://www.foreignpolicy2000.org/library/.

9. Statement on Defence at Campaign Rally in Kansas City, 22 Feb. 2000, accessed at http://www.foreignpolicy2000.org/library/.

10. CNN, 'Albright Blasts Rumsfeld Comments on Bosnia', 22 May 2001, accessed at http://www.cnn.com/2001/US/05/22/albright.rumsfeld/.

11. C. David Welch, Statement for the Record, Subcommittee on Commerce, Justice, State, and the Judiciary Committee on Appropriations, US House of Representatives, 10 May 2001, accessed at http://usinfo.state.gov/topical/pol/usandun/01051001.htm.

12. The Congress had conditioned the $582 million arrears payment upon successful completion of negotiations on assessments, including reduction in US peacekeeping assessments to 25 per cent. Although the agreement reached by the Clinton Administration at the UN did not quite reach the 25 per cent target, it did result in a substantial reduction in US assessments (with the expectation that Congress would accept the result). Welch's reference to the 'cap' referred to separate legislation, enacted by Congress in 1995, that unilaterally set payments of assessed peacekeeping operations at 25 per cent of the total cost. Thus, the Administration needed congressional action on two issues: first, action to permit payment of the $582 million in arrears despite the fact that the assessment rate had not been reduced to 25 per cent; and second, action to lift the 25 per cent cap on ongoing and future payments of US peacekeeping assessments.

13. One can fairly question whether Afghanistan under the Taliban constituted a 'failed state', given the considerable control over population and territory exercised by the Taliban leadership. However, the discussion and analysis in this section is relevant whether or not pre-11 September Afghanistan is regarded as a failed state.

14. Presiden Bush's speech on Global Development, Inter-American Development Bank, Washington DC, 14 March 2002.

15. Bush and Karzai press conference, accessed at http://www.whitehouse.gov/news/releases/2002/01020020128-13.v.smil.

16. Pamela Hess, 'US Attacks Reluctance to Fund Afghan Army', *UPI,* 28 Mar. 2002.

17. Alan Sipress, 'Peacekeepers Won't Go Beyond Kabul, Cheney Says', *The Washington Post,* 20 Mar. 2002.

18. Pamela Hess, 'US Attacks Reluctance to Fund Afghan Army'.

19. Interviews with Administration officials with responsibilities for peacekeeping policy.

20. Sally Buzbee, 'US Troops to Remain in Afghanistan', *Associated Press,* 28 Mar. 2002.

21. Ben Barber, 'US Resists Putting GIs Among Warlords', *The Washington Times*, 11 Mar. 2002.

22. Hess, 'US Attacks Reluctance'.

23. UN Security Council Resolution 1413. The resolution was an extension of the authorization provided under UN Security Council Resolution 1386.

24. 'Senator Biden Proposes $130 Million for Security in Afghanistan', press release issued by Senate Foreign Relations Committee, May 2002.

25. 'Lantos wins vote forcing Administration to address immediate Afghan security needs: Lantos Amendment to "Afghanistan Freedom Support Act" highlights shortcomings of Bush Afghanistan strategy', US House of Representatives, 21 May 2002, International Relations Committee, Democratic Office Press release accessed at http://www.house.gov/international_relations/democratic/press_afghan_amdt.html. Ultimately, the Bush Administration modified its position on ISAF expansion, indicating it did not oppose efforts to expand the force. The modification took place after this chapter was prepared.

26. Matthew Kaminski, 'Anti-Terrorism Requires Nation Building', *The Wall Street Journal*, 15 Mar. 2002, p. A10.

27. Statement as Delivered by Secretary of Defence Donald Rumsfeld, Brussels, Belgium, 18 December 2001, accessed at http://www.defenselink.mil/speeches/2001/s20011218-secdef1.html.

28. These sentiments were articulated most forcefully by the Australian Prime Minister in early September 1999. See for example, transcript of the Prime Minister's press conference, 10 Sept. 1999. At the time, Australian and American officials in Washington were in active dialogue about the nature of US support. As the senior White House advisor on peacekeeping policy, the author was deeply involved in those discussions.

29. See Under Secretary of State for Political Affairs Marc Grossman speech at CSIS, 6 May 2002, accessed at http://www.csis.org/events/grossman.PDF.

30. Colum Lynch, 'US Seeks Court Immunity For E. Timor Peacekeepers', *The Washington Post*, 15 May 2002, p. A22.

31. With the attainment of 60 ratifications, accomplished in April 2002, the treaty entered into force on 1 July 2002.

32. The US also had 78 civilian police deployed in East Timor as of 30 April 2002. Moreover, other US citizens may well have been among the UN personnel in East Timor. While press reports indicated that the US sought an exemption for *all* UN personnel (i.e. military and civilian), the author's conversations with US officials suggest that the principal US concern was US troops. For a discussion of the diplomacy surrounding this issue, see Colum Lynch, 'US Peacekeepers May Leave E. Timor', *The Washington Post*, 17 May 2002, p. A20; Somini Sengupta, 'US Fails in UN to Exempt Peacekeepers From New Court', *The New York Times*, 18 May 2002, p. A4; and Elizabeth Neuffer, 'US Pushes to Keep Its Troops Exempt from World Court', *Boston Globe*, 23 May 2002, p. A1.

33. In June 2002, these proposals were still under consideration by the US Congress.

34. Peace Operations Factsheet Series, 'US Funding for Peace Operations: A Look at the FY03 Budget Request & Selected State Department Programs', The Henry L. Stimson Centre, Feb. 2002, accessed at http://www.stimson.org/fopo/?SN=FP20011221175.

35. It should be noted that the fiscal year 2002 supplemental budget request did include monies for peacekeeping and related functions, but it was not clear how much of these funds would be available for 2003 requirements.

36. Discussions in Washington involving Administration officials.

37. Robert Burns, 'Army will close military's only office devoted to peacekeeping', *Associated*

Press, 31 May 2002. This decision was apparently reversed in mid-2003, just prior to publication (and well after preparation of this chapter).

38. *A Force for Peace and Security, US and Allied Commanders' Views of the Military's Role in Peace Operations and the Impact on Terrorism of States in Conflict*, Peace Through Law Education Fund (PTLEF), Washington DC, 2002. The project was led by Edith B. Wilkie and Beth C. DeGrasse, President and Executive Director, respectively, of PTLEF. Senior Fellow Colonel Richard Roan (USMC-ret.) was the primary interviewer, and General Wesley K. Clark (USA-ret.) acted as the project's senior advisor.

———◄◦►———

THREE

NATO's Shifting Priorities: From Peace Support Operations to Counter-Terrorism

Dick A. Leurdijk

The terror attacks on the territory of the United States on 11 September 2001 gave rise to a new appreciation of security threats: the scourge of war, which had been so characteristic for international relations in the previous century, had been replaced, at the beginning of a new millennium, by a newly identified 'scourge of international terrorism'. Moreover, simultaneously, it also led to a reinvigoration of the notion of the 'right to self-defence', a cornerstone of the international order, under completely new circumstances compared to the twentieth century.

The purpose of this essay is to identify the relevance of international terrorism as 'a new threat' for the North Atlantic Treaty Organization (NATO), as well as the possible shift from NATO's peace support operations to counter-terrorism activities.

Just like in the 1990s, when the Alliance, after the end of the cold war, had to adapt itself to a new security environment (and therefore to include 'peacekeeping' in its range of activities), in the aftermath of 11 September 2001, again, serious questions were raised about the relevance of an alliance that was originally conceived as a collective defence organization, built on the notion, as contained in the famous article 5, that an armed attack against one or more of the Allies shall be considered an attack against them all.

THE RIGHT TO SELF-DEFENCE: THE INVOCATION OF ARTICLE 5 IN NATO'S RESPONSE TO 11 SEPTEMBER

It is striking that in the immediate aftermath of the terror attacks of 11 September 2001, there was a broad, worldwide consensus within the international community, both in condemning the attacks and in supporting the justification for a response by referring to the right to self-defence. Within three days, the US Congress, arguing that the attacks of 11 September 2001 'render it both necessary and appropriate that the United States exercise its right to self-defence', basically, gave the President a blank cheque for the use of US armed forces, by authorizing him

> to use all necessary and appropriate force against those nations, organizations, or persons he determines planned, authorized, committed, or aided the terrorist attacks that occurred on September 11, 2001, or harboured such organizations or persons, in order to prevent any future acts of international terrorism against the United States by such nations, organizations or persons.[1]

Apart from the broad bi-partisan consensus among policy-makers in Washington on a US response, the United States initiated steps internationally to prepare the groundwork for the war on international terrorism. The decision-making process, at the time, thus had two functions: it had the effect of laying the basis for the legal justification of the use of force, while, simultaneously, providing the political support that the United States was seeking as part of its efforts to establish a so-called 'broad coalition' in the proclaimed military and non-military fight against international terrorism. On 12 September 2001, the UN Security Council, in adopting resolution 1368, recognized 'the inherent right of individual or collective self-defence in accordance with the [UN] Charter'. Although one can argue about the legal niceties of the text, the resolution, by referring to article 51 of the UN Charter, was widely interpreted as a tacit approval or consent by the permanent members of the Council of the US position. It did not provide for an explicit authorization of the use of force. At the same time, however, there is no requirement whatsoever for a UN member state, exercising its right to self-defence, to ask for such an authorization. This is not a disqualification of the UN, as some observers suggested, but fits exactly within the meaning of article 51, when it says that 'nothing in the present Charter shall impair the inherent right of individual or collective self-defence if an armed attack occurs against a Member State of the United Nations'. In this sense, article 51 is a cornerstone of the UN system of collective security, just like article 5 of the Washington Treaty is the backbone of NATO as a collective defence organization.

After three emergency sessions, the North Atlantic Council (NAC), NATO's main policy-making organ, adopted a declaration in which it established a link between the attacks on the United States and article 5 of the NATO Treaty. The Council stated that it had agreed that:

if it is determined that this attack was directed from abroad against the United States, it shall be regarded as an action covered by article 5 of the Washington Treaty, which states that an armed attack against one or more of the Allies in Europe or North America shall be considered an attack against them all.[2]

For the first time in its history, the Alliance took a decision, which potentially cleared the way for invoking NATO's most crucial article as a collective defence organization – a provision that had not been applied for some 52 years. The potentially far-reaching character of the NAC's position, however, also raised a couple of fundamental legal questions, both with respect to the issue of the modalities of the 'determination', including the 'quality' of the necessary evidence, and the question of how far the attacks could be considered 'armed attacks' in the sense of article 5. For the time being, the main function of the statement of 12 September was its political expression of solidarity of the Allies with the United States. At the same time, however, the Allies had made an explicit reservation in defining their first official statement, namely by underlining that article 5 would be invoked only 'if it is determined that this attack was directed from abroad against the United States'. Thus, the formal decision to invoke article 5 was made dependent on the evidence to be presented by the US government. The second issue was related to the identification of the terror attacks as falling under the terms of article 5. The Council, however, justified its concerns about the attacks in terms of a legitimate interest for the Alliance, by referring to its own earlier decisions related to terrorism, as part of its commitment to collective self-defence:

The commitment to collective self-defence embodied in the Washington Treaty was first entered into in circumstances very different from those that exist now, but it remains no less valid and no less essential today, in a world subject to the scourge of international terrorism. When the Heads of State and Government of NATO met in Washington in 1999 [on the occasion of NATO's fiftieth anniversary], they paid tribute to the success of the Alliance in ensuring the freedom of its members during the cold war and in making possible a Europe that was whole and free. But they also recognized the existence of a wide variety of risks to security, some of them quite unlike those that had called NATO into existence. More specifically, they condemned terrorism as a serious threat to peace and stability and reaffirmed their determination to combat it in accordance with their commitments to one another, their international commitments and national legislation.[3]

On 2 October, after a classified briefing of the Council by US representatives, NATO Secretary General Lord Robertson, in an official statement on behalf of the member states, declared that the worldwide terrorist network of Al Qaeda, headed by Usama bin Laden and his key lieutenants and protected by the Taliban, was responsible for the events of 11 September. It was further said that it had been 'determined that the attack against the United States ... was directed from abroad and shall therefore be regarded as an action covered by article 5 of the Washington Treaty'.[4]

While NATO, thus, invoked article 5, it seems that the justification for taking such a far-reaching decision, where Lord Robertson only spoke in terms of 'an Al Qaeda role' in the 11 September attacks, without any further clarification, is extremely weak and not convincing. It leaves room for doubts, and it leaves the observer with a continuing uneasy feeling about the formal authorization for invoking article 5, also because of its implications for the debates at the national level of each of NATO's member states, including the positions taken by different parliaments. This feeling of uneasiness was only strengthened by the remarkable comments Robertson made, in October 2001, after a meeting with President Bush and US Secretary of State Colin Powell, that NATO should obtain further proof to provide its support to military action against targets other than Afghanistan.[5] According to Robertson, NATO only supported 'action which is related to those who are responsible for the events of 11 September'.[6]

In the meantime, the decision to invoke article 5 had only to a limited extent a military-operational impact as far as the input of the Alliance as such was concerned. It was followed-up by a first presentation by the United States of a list of requests concerning the assistance by the Allies, and not NATO as such, in the fight against international terrorism. NATO's response became mainly a question of opening up airspace, allowing the use of military bases, logistical support and intelligence cooperation.[7] In early October, the Allies collectively agreed to deploy five Airborne Warning and Control System (AWACS) radar-aircraft, belonging to NATO, in US airspace to relieve American aircraft of the same type, engaged in the anti-terrorist campaign.[8] Meanwhile, NATO's Standing Naval Force Atlantic (STANAVFORLANT) deployed a nine-vessel fleet to the eastern Mediterranean to 'provide NATO presence in the area'.

NATO's involvement in the war on terrorism, however, was not the first time that the Alliance was confronted with a new security environment.

THE END OF THE COLD WAR: THE NATO MOVE TO
PEACE SUPPORT OPERATIONS

The end of the cold war resulted in a new political and strategic environment in Europe and the world. As the importance of NATO's classical collective defence task diminished, the Alliance had to adapt from deterring a clearly defined threat to coping with what emerged to be an unpredictable and unstable security environment. This led to a new conception of security-risks and the realization that NATO's preoccupations, from then on, might be containing the consequences of conflicts in eastern Europe. This perception was incorporated in NATO's New Strategic Concept, approved in November 1991.[9]

NATO's new security-perception required new conceptual thinking. At the beginning of the 1990s, 'peacekeeping' thus became a key concern for the Alliance, mainly as a consequence of the combined effect of two factors: the general policy debates on NATO's future tasks; and the implications of the war in the former Yugoslavia for the Alliance. As part of its re-orientation on its future relevance, in June 1992, NATO endorsed the principle of its participation in peacekeeping, in particular by making available its assets to the Conference on Security and Cooperation in Europe (CSCE). Six months later, on 17 December 1992, the Allies, responding to a letter from the UN Secretary General to his NATO counterpart, officially confirmed the

> preparedness of our Alliance to support, on a case-by-case basis and in accordance with our own procedures, peacekeeping oper-ations under the authority of the UN Security Council, which has the primary responsibility for international peace and security. We are ready to respond positively to initiatives that the UN Secretary General might take to seek Alliance assistance in the implementation of UN Security Council Resolutions.[10]

In its 1994 Brussels summit declaration, the North Atlantic Council reconfirmed its political willingness to support the UN in achieving its goals, as contained in relevant Security Council resolutions.[11] In this adaptation process, during the 1990s, NATO had to define its relationship with the UN, a development which led to a number of basic legal questions, related to the nature of NATO as a regional organization under Chapter VIII of the UN Charter or not, or to the legal competence of NATO to act 'out-of-area' and to engage in 'non-article 5 activities'. Conceptually, NATO's cooperation with the UN raised the question as to what extent its character as a collective defence organization could be reconciled with its function as an instrument of collective security.

THE PRIMACY WITHIN NATO'S
'DUAL-TRACK' POLICY

NATO's shift to 'peacekeeping' in the early 1990s illustrated a shift of priorities from a collective defence organization to a collective security instrument. Some authors concluded that the shift essentially marked the transition of the Alliance with an initial unilateral goal to an organization characterized by a dual-track policy. This is not to say that NATO lost its character as a collective defence organization. It never did. One could even argue that the willingness of NATO to support the UN in its involvement in the former Yugoslavia provided the Atlantic partners with a rationale in terms of a collective defence reflex, and an opportunity to combine the reflex to 'contain conflicts in Eastern Europe' with the achievement of collective security goals in the context of the United Nations. Indeed, predominant in NATO's position, even within the sub-contracting model as applied in the Balkans, was the Alliance's assessment of NATO's legitimate interest in developments along the periphery of its area of operation. NATO's involvement in Bosnia and Herzegovina (since 1995), Kosovo (since 1999) and, finally, Macedonia (since 2001), with all together no less than 60,000 soldiers at its peak, basically meant that the Balkans had been incorporated in, and had become an integral part of NATO's area of operation. In the meantime, NATO has dug itself into the region and has become part of the power balance in the area, to such an extent that it has become extremely difficult, if not impossible, to withdraw its troops completely. So, while NATO has, over the past years, extended its area of operation, it has simultaneously underlined that, even with its dual-track policy, the primacy lies at the collective defence level. It is also this status as a collective defence organization which ultimately determines its relationships with the UN: underlining its own autonomy, NATO rejects any notion that it would be a 'Chapter VIII regional organization' subject to the veto of the Security Council. While this can be seen as the main lesson learned from Kosovo and the New Strategic Concept, the discussions in 1998 and 1999 basically reflected the extensive discussions that took place at the end of the 1940s, preceding the establishment of NATO, an issue that was no less sensitive than 50 years later. As Sir Henderson, a member of the Treaty drafting team, observed: 'Listening to the bitter debates on the Preamble, it was difficult at moments to believe in that singleness of spirit of the North Atlantic community which the Preamble itself was meant to epitomise and proclaim.'[12]

THE AFTERMATH OF 11 SEPTEMBER: FURTHER ADAPTATION OF NATO'S MISSION

One of the key issues addressed in this book turns around the impact of the events of 11 September on the way peace operations are perceived, and conducted. What has been such an impact on NATO in general, and on NATO's missions more specifically?

From the 'historic' decision to the necessity to adapt

As already indicated, NATO's most immediate response to the attacks was its decision to invoke article 5. Potentially, the implications could be far-reaching. NATO would, for the first time in its history, be called upon to respond in its capacity as a collective defence organization; and second, the decision opened the possibility of NATO becoming active in Afghanistan, far away from its traditional 'area-of-operation'. However, the actual follow-up to this 'historic' decision, mainly restricted to 'back-filling' by providing some AWACS aircraft,[13] was by far not so far-reaching as some might have suspected. Thus, as Philip Gordon wrote, 'while the original idea may have been that any invocation of article 5 would necessarily trigger a military operation planned by NATO planners and carried out under the authority of the Supreme Allied Commander Europe (SACEUR), there was no automatic or legal obligation to do so'.[14] Furthermore, it became evident that the Bush Administration had no intention of asking NATO to lead or even be closely involved. The United States preferred to keep tight control of the war on terrorism, and not only because its own national security interests were at stake. This position also reflected the key lesson of Operation Allied Force as a model of 'warfare by coalition', as well as the US realization of the existence of an increasing military-technological gap between the United States and European countries. The follow-up by NATO to its invoking article 5, furthermore, led many observers to raise serious questions about NATO's marginalization or irrelevance. Stanley Sloan rightly indicated that the question of how the Alliance would recover from 'the perception of irrelevance' would depend on responses to two questions:

> The first is whether or not the United States is willing and able to lead the Allies toward further adaptation of NATO's mission to make it more relevant to the terrorist challenge. The second is whether the European Allies recognise the need for such an adaptation and put the resources to improve their ability to contribute to future counter-terror operations.[15]

It took some time before the Alliance started a more fundamental discussion on the implications of the events of 11 September, recognizing the need for an adaptation to a new security environment. In this respect, the terrorist attacks on the United States were indeed a 'wake-up call', in Robertson's words. NATO had to transform itself again, in order 'to preserve our collective security'.[16]

As a matter of fact, it appeared that 'terrorism' was already part of NATO's agenda since 1991. In its 1991 Strategic Concept, member states had indicated that 'Alliance security interests can be affected by ... actions of terrorism.' Eight years later, the 1999 Strategic Concept said, in a more or less similar wording:

> Any armed attack on the territory of the Allies, from whatever direction, would be covered by articles 5 and 6 of the Washington Treaty. However, Alliance security must also take account of the global context. Alliance security interests can be affected by other risks of a wider nature, including acts of terrorism, sabotage and organized crime, and by the disruption of the flow of vital resources. The uncontrolled movement of large numbers of people, particularly as a consequence of armed conflicts, can also pose problems for security and stability affecting the Alliance.[17]

Thus, in retrospect, one could argue that conceptually, the notion of terrorism through the years had hardly changed. After the 'wake-up call' of 11 September, NATO's first response was the invoking of article 5, followed only by a limited military operationalization of its key provision. It was only at a later stage that NATO started an internal assessment of the long-term implications of terrorism as a new threat for its position as a collective defence organization. A first indication of this new thinking came out of the ministerial meeting of NATO in December 2001. NATO defence ministers spent most of their semi-annual ministerial meeting on 18 and 19 December conferring on the US-led war against terrorism.[18]

The new 'job description'

The December 2001 meeting, thus, became the beginning of another transitional phase in NATO's existence, aimed at formulating a new 'job description' in the light of the new threats. In defining the threats, Lord Robertson identified a link between terrorism and globalization by underlining how the new security threats took advantage of the infrastructure of globalization: 'Al Qaeda was based in Central Asia, led by a Saudi, trained personnel in Europe, and carried out operations from Africa to the United States. It used the Internet, and powerful new encryption software, to communicate freely, anywhere in the world. ... civil war and terrorism have been facilitated and sustained by illicit financial networks embedded in the world's legal financial system.'[19] The challenge for the international community was to dismantle this network.

This should be realized by what Robertson described as the establishment of a 'global security network, in which NATO would be only one of the partners'.[20] It was evident that the discussion of NATO's role in the war on terrorism would dominate its agenda in the months to come. The implications of this process, both in conceptual, political and operational terms, could be potentially far-reaching, with consequences for its character as a collective defence organization. At the same time, it was clear that the new thinking would be to a large extent determined by the thinking among policy-makers in Washington. In his State of the Union address, in January 2002, President Bush presented his assessment of the link between international terrorism and the proliferation of weapons of mass destruction (WMD) as a direct consequence of the existence of 'an axis of evil', consisting of Iran, Iraq and North Korea.[21] At a later occasion, Syria, Libya and Cuba would be added to the list of countries suspected of having links with terrorist organizations, thus facilitating the use of nuclear, chemical and biological weapons by these groups.[22] A few months later, there were even reports stating that, under the Nuclear Posture Review, this threat assessment in Washington was considered to justify the use of nuclear weapons as a counter terrorist tactic by an unprecedented lowering of the traditional 'nuclear threshold'. And on the occasion of the six-month anniversary of the 11 September attacks, President Bush stated that 'Now that the Taliban are gone and Al Qaeda has lost its home base for terrorism, we have entered the second stage of the war on terror', which he defined as 'a sustained campaign to deny sanctuary to terrorists who would threaten our citizens from anywhere in the world'.[23]

The outcome of NATO's adaptation process, in the words of US Deputy Secretary of Defence Paul Wolfowitz, was aimed at finding a new 'job description' for the Alliance, which he summarized as follows: 'Fighting terrorism, which has been so clearly linked to weapons of mass destruction, is part of NATO's basic job description: collective defence. ... article 5 threats can come from anywhere, in many forms.'[24] This meant an effort at re-positioning the Alliance as a collective defence organization under completely new circumstances in comparison to the time of NATO's establishment in 1949, implying profound conceptual and political adaptations with respect to the concept of self-defence, including the extension of its traditional 'out-of-area' notion and the notion of 'pre-emptive attacks'.

After the discussions in the 1990s on NATO's legitimacy in acting 'out-of-area' (in peace support operations among other activities) along its periphery, NATO's possible involvement in the war on terrorism could now very well take on a global dimension. In several interviews in March 2002, Robertson explicitly indicated that the necessary adaptation would also include a capability to operate far beyond NATO's own borders, presenting this as a kind of logical extension of NATO's presence in south eastern Europe in the preceding decade.[25]

While the invoking of article 5 by NATO opened up the possibility for NATO to start an operation in or around Afghanistan, it was almost inconceivable to see the Alliance becoming active so far away from its own borders. Although the Alliance as such was only indirectly involved in Operation Enduring Freedom (by providing a number of AWACS), at NATO headquarters, some planning was done with a view to a possible NATO role in providing logistical support and means of transport for the distribution of humanitarian help to the Afghan people in the post-Taliban era. In early December, however, the UNHCR announced that it did not need allied assistance. Furthermore, in April 2002, NATO offered help to Turkey to carry out the planning, in terms of force generation and force planning, for the International Security Assistance Force (ISAF), after Turkey agreed to take over the command from the United Kingdom in June 2002. 'It shows imagination on the part of the Allies', one Western diplomat said, adding that 'NATO doesn't have to choose between running the mission itself or doing nothing. There are other things it can do.'[26]

Now, in anticipation of the outcome of its present adaptation process, the prospect of NATO acting as a global player (a discussion that was preceded by similar talks on NATO's New Strategic Concept in 1999) is explicitly mentioned in the statements of Lord Robertson.

Towards a 'pre-emptive' strategy as a new approach to self-defence

Another conceptual adaptation could involve the acceptance of 'pre-emptive action' as part of NATO's strategy and as a consequence of a new approach to self-defence. Such an extension of the notion of self-defence was already implied in the letter to the UN on 7 October 2001, in which the Bush Administration wrote that the United States 'may find that our self-defence requires further actions with respect to other organizations and other States'.[27] In statements made by other members of the Administration in the following months, authorities like Rumsfeld and Wolfowitz elaborated on the issue of a so-called 'right of anticipatory self-defence', by saying, respectively, that 'Our goal is not simply to fight and win wars, it is to prevent them'[28] and, 'Self-defence requires prevention and sometimes pre-emption.'[29] In early June 2002, President Bush, speaking at West Point, stressed that the cold war doctrines of deterrence and containment had become obsolete, and required new thinking: 'the war on terrorism will not be won on the defensive. We must take the battle to the enemy, disrupt his plans, and confront the worst threats before they emerge', necessitating 'pre-emptive action when necessary to defend our liberty and to defend our lives.'[30] Like the US officials, Robertson completely disregarded the international legal questions that are being raised by such a broad conception of self-defence, explicitly included pre-emption as part of NATO's response to the threats of terrorist attacks, by saying that NATO forces should also be better able 'to deter, pre-empt and defeat' attacks, thus underlining the need to accelerate the development of new military capabilities.[31] Given the urgency of preventing the use of weapons of mass destruction against targets on the territory of the allies, it is believed that a traditional, purely reactive policy to future terrorist attacks would be inappropriate and necessitate preventive measures, ranging from sharing intelligence to pre-emptive attacks on states suspected of complicity in preparing terrorist activities, and including the possible use of weapons of mass destruction by terrorist groups.

The capability gap

For many now, there is general consensus that, from a military-operational point of view, one of the most persistent points of concern for NATO is the gap in military capabilities between the United States and its European allies. The Defence Capabilities Initiative (DCI) was specifically aimed at correcting this imbalance, but could not prevent the gap from becoming wider, threatening to become a constraining factor as far as NATO's military effectiveness is concerned. While this was already fully recognized before 11 September, the terror attacks only contributed to the realization of the urgency to correct this imbalance in the light of the war on terrorism.

In May 2002, Robertson said that NATO would 'guide and accelerate the development of new military capabilities', underlining that, 'in the face of new threats, our forces must be better able to deter, pre-empt and defeat attacks, and sustain operations over distance and time'.[32]

At the meeting of the NATO Military Committee in Chief of Staff session in early May 2002, NATO's member countries decided to develop a conceptual document on the common fight against terrorism (with national and international 'input'), to be submitted during the Prague Summit in

November 2002.[33] Among other things, the idea is to protect forces and populations against attacks from weapons of mass destruction and to provide for prevention capacities (above all consisting of intelligence sharing). At a NATO meeting in Reykjavik, in May 2002, it was agreed that NATO would no longer focus on the earlier 58 identified shortcomings as part of the DCI, but concentrate its efforts on five or six insufficiencies like heavy transportation material, communications, intelligence and precision-guided weapons.

The impact on NATO–Russia relations

The war on terrorism, as proclaimed in the aftermath of 11 September, would also have consequences for the relationship between NATO and the Russian Federation. Recognizing that international terrorism was a shared concern threatening their common security interests led to the official launching in May 2002 of a new relationship by the establishment of a new cooperation body, the NATO–Russia Council (NRC) 'at 20', in which the parties would sit around the table on an equal footing. The new council would deal with all non-article 5 topics of common interest, including counter-terrorism and the proliferation of WMD, and also peace operations. Decisions would be taken on the basis of consensus. The NRC would not deal with article 5 issues, this being the prerogative of NATO's membership.

Just like the issue of NATO's relationship with Russia, the question of the extension of NATO's membership was already on the Alliance's agenda before 11 September. One could argue that the events of 11 September, finally, were used to underline the need for both better relationships with Russia and to prepare NATO for a 'big bang', by admitting new members. The Bush Administration, arguing that a larger membership could be seen as an asset in the war on terrorism, wanted a robust enlargement. Late March 2002, after the Bucharest summit of countries seeking NATO membership, US Deputy Secretary of State, Richard Armitage, indicated that the United States wanted 'the most robust enlargement possible' at the Prague Summit in November.[34] At a meeting in Reykjavik, two months later, US Secretary of State, Colin Powell, using the same language, indicated that Washington wanted a robust NATO enlargement.[35]

The fight against terrorism: from first to second phase

The debate on NATO's contribution to the international campaign against terrorism dominated the Alliance's agenda in anticipation of the Prague Summit in November 2002. Simultaneously, however, that discussion was overshadowed by the perspective of the transition from the first phase in the war on terrorism (Afghanistan) to the second, and politically most sensitive, phase, a possible attack on Iraq, aimed at the removal of Saddam Hussein's regime ('regime change') and the dismantling of his weapons of mass destruction capabilities. While the idea of such an attack was strongly favoured by the Bush Administration, the European allies were much more hesitant, fearing the possible repercussions for the stability of the region and the situation worldwide. Instead, they favoured the return of UN weapons inspectors to the country, in an effort to prevent a possible large-scale military conflict with Baghdad. The discussion is also related to the issue of the justification for an attack on Iraq and NATO's possible involvement. In October 2001, Robertson, after high level talks in Washington, made it clear that, by invoking article 5 on 3 October, NATO only supported 'action which is related to those who are responsible for the events of 11 September'.[36] In other words, NATO should obtain further proof (further to the earlier evidence provided by the United States in October) before giving its support to military action against targets other than Afghanistan.[37]

The issue of NATO's position is the more sensitive since it became clear, given the statements made by the Bush Administration, that the question is no longer whether an attack on Iraq will take place, but only when. It is this perspective that leads many to believe that the transatlantic relationship will come under heavy pressure.

PEACE SUPPORT OPERATIONS IN THE BALKANS: NOT MUCH HAS CHANGED AFTER 11 SEPTEMBER

In the meantime, however, NATO members were still closely involved with the developments in the Balkans as a result of the presence of three ongoing peace support operations in Bosnia-Herzegovina, Kosovo and Macedonia. In all these cases, the Alliance both used its military presence in the area and its capacity to apply strong political pressure on parties to agree on a peaceful settlement of the inter-ethnic relationships.

A renewed yet adapted commitment

As a result, the security environment, as perceived by NATO, improved significantly, and was hardly influenced by the events of 11 September, with only one exception. Late in October 2001, SFOR arrested several people 'suspected of terrorist activity' in Bosnia and Herzegovina in connection with the threat against the US embassy in Sarajevo, which had caused the US and British embassies to close down momentarily. According to the *Sunday*

Times, the arrested men had plotted suicide attacks, with helicopters and small aircraft, against SFOR bases and mainly the Eagle Base where a majority of the 3,000 US soldiers of SFOR were located.[38] Realizing their vulnerability to attacks has only increased, force protection, since then, has become a major concern for NATO's peace support operations, requiring additional precautionary measures.

NATO's public statements on the situation in the Balkans, including in the aftermath of 11 September, have only underlined its continued determination to 'finish the jobs' there. Still, in June 2002, on the occasion of the regular half-yearly meetings of the North Atlantic Council in Defence Ministers Session, the Alliance issued a separate statement on NATO's continuing commitment to the region, saying, among other things:

> We remain committed to the territorial integrity and sovereignty of all countries in the Balkans and, in cooperation with Partners and other international organizations, to the pursuit of a peaceful, democratic and stable region. The continued presence of the NATO-led forces demonstrates our firm support for the rule of law, democratic institutions, basic human rights, return of refugees, tolerance, reconciliation and the peaceful resolution of disputes, and embodies our determination to oppose all violence, whether ethnically, politically, or criminally motivated.[39]

Yet, in the post-11 September environment, NATO was forced to balance its assessments of the progress made so far and the scope for rationalizing its missions in the region, while, at the same time, acknowledging the need to focus on and respond to new security threats, such as terrorism. The improved security situation in the region led NATO to decide to withdraw most heavy war fighting equipment, together with a reduction in the overall numbers of troops 'without weakening NATO's engagement'. NATO approved a series of changes to SFOR and KFOR, based on what was termed the 'Joint Operational Area Review',[40] with a view to 'providing a smaller, lighter, more mobile and flexible force posture, that will be more cost effective and better able to meet current challenges'.[41] After expiry of the 'silent procedure', NATO officially decided, on 10 May 2002, to carry out a restructuring of forces, including a phased reduction of both SFOR (12,000 troops by the end of 2002) and KFOR (29,000 by the end of June 2003).[42] These measures were presented as 'a sign of the achievements to date and the Alliance's confidence in the process' toward self-sustaining stability, suggesting the gradual handing-over of responsibilities to the local authorities.[43]

The need for regional and inter-institutional cooperation

The Alliance's determination to continue to contribute to the achievement of the international community's objectives is based on a number of pillars, such as engaging the Balkan countries politically, promoting regional cooperation, and focusing more strongly than before on cross-border problems, including terrorism. NATO's intentions to place a greater emphasis on engaging the countries in the region politically is taking place in the context of 'cooperative security' mechanisms, such as the Euro-Atlantic Partnership Council and the Partnership for Peace, earmarked as first steps on the road that, ultimately, would lead to full NATO membership. In a speech given in Zagreb, in June 2002, Robertson furthermore stressed the role of the regional governments, whom he considered to be 'primarily responsible for getting their house in order, for offering their populations a better future, and anchoring their countries in the Euro-Atlantic community'.[44]

This explains why NATO has been 'eager' to assist in the development of such regional initiatives as the 'Stability Pact for South East Europe'.[45] The Pact's main feature, indeed, is its broad approach. It is not restricted to separate flashpoints, like Kosovo, but directed at the region of south east Europe as a whole. It covers the whole spectrum of the necessary economic, political and security issues. And it is supported by a broad range of countries and organizations that would be able to provide a contribution. In this context, Lord Robertson, in his speech in Zagreb, gave an indication of NATO's contribution by pointing out that 'NATO has helped to set up programmes to assist discharged officers make the transition from military to civilian life, and projects to close military bases and convert them to civilian uses.'[46]

Furthermore, the whole range of NATO activities aimed at enhancing regional cooperation in the Balkans basically reflected an increasing cooperation between NATO and other international organizations in the field. In the 1990s, the Balkans had already become a testing ground for close cooperation between NATO, the United Nations, the OSCE and the European Union (EU). The unique cooperation between NATO and the EU in Macedonia in 2001, aimed at preventing the outbreak of a civil war, was seen as a first successful effort at common 'preventive diplomacy'. In June 2002, NATO participated in an OSCE conference on conflict prevention and the fight against terrorism, the first of its kind since 11 September, meant, among others, to identify areas where international organizations could be more proactive and work together.

Terrorism as a 'current security challenge'

The most immediate impact of the events of 11 September on NATO's peace support operations in the Balkans – apart from SFOR's earlier mentioned involvement in the apprehension of suspected terrorists in Bosnia – probably has been a stronger focus on security threats in the region with a cross-border character, which, indeed, also included terrorism. In NATO's December 2001 statement on the situation in the Balkans, there was only one reference to 'terrorism' in very general terms:

> Over the past six years, the challenges and threats have radically altered and operational areas are increasingly affected by common problems. Against this background we believe there is scope for developing a more regional approach to specific aspects of Balkan operations, including refugee returns, border security and combating organized crime, extremism and terrorism.[47]

Half a year later, in June 2002, in a similar statement on the Balkans, NATO's Defence Ministers became more specific and dedicated a separate paragraph to the issue of terrorism:

> We will ensure that our forces continue to pursue, within their current mandates and capabilities, actions against persons suspected to be terrorists, in coordination with appropriate civil authorities and other international organizations. The Alliance will remain engaged with local authorities to ensure that the region does not become a safe haven or way station for terrorists.[48]

Lord Robertson, emphasizing in his June 2002 statement, the (political and military) regional dimension of NATO's continued involvement, presented terrorism not as an isolated phenomenon, but as part of NATO's 'current security challenges' with a regional, cross-border character:

> The challenges I am referring to are of a regional, cross-border character [that] include the illegal movement of people, arms and drugs; criminal and terrorist gangs feeding from such criminal activities; and the way these gangs encourage both criminal aggression and ethnic and political violence.
> This is not a new task for NATO. For several years, KFOR has detected, disrupted and deterred the transfer of people and

matériel along Kosovo's borders and internal boundaries. The
Alliance has also been working with governments throughout the
region to help them address border security issues. And in the
wake of 11 September, our troops have clamped down hard on
terrorist cells.

The Alliance will increase its efforts in these areas in the future.
Because they are areas that are crucial to the security of South-
East Europe, and that of the wider Euro-Atlantic community.

Generally speaking, one can conclude that NATO's policy on the Balkans,
in the aftermath of 11 September, while remaining committed to the
implementation of the peace settlements, basically did not change. NATO's
involvement in the dismantling of terrorist cells is being presented in
a broader context, covering security threats of a regional, cross-border
character, in which SFOR and KFOR were already involved in the period
before 11 September. While NATO, rightly, is thus inclined to tone down
the impact of 11 September in its performance on the Balkans, the Alliance
certainly would not deny that, by promoting stability, it helps 'to deny
terrorist organizations the opportunity to take root', like the European
Council declared in June 2002. This argument is implied in NATO's analysis
that counter-terrorism action is only part of a broader set of cross-border
security challenges that should be tackled as a necessary precondition for
stability. In incorporating actions against suspected terrorists in its tasks,
NATO adopted an approach that might be applauded as pragmatic and
justified under the circumstances.

At the same time, however, it also raised questions, such as how far
NATO's counter-terror actions in the Balkans set a precedent. The most
pertinent question has to do with the easiness with which NATO accepted
its involvement in counter-terrorist actions as part of its mandate in the
Balkans, without opening up a discussion on 'mission creep', like in the case
of the extensive debates about SFOR's policy with regard to the apprehension of indicted war criminals.[49] It should be stressed, however, that all these
issues are only relevant as long as NATO is still willing to stay in the area.
Withdrawal and discussions about an exit strategy would be, under the
present circumstances, premature. At the same time, it cannot be taken for
granted that the presence of NATO in the Balkans is an automaticity,
both for military and political reasons, taking into account the possibility of
serious disagreements between the United States and its European allies. In
the aftermath of Operation Allied Force, serious disagreements came to the
surface among the member states in terms of 'coalition warfare', capability
gap and burden-sharing. In the US Congress, in spring 2000, the unease

about the open-ended US commitment to the Balkans culminated in the introduction of an amendment that urged the withdrawal of US forces by July 2001, as a result of the belief on Capitol Hill that stability in the Balkans is ultimately a concern for Europe rather than for the United States.[50] In June 2002, finally, the Bush Administration threatened to disengage itself from SFOR (and, by implication, any future UN peacekeeping operation as well as any multinational force authorized by the UN Security Council, including KFOR) if its service personnel did not get full immunity from surrendering or otherwise transferring to an international tribunal, such as the International Criminal Court (ICC), due to start its operations from 1 July 2002.

CONCLUSION

'There is no question that this is a defining, transformational year for NATO', declared the US ambassador to NATO, Nicholas Burns, in May 2002.[51] NATO's response to 11 September, first by invoking and operationalizing article 5, and then starting an adaptation process that is supposed to be finalized in November 2002, basically is aimed at re-positioning the Alliance as a collective defence organization with a new face. In historical perspective, the outcome of this process would bring NATO, after shifting its priorities in the 1990s from collective defence to collective security (through peace support operations), back again to its core business: collective defence, though in a new security environment and format. Strongly supported by Lord Robertson, all too eager to ensure the relevance of the organization under the motto 'modernise or marginalise', and linked to NATO's ongoing agenda, NATO has started a process of adaptation in several directions, conceptually and operationally.

Conceptually, the broad interpretation of self-defence, as proposed by the present US Administration, could change quite dramatically the traditional collective defence character of NATO. Operationally, in terms of the identification of new threat assessments and the required responses, the Alliance is in the process of defining its role in combating international terrorism, including the Al Qaeda network, the so-called sponsor states, and the linkage with weapons of mass destruction, while adapting its military capabilities. In geographical terms, it is considering an extension of its role far beyond its own borders, presenting itself as a global player, while extending its membership and establishing new relations with Russia.

Although this assessment still has to be confirmed by further developments, there are at least three moments that will have an impact on NATO's future status: the NATO summit in Prague in November 2002; a possible second terrorist attack, similar to or even greater than the events on 11 September, on the territory of one or more of the Allies; and the second phase in the war on international terrorism, focused on Iraq. It seems probable that NATO's agenda, for the longer term, will be dominated by its pre-occupation with counter-terrorism measures, a debate in which the United States already has taken the lead. Disagreements have emerged among the allies about the next steps in the campaign against terrorism, and are bound to stay there as long as NATO exists. The big challenge will be how to define NATO's continued *raison d'être* as a credible collective defence organization, working for the collective security good of its membership.

While NATO finds itself, generally speaking, in the process of shifting its priorities from peace support operations back again to 'article 5 pre-occupations', conceptually, its involvement in the current peace operations in the Balkans can be described as combining elements of collective defence, cooperative security and collective security. Although for the time being, the Alliance will certainly remain committed to maintaining stability in the Balkans, it seems likely that, as part of its adaptation process, it is aiming at disengaging itself, wherever possible and as soon as the situation permits, while being reluctant to accept new deployments. This explains both its eagerness to diminish its presence in the region and to leave the task of Operation Amber Fox in Macedonia to the European Union, if an agreement on EU–NATO relations is reached.

In the meantime, NATO's willingness to provide logistical assistance for humanitarian purposes in Afghanistan and its offer to help Turkey in planning its ISAF-command in Kabul provide illustrations of the kind of operations (while operationally more or less similar to the 'peace support operations' of the 1990s) that NATO is prepared, as part of its adaptation process, to execute in the new security environment, as long as there is a link to the fight against terrorism. The conclusion must be that peace support operations will probably have a much less prominent place in NATO's performance than in the 1990s. In other words, the biggest challenge for future peace support operations, probably, will be the war on terrorism.

NOTES

1. For the official text of the 'Joint Resolution', see my contribution, 'The Fight Against International Terrorism: the Right to Self-Defence, and the Involvement of the UN and NATO', in *Terrorism and Counter-terrorism: Insights and Perspectives after September 11*, The Hague: Netherlands Institute of International Relations ('Clingendael'), Dec. 2001, pp. 31–46.

2. Statement by the North Atlantic Council, Communiqué PR/CP (2001)124, 12 Sept. 2001.

3. *NATO Press Release* 124, 12 Sept. 2001.

4. Statement by NATO Secretary General, Lord Robertson, 2 Oct. 2001.

5. *Atlantic News*, No. 3328, 12 Oct. 2001.

6. *NRC Handelsblad*, 11 Oct. 2001.

7. *Atlantic News*, No. 3326, 5 Oct. 2001.

8. These aircraft are equipped by specialists from about ten allied countries. NATO also possesses a network of pipelines and several headquarters. In order to be able to use these capabilities, prior agreement of the North Atlantic Council is needed.

9. See David S. Yost, *NATO Transformed. The Alliance's New Roles in International Security*, Washington DC: United States Institute of Peace Press, 1998.

10. Final Communiqué of the Ministerial Meeting of the North Atlantic Council, Brussels, 17 Dec. 1992.

11. See Brussels Summit Declaration, Brussels, 11 Jan. 1994.

12. Sir Nicholas Henderson, *The Birth of NATO*, Boulder, CO: Westview, 1983.

13. On 30 April 2002, NATO Secretary General Lord Robertson announced that the US no longer needed NATO AWACS, by making the following statement: 'On the basis of material upgrades to the US air defence posture and enhanced cooperation between civil and military authorities, and following a recent US evaluation of homeland security requirements, the North Atlantic Council today agreed to terminate Operation Eagle Assist effective 16 May 2002. This decision concludes NATO's historic first deployment of assets in direct support of operations in the continental United States. It also reflects the North Atlantic Council's great satisfaction with the significant contribution to counter-terrorism efforts that the Allied Airborne Early Warning and Control (AWACS) aircraft have made. Operation Eagle Assist began on 9 October 2001 following the North Atlantic Council's 4 October decision to take measures to operationalize article 5 of the Washington Treaty. To date, 830 crew members from 13 NATO nations have patrolled US skies in the NATO AWACS for nearly 4,300 hours in over 360 operational sorties. This operation has been a concrete demonstration of Allied solidarity.' *Atlantic News*, No. 3381, 3 May 2002.

14. Philip H. Gordon, 'NATO after 11 September', *Survival*, Vol. 43, No. 4, Winter 2001–02, pp. 89–106.

15. Stanley R. Sloan: 'Crisis Response', *NATO Review*, Spring 2002.

16. Opening Statement by NATO Secretary General, Lord Robertson, at the Opening Session of the Meeting of the Council in Ministerial Session, Reykjavik, 14 May 2002.

17. The 'Alliance Strategic Concept', 24 Apr. 1999, para. 24.

18. See Opening Statement by NATO Secretary General, Lord Robertson, Meeting of the NAC in Defence Ministers Session, 18 Dec. 2001.

19. Lord Robertson, 'A New Security Network for the 21st Century', Speech at the Economist Conference, Athens, 17 Apr. 2002.

20. Ibid.

21. President Bush State of the Union Address, Washington DC, 29 Jan. 2002.

22. See for example 'Beyond the Axis of Evil', speech by Under Secretary of State John Bolton at the Heritage Foundation, 6 May 2002.

23. Remarks by the President on the Six-Month Anniversary of the 11 September Attacks, Washington DC, 11 Mar. 2002.

24. Speech by Paul Wolfowitz at the Munich Conference on Security Policy (Wehrkunde),

Munich, 2 Feb. 2002.

25. *De Volkskrant* (Dutch newspaper), 7 Mar. 2002.

26. *International Herald Tribune*, 12 Apr. 2002. Interestingly enough, this initiative coincided with proposals to deploy a NATO-led multinational force in the Middle East to supervise a cease-fire or peace agreement between Israelis and Palestinians, as the outcome of the second intifada. See, e.g.: Thomas L. Freedman, *International Herald Tribune*, 5 Sept. 2001; Fredrick Bonnart, *International Herald Tribune*, 16 Apr. 2002; and UN Secretary General, Kofi Annan, in *Financial Times*, 19 Apr. 2002. In an article in *The World Today*, in May 2002, Christopher Brewin, writing about the 'Endgame' in Cyprus, suggested that NATO could lead an international force to supervise a peace agreement on the island.

27. Letter dated 7 October 2001 from the Permanent Representative of the USA to the UN addressed to the President of the Security Council, S/2001/946, 7 Oct. 2001.

28. Donald Rumsfeld, National Defence University speech, Washington DC, 31 Jan. 2002.

29. Paul Wolfowitz quoting Donald Rumsfeld, Remarks made at the Munich Conference on Security Policy (Wehrkunde), 2 Feb. 2002.

30. Remarks by the President at 2002 Graduation Exercise of the US Military Academy, West Point, New York, 1 June 2002.

31. Opening Statement by NATO Secretary General, Lord Robertson at the Opening Session of the Meeting of the Council in Ministerial Session, Reykjavik, 14 May 2002.

32. Ibid.

33. *Atlantic News*, No. 3383, 11 May 2002.

34. *Atlantic News*, No. 3373, 4 Apr. 2002.

35. An eastern European diplomat was quoted as saying: 'He told us the enlargement should be a robust one, without saying what that means in terms of numbers. But the message was clear.' *International Herald Tribune*, 16 May 2002.

36. *NRC Handelsblad* (Dutch newspaper), 11 Oct. 2001.

37. *Atlantic News*, No. 3328, 12 Oct. 2001. In May 2002, at a classified NAC meeting, the United States reported on Iraq's activities to regain weapons of mass destruction since the UN weapons inspectors had to leave the country. According to diplomats, US Under-Secretary of State Richard Armitage acknowledged that the United States had no evidence concerning cooperation between Al Qaeda and Iraq with respect to weapons of mass destruction.

38. Most of those arrested had arrived in Bosnia after the 1992–95 war. See *Atlantic News*, No. 3333, 31 Oct. 2001.

39. Final communiqué of the meeting of the NAC in Defence Ministers Session held in Brussels on 6 June 2002. *Atlantic News*, No. 3391 (Annex), 8 June 2002.

40. 'Joint Operational Area Review', NATO, May 2002.

41. 'Statement on the Balkans', meeting of the NAC in Defence Ministers Session, Brussels, 6 June 2002.

42. The 'Statement on the Balkans' contains the details of the implementation plan for the restructuring in three phases, based on the Joint Operations Area (JOA) review for SFOR and KFOR. See *Atlantic News*, No. 3392 (Annex), 11 June 2002.

43. *Atlantic News*, No. 3383, 11 May 2002.

44. Speech by NATO Secretary General Lord Robertson at the international conference on 'Regional Stability and Cooperation: NATO, Croatia and South East Europe', Zagreb, Croatia, 24 June 2002.

45. The 'Stability Pact for South East Europe' is a broad-based international programme,

adopted after the Kosovo crisis in 1999 at the initiative of the European Union, and aimed at establishing stability in the Balkans, thereby, ultimately, creating the conditions for an integration of the region both into the European Union and the Euro-Atlantic (NATO) structures.

46. Speech by NATO Secretary General Lord Robertson at 'Regional Stability' Conference.
47. Statement on the Situation in the Balkans, meeting of the NAC in Defence Ministers Session, Brussels, 18 Dec. 2001. *Atlantic News*, No. 3347 (Annex), 20 Dec. 2001.
43. 'Statement on the Balkans', *Atlantic News*, No. 3392 (Annex), 11 June 2002.
49. See my contribution, 'Arresting War Criminals. The Establishment of an International Arresting Team: Fiction, Reality or Both?', in W. A. M. van Dijk and J. I. Hovens (eds), *Arresting War Criminals*, Special publication by the Royal Dutch Constabulary in cooperation with Wolf Legal Publishers, Nijmegen, 2001.
50. Ivo H. Daalder and Michael E. O'Hanlon, 'The United States in the Balkans: There to Stay', *The Washington Quarterly*, Vol. 23, No. 4, Autumn 2000.
51. *International Herald Tribune*, 21 May 2002.

⎯⎯⎯◄◦►⎯⎯⎯

FOUR

The European Union, Peace Operations and Terrorism

Jolyon Howorth

The central question to be addressed in this chapter is the following: have the events of 11 September 2001 brought about a re-appraisal by the European Union (EU) of the definition and requirements of 'peace operations'? The concept of 'peace operations' will take as a base-line the Petersberg tasks: 'humanitarian and rescue tasks; peacekeeping tasks; tasks of combat forces in crisis management, including peacemaking'. These tasks were devised in 1992 to cover the type of security policy operation which had become necessary in the Balkans and they have essentially (to date) been restricted to that type of operation, ranging from low intensity missions such as the policing of Mostar to high intensity combat such as in Kosovo.

However, the terrorist attacks on New York and Washington introduced into the security equation a new element which does not easily fit with crisis management tasks as traditionally defined. Petersberg tasks have tended to assume the identity and localization of an adversary (or at least of a problem or crisis to be 'managed'), the availability of appropriate instruments, a clear operational plan and an eventual political objective. They have also assumed on the part of the 'adversary' a clear political objective, which can be countered through a strategic plan. It is not obvious that combating terrorism fits easily into these parameters.

This chapter takes it as axiomatic that, since 11 September 2001, the EU must factor into its security policy – and indeed into its defence policy – the prospect of a terrorist attack, somewhere on the territory of the member states, either by organized terror networks such as Al Qaeda or by state actors making weapons of mass destruction available to non-state actors. At the extraordinary meeting of the European Council on 21 September 2001, it was declared that 'Terrorism is a real challenge to the world and to Europe. The European Council has decided that *the fight against* terrorism will, more than ever, be a priority objective of the European Union' (author's italics).[1]

The chapter therefore addresses three interconnected issues. First, in what ways has 11 September 2001 changed anything fundamental in the EU's approach to security and defence? Second, assuming that there will now be a focus on combating terrorism, does such a focus call on a different range of instruments and processes from those considered appropriate for conducting traditional Petersberg tasks? In other words, is the Union now faced with two interconnected but distinct security tasks, one linked to Petersberg and one linked to the fight against terrorism? Third, how does this new terrorist factor affect cooperation between the EU and the US and what impact will it have on European Security and Defence Policy (ESDP) and on NATO?

WHAT CHANGED ON 11 SEPTEMBER?

Some have argued that very little has changed, and that, despite the surface drama, the basic problems in international relations (of which coping with terrorism and the sources of terrorism have always been, and are still, but one) remain as before.[2] Others have insisted that the world changed fundamentally on 11 September, especially when combined with and set in the context of the (recent) end of the cold war.[3] A third school of thought interprets 11 September more as a factor of intense acceleration of already emerging trends than as an abrupt and qualitative leap into a new and unfamiliar security context.[4] Although there are elements of truth in all three of these interpretations, the reality probably lies somewhere between the second and the third approaches.

The fundamental problems driving international relations (such as the Middle East, world hunger, socio-national inequality, environmental crisis, and regional conflict in Asia and Africa) did not of course disappear on 11 September. But the attacks did bring to the world's attention the direct and immediate connection between these problems and the overall vulnerability of 'the west'. That connection poses many questions at the level of security and defence policy. First, how can nation states and regional regimes such as the EU go about interpreting the new situation and assessing the dominant threats to their citizens, resources and way of life? A serious exercise in threat assessment was, until June 2003, the major absentee at the Common Foreign and Security Policy (CFSP) and ESDP table. The Seville European Council in June 2002 recognized the urgency of conducting such an exercise.[5] Moreover, what does 11 September tell the EU about the territorial space which must henceforth be regarded as pertinent to the vital security interests of the member states? After the end of the cold war, there was an assumption that there was no longer any real *threat* to the EU and its member states emanating from beyond the frontiers of the Union. At most, *risks* of destabilization arising from ethnic violence and/or civil war were considered to lie along the entire periphery of the Union, from the Baltic Sea to Mauritania. Experience in the Balkans, giving rise to responses such as Petersberg, has been the unique model for managing this type of risk. Focus on the 'near abroad' was seen more in terms of managing stability than in terms of combating threats. The EU must now cast its eyes further afield to assess the reality of externally projected threats. Has the EU been forced to 'go global'? Second, in light of the threat assessment, the EU must reassess the nature of the instruments most appropriate to counter whatever threats are perceived. Given the explicit post-11 September erosion of the time-honoured distinction between external and internal security, and given the potential urgency of decision-making in an emergency, how best can nation states reorganize themselves and their different agencies so as to ensure effective security for all citizens? The EU will also need to reassess its institutional procedures to ensure that the current mix of the intergovernmental and the supranational is optimally configured to enhance rapid decision-making in the event of a crisis arising from newly perceived threats.

THREAT ASSESSMENT AND CFSP/ESDP GRAND STRATEGY

The *Presidency Report on European Security and Defence Policy* adopted at the Laeken European Council in December 2001 stated that the events of 11 September 'demonstrated that terrorism was a real challenge for Europe' and added that 'it is essential to speed up resolutely implementation of the ESDP'.[6] At Seville, in June 2002, the EU Council issued a 'Draft Declaration on the Contribution of CFSP, including ESDP, in the Fight against Terrorism' (Annex V). At the Thessaloniki EU Council meeting in June 2003, the EU finally adopted a 'Report on EU External Action in the Fight Against Terrorism (including CFSP/ESPD)'.[7] The EU's special Committee on Terrorism (COTER) finalized threat assessments for nine regions and 55 countries. A report on the links between extreme fundamentalism and terrorism was under discussion. Discussions with third countries both on political issues and on technical assistance were henceforth explicitly linked to counter-terrorism. Priority for technical assistance was accorded to Indonesia, Pakistan and the Philippines. Further work was undertaken on the freezing of terrorist assets and the list of target persons, groups and entities is regularly updated. Intense coordination was undertaken with international agencies such as the UN, regional fora such as ASEAN (Association of Southeast Asian Nations) and the Barcelona process, and other partners, such as NATO. Concrete cooperation intensified with Russia. A cross-pillar Compendium on threat assessment was undertaken, linking, notably ESDP and JHA. Less impressive progress was recorded in the possible interaction between the military capabilities under ESPD and the fight against terrorism, other than in the realm of civilian protection. The Council Secretariat prepared an assessment on chemical, biological, radiological and nuclear (CBRN) terrorism. All this work remained ongoing.

The approach to security policy post-11 September must begin with a robust EU-wide threat assessment. That the attacks took place against New York *and not* against Paris, London or Rome is not totally insignificant (all previous 'warning shots' with a clear Al Qaeda signature had targeted the United States). But this should not lull Europeans into a false sense of security.[8] Since 11 September, there has been a strange silence from the EU about the potential consequences for Europeans of the new age of terror. In a sense, while the US has discovered vulnerability and has fomented the war on terror, the EU has seemed to wish to avoid discussing it. Yet it is known that a hijacked Air France Airbus A-300 with 227 passengers on board was intended to crash into the Eiffel Tower in December 1994. Owing to a French intelligence breakthrough, the plot was discovered and the plane stormed by special forces while refuelling in Marseille.[9] Claims exist that a 'fifth' terrorist attack was planned for 11 September 2001 involving Indian pilots prepared to crash a British Airways jetliner onto the House of Commons in London.[10] Emergency measures have been taken to step up defences around the major oil refineries in Rotterdam and the nuclear reprocessing plants at Sellafield (UK) and La Hague (France), the latter now being protected with ground to air missiles.[11] But no concerted attempt has yet been made to determine the nature, degree and likelihood of any future terrorist attacks against the territory of an EU member state. And there has been all too little public discussion of threat assessment.

The terrorist networks, which carried out the 11 September attacks are more widespread, more organized and more ruthless than was previously suspected. Rarely since the formation of the modern state system have states perceived such a threat from overseas non-state actors. The ability of such non-state adversaries to fight 'netwars' is a totally new parameter in security planning.[12] The type of attack to which EU member states might be vulnerable can be either totally unexpected (the use of a passenger liner as a cruise missile[13]) or anticipated but difficult to prevent (documents captured in Afghanistan make it clear that Al Qaeda members have had extensive training in biological and chemical warfare[14]). States and regional regimes such as the EU now have a clear responsibility to provide for effective civil protection. This is all the more delicate a task in that the experience of 'sleeper cells' in the United States, and the surprising number of western passport-holders known to have fought for the Taliban and Al Qaeda suggest the need for greater internal intelligence, surveillance and preparedness. The concept of 'asymmetric warfare' was, prior to 11 September, essentially an abstraction. Since that date, it has become a dreadful reality.[15] Strategic surprise is the new challenge of the new century.

The third issue which will need to be addressed by the ongoing threat assessment exercise would be the potential strategic unity or disunity of the Euro-Atlantic area as suggested by 11 September. President Bush had no doubts in his address to Congress: 'Either you're with us or you're with the terrorists.'[16] If it is true that this is 'globalization's first war',[17] then EU member states may in some measure be forced into the 'for us or against us' mould which Bush announced. But it should not be overlooked either that most EU member states have tried, in one way or another, to persuade the US Administration that the solution to the problem cannot be sought exclusively *via* military instruments. The virtual 'war of words' which took place between the Europeans collectively and the Americans in the wake of the *Wehrkunde* and 'axis of evil' speeches of February 2002,[18] aggravated by the escalation of violence in the Middle East, simply revealed yet again that the two sides of the Atlantic do not view the world through the same strategic lens.[19] The issue of EU–US 'strategic wavelength' will continue to be a key factor in the long-drawn out struggle against terrorism which has just begun. It has recently been severely tested both in the Middle East and in the Gulf. In this context, it is all the more necessary for the EU member states to develop a lucid view of their real level of vulnerability relative to that of the United States. This will be a crucial factor in taking forward the embryonic CFSP (as distinct from, but not as opposed to, the ESDP).

In this regard, the broader international context will need to be properly evaluated. While it is true that 'the west' as a whole must feel more threatened from one source, the surprising international coalitions thrown up by 11 September have changed the strategic parameters in terms of threat assessment from other sources. The fact that the US military response in Afghanistan was 'authorized' by the UN Security Council (Resolution 1368) with the support of both Russia and China is an innovation in the history of 'the international community'. While there are those who are sceptical about the US commitment to durable coalition-building and nation-building,[20] no one can doubt that the EU will continue to view the preservation of international coalitions as the alpha and omega of foreign policy. The EU favours 'nation building' and helping 'failed states'[21] to rejoin the international community. The extraordinary meeting of the European Council on 21 September noted: 'The integration of all countries into a fair world system of security, prosperity and improved development is the condition for a strong and sustainable community for combating terrorism.' The policy implications of this stance – particularly as concerns EU–US relations – are considerable, but, to date, very uneven. The EU played a negligible role in the 2002 de-escalation of the India–Pakistan crisis (particularly odd given Britain's links with the area), but has, since early 2002, played a crucial and ever growing role in the stabilization of Afghanistan – a mission which the US government was at first reluctant even to countenance. In addition to the key UK and German–Dutch leadership of the International Security Assistance Force (ISAF), hundreds of German special forces and thousands of French troops were involved. Indeed, one of the more positive features of the EU's response to 11 September has been the willingness of member states not only to commit forces to unplanned-for hostile theatres, but also to be very flexible as to the type of commitment made.[22] EU relations with the Middle East, with the Gulf region, with Russia, South Asia, China and even Japan are bound to be different from the US relationship with these same areas. This will not fail to provoke significant ructions with the United States.[23] At the far end of the current EU self-interrogation over 11 September must lie a fundamental political question which at the time of writing remained unformulated. Does the EU simply wish to respond – in purely reactive mode – to crises not of its own choosing, as and when they arise? Or does it genuinely seek, as stated in the Saint-Malo Declaration, to 'play its full role on the international stage', in other words, to be able to help set the agenda of international crisis management?

As an integral part of the entire threat assessment exercise, the EU will need to devise a comprehensive, foreign-policy-driven 'grand strategy', based on a lucid analysis of the nature of terrorism in the contemporary world. Is Al Qaeda the modern equivalent of late nineteenth-century anarchism – a 'demonstration of nihilistic theological despair', striking blindly with a view to causing maximum destruction and destabilization but with no clear political ambition, the product of political failure and weakness rather than of successful proselytism and strength?[24] In that case, the only real strategic response (beyond addressing its social and economic roots) is to seek to contain it and to minimize its impact – while hunting it down. Or is it closer to a global form of early nineteenth-century socialism, based on inchoate ideology, angered by socio-economic injustice, fuelled with theological fervour and confident of stirring up a socio-religious war?[25] If so, then 'the west' (in addition to addressing the root causes) will be able to play on the divisions within the movement between 'revolutionaries' or maximalists and 'reformists' or compromisers. Or is Al Qaeda above all the manifestation of a power struggle within Islam?[26] The answers to these questions will inform the necessary grand strategy, and will allow for optimal integration of the entire panoply of instruments the EU can bring into play in its support: economic, financial, commercial, administrative, civil and diplomatic instruments as well as military.

In the elaboration of such a strategy, the EU will once again find itself in a state of tension with the US. This tension should not be exaggerated.[27] But nor should it be ignored. The EU will have to develop the confidence to stick to its guns in such situations. There will be times when choices will have to be made between the European approach and the US approach. This will be particularly tough for the UK, whose foreign policy preferences are explicitly predicated on the avoidance of any such choice. But the chances of continuing indefinitely with such a fence-sitting approach have diminished since 11 September. A leading UK commentator, Will Hutton, a long-time supporter of the British prime minister, sounded a dramatic warning note: 'Mr Blair should beware. Trying to be both pro-European and pro-American will no longer work. There is a choice and, if he does not make it, ultimately it will wreck his premiership. The Tories broke over Europe. Labour will break over too-slavish fealty to this US. This is the new political drama.'[28]

The EU's post-11 September threat assessment must therefore lead to a lucid analysis of the extent to which the interests of the United States and those of the EU are – and are not – compatible. While the EU may, as a result of 11 September, have no alternative but to go global, it should not do so by blindly following the US wherever it leads, as was sometimes implicit in the 'globalizing NATO debates' of the 1990s.[29] The formulating of a grand strategy must then necessarily lead to a review of needs, assets, capabilities and procedures.

FROM THREAT ASSESSMENT TO CONCRETE MEASURES

There are those who argue that 11 September will simply highlight the previous inadequacies of the ESDP, hamper its further development and accelerate the pace of EU–US 'resolidarization'.[30] Others argue that 'the impact of September 11 is likely to strengthen Europe's foreign and defence policies'.[31] This discussion is inexorably linked to the parallel debate on the future of NATO. In 2002 a new consensus seemed to emerge around the notion that the Alliance, while remaining in business, would cease to exist primarily as a military organization and would evolve into more of a political and diplomatic problem-solving forum. This seemed more likely to be the case as the United States shifted its military resources elsewhere in the world, as NATO enlargement embraced the remaining central and eastern Europe candidate countries and as the Alliance worked out some new kind of relationship with Russia.[32] Others saw NATO retaining a central military role.[33] The evidence for the former interpretation, notwithstanding the 2003 launch of the NATO Response Force, is considerable, but, for the moment, virtual rather than actual, theoretical rather than practical. The fact that the US military is likely to be less present in the European theatre than at any time since the Second World War can hardly act otherwise than as a stimulant to the development of the EU's own Rapid Reaction Force (RRF). The US decision in late June 2002 to withdraw its peacekeeping troops from Bosnia, if they were not granted immunity under the terms of reference of the newly established International Criminal Court, offered yet another illustration of this trend.[34] The package of Justice and Home Affairs (JHA) measures adopted by the EU on 21 September 2001 had profound integrationist implications.[35] The intense efforts by the EU at the Barcelona European Council in March 2002 and (less convincingly) at the Seville Council in June 2002 to formulate a coherent and constructive approach to the resolution of the Middle East crisis[36] failed to have any direct impact owing to the overwhelming importance of the US in the process. They nevertheless broke new ground for two reasons. First, because they demonstrated that the EU is capable of transcending its own internal divisions on the issue, and second because they posited the indivisibility of the international community's overall approach to a solution, highlighting the cohesion between the Mitchell Report/Tenet Plan,[37] the Russian involvement, and the role of the United Nations. In summer 2003, such community of purpose was finally noticed – and taken notice of – in Washington.

Notwithstanding European divisions over the Iraq war, ESDP made real progress in 2003. In May 2002, it successfully conducted its first crisis management exercise (CME02) testing procedures in the area of cross-pillar coherence of its many policy instruments. December 2002 saw resolution of the long-standing conundrum of cooperative relations between the EU and NATO ('Berlin Plus'); January 2003, the launch of an EU police mission in Bosnia; March 2003 the launch of 'Operation Concordia' in Macedonia. June 2003 witnessed the launch of 'Operation Artemis' in the Democratic Republic of Congo, the drafting of a document outlining a European Security Strategy and the adoption of an EU action plan to combat the proliferation of weapons of mass destruction (WMD). The EU also contributed to the launch of the Middle East 'Road Map'. Given that the ESDP is still in its infancy, that is not bad.

Yet progress on the military hardware of the European RRF was slow. There was little attempt to reassess the Helsinki Headline Goal targets in light of 11 September or indeed in light of the EU's own statements on terrorism of 21 September 2001. It remains the assumption that the Headline Goal 'force catalogue' from which might be drawn the elements of a European RRF constitutes the optimum range of the military instruments which might one day be required. The failure to review that assumption in light of 11 September is curious. The UK government initiated a 're-evaluation' of the 1998 Strategic Defence Review, but no other government followed suit. The December 2001 'Statement on Improving European Military Capabilities' – introducing the European Capability Action Plan (ECAP) – which was unveiled at Laeken is a blandly conservative (and highly optimistic) assessment of progress towards the basic Headline Goal.[38] Moreover, neither the 'Statement on Improving European Military Capabilities' nor the parallel 'Ministerial Police Capabilities Conference Declaration' issued at Laeken made the slightest reference to 11 September. The May 2003 Capabilities Conference plugged some gaps but acknowledged the persistence of others. An animated debate exists as to precisely what the EU's military 'operationality', which was trumpeted in December 2001, might amount to if a genuine crisis situation arose.[39] Some argue that 90 per cent of the military hardware called for by Helsinki has now been assembled and that the real problem is not military capacity but political will. Others insist that the Helsinki process has generated no new EU military hardware other than that which would have existed without it. While it is undoubtedly unrealistic to expect 'procurement miracles' to happen overnight, there is a growing consensus among independent defence experts that the EU's biggest failing is in the area of military hardware, not so much in the raw assets as in their coherence.[40]

In a situation where there are still no signs of defence ministers beginning to win the battle for resources against finance ministers, the amount to be allocated needs to be recalculated in light of 11 September. Rob de Wijk has demonstrated that the types of weapons systems required for conducting Petersberg tasks are very different from those which might be useful for combating terrorism.[41] And while it may be true that the Balkans are not yet entirely stabilized, that in a few years' time the EU may require the conventional capabilities currently planned under the Headline Goal, or that further force projection operations in Africa cannot be excluded (in other words, that Petersberg still remains a live issue), it is nevertheless essential sooner rather than later to take a critical approach to the coherence of force provision in the new context. The 17 working groups established in 2002 under the aegis of the European Union Military Committee essentially focused on traditional capabilities identified by the Improvements Conference as being in need of strengthening.[42] Some experts have argued in favour of de-emphasizing the procurement process defined by Petersberg (essentially product-driven) and of focusing instead on a new approach deriving from the threat assessment (essentially mission-driven or 'market-driven').[43] Such an approach might concentrate on assets such as special forces, elite forces, specialized forces such as follow-on forces for holding terrain, human intelligence and signals intelligence, and assets for engaging in network-centred warfare. While other experts continue to argue that the Headline Goal remains as valid as ever,[44] the events of 11 September have forced onto the agenda the ultimate heretical question: did the Headline Goal force catalogue (essentially a miniature version of the US arsenal) ever make sound military sense? Could the sort of war the US conducted in Afghanistan and Iraq be successfully conducted with a simpler scaled down version of US assets? Does the EU really need cruise missiles, aircraft carrier groups, the next generation of (possibly pilotless) fighter aircraft? For what? Such critics insist that it is increasingly difficult to envisage the core level Headline Goal forces ever being deployed in the way initially envisaged. What is more appropriate, in this view, are small, highly mobile, elite forces for limited high-intensity operations.[45] The EU, such analysts argue, is currently planning to fight today's conflicts with yesterday's weapons, whereas the real challenge is to plan, today, to fight tomorrow's conflicts with the day-after-tomorrow's weapons. A radical review of the genuine military needs of the EU in the post-11 September context could also go some way towards solving the budgetary problem in that savings in the high-technology area might allow for effective provision in the low-technology area.

There is a danger here that the EU, which replaced the Western European Union (WEU) precisely because of the latter's political and military inadequacy, will eventually replicate the WEU story, but with a different outcome. Faced with yet another incoherent and potentially useless military structure, EU member states might revert to nationalism or indeed seek to reinvent NATO (a NATO which was no longer the same organization as the one they edged away from in 1999).[46] This paradox has led some to suggest that concurrent moves within NATO, crystallized at the November 2002 Prague Summit with the launch of the multinational highly mobile NATO Response Force for deployment to overseas trouble-spots might constitute an overt challenge to the European RRF: if the EU proves incapable of mobilizing effective military intervention forces, NATO could well take over that role.[47] While the EU appears to dither, NATO is actively addressing both the war on terrorism and the reconfiguration of fighting units.[48] There is therefore a possibility that if the EU fails convincingly to deliver its promises on the capacities front, the 'autonomous' ESDP project could fizzle out and there might be a return to the ESDI-type scenarios of the mid-1990s, but in more favourable circumstances, avoiding the mistakes which led to the collapse of ESDI in 1997.[49]

History alone will tell. But the main problem for EU–US cooperation is likely to be technological incompatibility as the US widens the already yawning capabilities gap in the wake of the US *Quadrennial Defence Review* and the 2002 defence budget increases.[50] The task now is not so much to close the capabilities gap as to manage it. The main objective, as Lindley-French has argued, might well no longer be *interoperability*, since it is highly unlikely that the US military will be expecting significant inputs from allies, but *compatibility* along the entire mission spectrum from the strategic and mid-strategic levels for which the US army is planning, to the sub-strategic and 'Petersberg' levels for which the EU is preparing.[51] The March 2002 dispute over the replacement of the NATO mission in Macedonia by an EU mission exemplified perfectly the need for such a novel approach to the mission spectrum. It is unreasonable for US troops to be tied up in Macedonia. And it is incomprehensible that the EU should be so diffident about taking on a low-level Petersberg mission. Forging a new partnership with the United States will be a major – and highly sensitive – task in the years ahead.[52] But such a new partnership will entail drastic force and institutional restructuring. Again, this highlights the urgency of the EU's re-evaluation of its specific military requirements.

MILITARY AND NON-MILITARY INSTRUMENTS AND PROBLEMS OF COORDINATION

In evaluating the EU's absorption of the 'lessons of September 11' for the development of appropriate instruments with which to respond to new crisis scenarios, non-military instruments must of course also be factored in. The civilian instruments pre-existing in the form of EU aid and investment programmes, plus the new civil measures projected during the Swedish presidency (5,000 police officers for international assignments; strengthening – in crisis zones – of the rule of law, civilian administration and civil protection) are clearly important elements of nation-building, the necessary follow-up to any military intervention (or indeed an alternative to military instruments). Since 11 September, an entire new array of measures, mainly in the field of justice and home affairs, has been adopted to counter terrorism.[53] At the Seville European Council in June 2002, the main areas of progress recorded under ESDP were in the field of civilian instruments. A

'Rule of Law Commitment' conference held in Brussels on 16 May 2002 generated 282 officials (judges, prosecutors and administrators) deployable to post-conflict regions. Similar progress was reported on the Police Action Plan, but – curiously – little substantial progress was evident in the two other civilian areas – civil administration and civil protection. An ambitious systematic, cross-pillar approach to conflict prevention is being developed, emphasizing cooperation with international organizations and NGOs, intercultural dialogue, a new approach to trade ('everything-but-arms' – humorously referred to as the *Venus de Milo* approach), environmental policy, human and minority rights policies, international financial policies and new approaches to non-proliferation, disarmament and arms control. One of the most important future tasks for ESDP noted by the Seville Council will be 'developing the conceptual and practical aspects related to civil-military coordination'. The greatest danger for the ESDP would derive from tipping the balance too far in the direction of what are misleadingly labelled 'soft' policy instruments.[54] The 'carrot' is an extremely important instrument of international policy, but as history has shown time and again, deployed on its own it is considerably less effective than when backed by the stick. Coordination will be the greatest ESDP challenge of the future. This has obvious institutional implications.

Any wholesale review of needs would have to be conducted across the pillars in a variety of new inter-agency fora. For example, the High Representative for the CFSP, Javier Solana, has examined a proposal for the creation of an EU Intelligence Unit. Quite apart from the political and diplomatic problems involved in establishing such a unit,[55] it is obvious that it could only be done through tight coordination between ministries of Foreign Affairs, Defence, Interior, Justice and Finances.[56] Given the urgency of the post-11 September situation and the likelihood of the EU's having to take emergency measures rapidly, a comprehensive review of the institutional and procedural practices of the EU itself is also required. Some work was recorded on this at the Seville European Council, but it remained piecemeal and very limited. Attempts on the part of some member states – led by the Spanish presidency and strongly supported by Javier Solana – to create a new External Relations Council separate from the General Affairs Council (GAC) aroused the suspicion of others and the plan was watered down to one in which the GAC now meets in two separate guises, one to deal with CFSP proper and the other to deal with the remaining items on the agenda. Proposals formulated under the Giscard convention by France, Britain, Spain and Italy to replace the rotating presidency with a permanent President of the Council were strongly resisted by the smaller member states. And proposals put forward by the Commission and Germany to increase the use of qualified majority voting were blocked by France and the UK.[57] Everybody agrees on the need for greater ESDP efficiency in the post-11 September era, but there is precious little agreement on how to achieve it.

Several blueprints for a comprehensive review of institutional procedures have been published, based on debates which have been going on for some time within European think-tanks and other agencies.[58] The complex overlapping ESDP agencies of intergovernmentalism[59] require significant rationalization, including, in most scenarios, the abolition of the rotating presidency; the merging of the functions of High-Representative for CFSP and the Commissioner for External Relations, in order to create a position combining those of vice-president of the Commission and Secretary General of the Council; the creation of a Foreign Affairs Council to focus Ministry of Foreign Affairs (MFA) minds on foreign and security issues; the transformation of the General Affairs Council into a Council of European Ministers permanently based in Brussels; the institutionalization of the Council of Defence Ministers and of a permanent Brussels-based co-ordinating conference of higher officials from ministries of both Justice and the Interior; and the upgrading of both the Political and Security Committee (PSC) and the Policy Unit. The lack of progress on formalizing meetings of the Council of Defence Ministers[60] – albeit a task mandated by Laeken to the Spanish presidency – has highlighted the continuing strength of the interagency turf wars within each nation state. Such institutional blueprints are intended as much to galvanize discussion on the implications of 11 September as they are to instrumentalize reform. Most of the proposals currently being canvassed are vigorously opposed by more than one national capital. What is required above all is an assertion of political will. It is to be hoped that it will not take a devastating attack on an EU member state before such political will is refocused in the way it was (all too briefly) in the days and weeks immediately after 11 September.

CONCLUSION

The events of 11 September, rather like the break-up of Yugoslavia, were particularly ill-timed for the infant ESDP. Barely had the new structures been formed – essentially to deal with regional crisis management as under-stood in the context of Balkan peacekeeping – when a new and potentially more deadly global threat reared its head. It was not surprising that the EU, while making largely declaratory policy on counter-terrorism, should predominantly continue to develop its existing projects. But the questions thrown up in the wake of 11 September – questions about threat assessment, about the range and type of instruments required to deal with those threats, about relations with most regions and major countries in the world, and above all with the United States, about cooperation between ESDP and NATO, and about institutional reform – are so far-reaching and so interconnected that it will only be possible to tackle them progressively over a reasonable period of time. In the summer of 2003, ESDP was again at a turning point. Either it would get firmly to grips with the new challenges posed by 11 September and move robustly forward on the road to autonomy in a new partnership with NATO, or it would baulk at the enormity of the challenge and revert to earlier plans to deliver its military security exclusively as a junior partner in a hegemonic US-dominated Alliance. Time was of the essence. The Alliance was reforming rapidly and planning, in 2004, to incorporate seven new members. The future of ESDP, in summer 2003, hinged crucially on the political willpower of its member states both to learn and to apply the lessons of 11 September.

NOTES

1. Brussels Extraordinary European Council, 21 September 2001, *Conclusions and Plan of Action*, p. 1. At the Seville Council on 21–22 June 2002, a 'Draft Declaration on the Contribution of CFSP, including ESDP, in the Fight against Terrorism' was annexed to the *Presidency Conclusions* (Annex V, pp. 31–4). Both documents can be found on the Council website at www.europa.eu.int.
2. Pascal Boniface, *Les Leçons du 11 Septembre*, Paris: PUF, 2002; William Hopkinson, 'What is Security Now?', *Institute for Security Studies, WEU Newsletter*, No. 35, Oct. 2001.
3. François Heisbourg, *Hyperterrorisme: la nouvelle guerre*, Paris: Odile Jacob, 2001; Thérèse Delpech, *Politique du Chaos. L'autre face de la mondialisation*, Paris: Seuil, 2002.
4. Dominique David, *Sécurité: l'Après-New York*, Paris: Presses de Sciences Po, 2002.
5. The assessment exercise called for by Annex V to the *Presidency Conclusions* (para. 7) included a 'common evaluation of the terrorist threat against the Member States or the forces deployed under ESDP outside the Union in crisis management operations, including the threat posed by terrorist use of weapons of mass destruction'.
6. Council of the European Union, 'Draft Presidency Report on European Security and Defence Policy', Laeken, December 2001, para. 4.
7. Annex 1 to the *Presidency Conclusions*, Thessaloniki European Council, June 2003.
8. While in the immediate aftermath of 11 September opinion polls showed Europeans to be very concerned for their own security (according to *Le Figaro* of 15 Oct., 80 per cent of respondents were '*très inquiets*' or '*plutôt inquiets*' about European security, and 75 per cent feared a terrorist attack in France), a straw poll of doctoral students at *Sciences Po* in Paris in March 2002 revealed deep-rooted scepticism about the notion that France was in any way threatened.
9. Interview with senior French official. This incident is recounted in some detail in Rohan Gunaratna, *Inside Al Qaeda, Global Network of Terror*, London: Hurst, 2002, p. 123.

10. See Gunaratna, *Inside Al Qaeda*, pp. 119–20. Gunaratna also claims that further 11 September attacks were planned against the US embassy in Paris and, using nerve gas, against the European Parliament. All were foiled.

11. Interviews with EU and French officials. 'Nuclear Sites Get Armed Police', *The Times*, 5 July 2002.

12. David Ronfeldt and John Arquilla (eds), *Networks and Netwars: The Future of Terror, Crime and Militancy*, Santa Monica: RAND, 2001. On Al Qaeda's networks and strategy, see Gunaratna, *Inside Al Qaeda*, chs. 2 and 3, and Peter L. Bergen, *Inside the Secret World of Osama Bin Laden*, London: Weidenfeld & Nicholson, 2001.

13. However this is one form of attack whose success depended overwhelmingly on its unexpectedness. It would now be difficult to repeat the 11 September suicide hijackings in the same form.

14. Moreover, although the source of the anthrax attacks in September 2001 is still unknown, the author(s) of those attacks demonstrated beyond any doubt their effective lethality.

15. An enemy with no 'centre' can strike at the very heart of the west; killing thousands of civilians at a time when US war-fighting objectives involved 'zero death'; destroying the myth of US invulnerability not with Inter-Continental Ballistic Missiles (ICBMs) but with the most rustic of methods; offering the type of combat the west most dreads – based on an invisible enemy. On these elements of asymmetry, see Thérèse Delpech, 'The Imbalance of Terror', *The Washington Quarterly*, Winter 2002, Vol. 25, No. 1, pp. 31–40.

16. Newt Gingricht put this even more bluntly: 'There are only two teams on the planet for this war. There's the team that represents civilization and there's the team that represents terrorism. Just tell us which. There are no neutrals,' cited in Steven E. Miller, 'The End of Unilateralism. Or Unilateralism Redux?', *The Washington Quarterly*, Vol. 25, No. 1, Winter 2002, p. 19. See also R. W. Apple Jr., 'Stark Choice from Washington: Ally or Enemy in Global Assault', *International Herald Tribune*, 15–16 Sept. 2001.

17. Kurt M. Campbell, 'Globalization's First War?', *The Washington Quarterly*, Vol. 25, No. 1, Winter 2002, pp. 7–14.

18. For the February 2002 *Wehrkunde* speeches, see www.securityconference.de/anfang.asp. For George W. Bush's 2002 address on the State of the Union, see http://www.whitehouse.gov/news/releases/2002/01/20020129-11.html.

19. Chris Patten, 'Jaw-Jaw not War-War', *Financial Times*, 14 Feb. 2002; David Ignatius, 'The Transatlantic Rift is Getting Serious', *The Washington Post*, 15 Feb. 2002; Steven Erlanger, 'Europe Seethes as US Flies Solo in World Affairs', *The New York Times*, 23 Feb. 2002; William Pfaff, 'The NATO Allies are Drifting Apart', *International Herald Tribune*, 18 April 2002.

20. For Stephen E. Miller, 'The antiterrorist coalition is neither so necessary nor so valuable as to make those who set US policy likely to alter fundamental beliefs about international politics or abandon deeply-rooted policy priorities.' 'The End of Unilateralism', pp. 26–7. Many in the Bush Administration would subscribe to Charles Krauthammer's assertion that 'The American military is the world's premier fighting force. Peacekeeping is for others' ('We Don't Do Peacekeeping', *International Herald Tribune*, 10 Jan. 2002).

21. There is nothing purely idealistic about this. Raw interest is also involved since the EU is actually surrounded by failed states.

22. Interviews with senior British officials in the Foreign and Commonwealth Office (FCO) and the Ministry of Defence (MOD), Whitehall, July 2002. Most countries wished, for reasons of prestige, to send ground troops. But they proved equally willing to send trucks,

medical teams or other assets as required.

23. See, on this, Julian Lindley-French, 'Terms of Engagement: The Paradox of American Power and the Transatlantic Dilemma post-11 September', *Chaillot Paper* 52, Paris: EU-ISS, 2002.

24. Gilles Kepel, *Jihad: the Trail of Political Islam*, Berlin, IB Tauris, 2002; Malise Ruthven, *A Fury for God*, London: Granta, 2002; see also the recent analyses of Lawrence Freedman, 'The Coming War on Terrorism', in Lawrence Freedman (ed.), *Superterrorism: Policy Responses*, Oxford: Blackwell, 2002.

25. Clement M. Henry and Robert Springborg, *Globalization and the Politics of Development in the Middle East*, Cambridge University Press, 2001; see, for a discussion of these issues, Duncan Green and Matthew Griffith, 'Globalization and its Discontents', *International Affairs*, Vol. 78, No. 1, Jan. 2002, pp. 49–68.

26. Gunaratna, *Inside Al Qaeda*; James Piscatori (ed.), *Islamic Fundamentalisms and the Gulf Crisis*, University of Chicago Press, 1991. For an interpretation informed purely by cyclical trends in the history of Islam, see Malise Ruthven, 'The Eleventh of September and the Sudanese Mahdiya in the Context of Ibn Khaldun's Theory of Islamic History', *International Affairs*, Vol. 78, No. 2, April 2002, pp. 339–51.

27. Lawrence Freedman has argued that the 'anti-American litany in the West is fuelled by an old-left reading of US foreign policy that does not bear scrutiny – neither policy on Iraq, nor support for Israel fit the charges'. 'Blaming America', *Prospect*, Dec. 2001, pp. 34–7. For an alternative view, see Lindley-French, 'Terms of Engagement'.

28. *Observer*, London, 17 Feb. 2001. Hutton elaborates on this theme in his book, *The World We're In*, London: Little Brown, 2002.

29. Jenny Medcalf, 'Going Global? NATO, the EU and the "out-of-area" disputes in the 1990s', unpublished PhD dissertation, University of Bath, 2002.

30. Robert Dover, 'Reflections on the Role of the EU and the War against Terrorism', *Foreign Policy Network Newsletter*, Nov. 2001, pp. 2–3; Anand Menon, 'Why ESDP is Dangerous for the EU and the Atlantic Alliance', in Jolyon Howorth and John Keeler (eds), *Defending Europe: NATO and the Quest for European Autonomy*, London: Palgrave, 2003.

31. See Charles Grant, 'A Stronger European Foreign and Defence Policy', in Edward Bannerman et al., *Europe After September 11th*, London: Centre for European Reform, 2001, pp. 31–48; Hanna Ojanen, *Theories at a Loss. EU–NATO Fusion and the 'Low Politicisation' of Security and Defence in European Integration*, Helsinki: Finnish Institute of International Affairs, UPI Working Papers 35, 2002. See also my own alignment with this more positive interpretation (albeit for different reasons): 'CESDP after 11 September: from Short-term Confusion to Long-term Cohesion?', *EUSA Review*, Vol. 15, No. 1, Jan. 2002, pp. 1–4.

32. Anatole Lieven, 'The End of NATO', *Prospect*, Dec. 2001, pp. 14–15; Anthony Forster and William Wallace, 'What is NATO for?', *Survival*, Vol. 43, No. 4, 2002, pp. 107–22. See also, on the 'death of NATO' thesis, Christopher Layne, 'Death Knell for NATO?', *Policy Analysis*, Cato Institute, No. 394, 4 April 2001.

33. Philip H. Gordon, 'NATO After 11 September', *Survival*, Vol. 43, No. 4, Winter 2001–02.

34. See, on this incident, *Atlantic News*, No. 3397, 28 June 2002.

35. Heather Grabbe, 'Breaking New Ground in Internal Security', in Bannerman, *Europe After September 11th*, pp. 63–75.

36. The 'Declaration of Barcelona on the Middle East' appears as Annex I to the *Presidency Conclusions*, pp. 28–30. The Seville 'Declaration on the Middle East' appears as Annex VI of the *Presidency Conclusions*, pp. 35–6.

37. The Mitchell Report (officially called the Sharm El-Sheikh Fact-Finding Committee Final Report, released in April 2001) examined the causes of violence in Israel/Palestine and made recommendations on how to stop it. The Tenet Plan (officially called the Israeli–Palestinian Ceasefire and Security Plan, released in June 2001) is based on the Mitchell Report.

38. The 'Statement on Improving European Military Capabilities' appears as Annexe I to the *Draft Presidency Report on European Security and Defence Policy* which can be found at http://ue.eu.int/newsroom/newmain.asp?lang=1. The 'Declaration on the Operational Capability of the CESDP' is to be found as Annexe II to the *Presidency Conclusions*, pp. 27–9.

39. As exemplified by the lively but inconclusive exchanges between senior officials, military officers and security experts at the 4th Franco-British Defence Cooperation Conference held at Lancaster House, London, 3 July 2002.

40. 'Achieving the Helsinki Headline Goal', *Centre for Defence Studies Discussion Paper*, Kings College, University of London, Nov. 2001; International Institute for Strategic Studies, 'The European Rapid Reaction Force', *The Military Balance 2001–2002*, Oxford: Oxford University Press, 2001, pp. 283–91; Michael Alexander and Timothy Garden, 'The Arithmetic of Defence Policy', *International Affairs*, Vol. 77, No. 3, July 2001.

41. Rob de Wijk, 'The Limits of Military Power', *The Washington Quarterly*, Vol. 25, No. 1, Winter 2002, pp. 75–92.

42. Details in *Nouvelles Atlantiques*, No. 3364, 27 Feb. 2002, p. 4 and an update in Ibid., No. 3384, 16 May 2002. The groups were examining 24 of the 40 identified 'gaps' where EU inadequacy is considered most significant. It is true that some of these working groups are focusing on assets that are relevant to the new context (use of drones, strategic imagery, protection against ABC attacks, etc.) but this is not being coordinated with developments in other pillars.

43. Among others, Julian Lindley-French, Thomas Ries, Rob de Wijk, Thérèse Delpech at a conference of the EU Institute for Security Studies, 'European Defence after 11 September', 18 Mar. 2002. These views are exemplified by Maartje Rutten, 'Stagnation of the ESDP', *European Union Institute for Security Studies Newsletter* No. 1, Feb. 2002, pp. 2–3. Lindley-French has pioneered the distinction between 'product-led and market-led approaches', arguing in his *Chaillot Paper*, 'Terms of Engagement', that 'for the past ten years Europe has acted as though it only seemed prepared to recognise as much threat as it could afford' (p. 63).

44. Sir Timothy Garden, Lord John Roper, William Hopkinson, Stefano Silvestri, Gilles Andréani. Lindley-French himself – whose worries are more focused on the approach than on the outcome – also argues in favour of delivering the Headline Goal.

45. See Michael Clarke, 'War in the New International Order', *International Affairs*, Vol. 77, No. 3, July 2001.

46. The 'WEU-ization of the EU' paradox was originally formulated by Nicole Gnesotto.

47. David Wastell, 'US Plans NATO Rival to Blair's "Euro-army"', *Daily Telegraph*, 2 June 2002; 'Europe Joins Drive to Build NATO's Military Muscle', *The New York Times*, 4 June 2002; Bronislaw Geremek, Jacques Lanxade, Peter Mandelson, Margarita Mathiopoulos and Klaus Naumann, 'A Global Future for a Balanced NATO', *International Herald Tribune*, 6 June 2002.

48. In February 2002, the NATO Defence College in Rome held a conference on 'Military Role in Combating Terrorism' and later that month the EAPC held a similar seminar in Warsaw. For developments at the June ministerial meeting, see *Final Communiqué*

and *Statement on Capabilities*. Meeting of the North Atlantic Council in Defence Ministers Session, 6 June 2000 at http://www.nato.int/docu/pr/2002/p.02–172e.htm and http://www.nato.int/docu/pr/2002/p.02–174e.htm.

49. On the shift from ESDI to ESDP, see my 'European Integration and Defence: the Ultimate Challenge?', *Chaillot Paper* 43, Paris: WEU-ISS, 2000, pp. 22–30.

50. Etienne de Durand, 'The QDR and the Euro-US Capabilities Gap', Paper at IFRI Colloquium on Franco-American Relations, 21 Jan. 2002.

51. Lindley-French, 'Terms of Engagement', ch. 5, 'Re-engaging Transatlantic Security Relations'.

52. On this, see Robert E. Hunter, *The European Security and Defence Policy: NATO's Companion – or Competitor?*, Santa Monica: RAND, 2002.

53. Heather Grabbe, 'Breaking New Ground'. The measures include: intensified judicial and police cooperation; improved external border controls; common definition of terrorism; prevention of financing of terrorism; adoption of European arrest warrant; pooling of intelligence; common system of penalties.

54. In reality not 'soft' at all, but extremely difficult to implement, involving far more inputs over a far longer time period than 'simple' military campaigns.

55. The role of the UK would once again be sensitive since London benefits enormously from US intelligence – much of which it is explicitly prohibited from passing on to its EU partners. And yet an EU Intelligence Unit without the UK would be difficult to imagine.

56. See, on the need for cross-pillar coherence, Antonio Missiroli (ed.), *The Coherence of the CFSP*, WEU-ISS Occasional Paper No. 30, 2001; and Claire Piana, 'September 11th 2001: What Implications for the EU's CFSP/ESDP?', *Foreign Policy Network Newsletter*, Feb. 2002.

57. See Euractiv website (Euractiv.com), June 2002. Also see 'A Project for the European Union', Communication by the European Commission, Brussels, 22 May 2002, COM(2002) 247 final.

58. Steven Everts, *Shaping a Credible EU Foreign Policy*, London: CER, 2002; Jolyon Howorth, *The European Security Conundrum: Prospects for ESDP after 11 September 2001*, Paris: Notre Europe, 2002; Venusberg Group, *Enhancing the European Union as an International Actor*, Gütersloh: Bertelsmann, 2000. A broader reform programme is suggested by Heather Grabbe, 'Preparing the EU for 2004', *Centre for European Reform Policy Brief*, 2002. These issues are also, of course, at the heart of the work being carried out by the European Convention headed by Valéry Giscard d'Estaing.

59. Of which there are currently no fewer than *nine* involved in CFSP/ESDP decision-making. See Howorth, *The European Security Conundrum*, pp. 3–4.

60. A first formal meeting of the defence ministers had been scheduled in the wake of the Barcelona European Council in March 2002, but was vetoed by a handful of powerful foreign ministries reluctant to cede authority. The first formal meeting took place on 13 May in the context of the General Affairs Council, but no plans were laid to hold formal meetings of defence ministers independently of the GAC.

Part II:
Inside Peace Operations

Peace Operations and Governance: Lessons Learned and Perspectives

Winrich Kühne

In the weeks following 11 September 2001, debate in western countries seemed to lead to two agreed basic points. First, fighting terrorism is now of vital interest, not only for the United States, but also for its allies and the international community at large; resources, strategies, political will have to be focused accordingly. Second, fighting terrorism is not just about the pursuit and elimination of terrorists, their networks and supporting regimes, such as the Taliban in Afghanistan; it is also about tackling the basic causes of widespread frustration and anger in the Muslim world. Obviously, terrorist groups like Al Qaeda are prospering because of these frustrations.

There is less consensus between Americans and Europeans when it comes to the general root causes of terrorism by Muslim groups. European, but also many American analysts, point to the unresolved question of Palestine, the stationing of US troops on so-called holy Islamic soil in Saudi Arabia and the negative effects of globalization, particularly the widening gap between rich and poor, as such causes. These reinforce a feeling of anger and of being attacked by US-dominated forces of globalization – a feeling that Usama bin Laden successfully mobilized for justifying the 11 September attacks on the World Trade Center.

The United States and European states, however, agreed on another point: taking better care of war-torn, failed states is an important element of successfully fighting international terrorism. The total breakdown of governance and rule of law provides ideal operating conditions for terrorist networks. Apart from Afghanistan, forgotten conflicts like those in Somalia and Sudan returned to the international limelight. It was President Bush who then declared, after the bombing in Afghanistan had started, that America should have learned from past interventions in Afghanistan that it cannot simply withdraw when the military goal is achieved. European leaders agreed wholeheartedly.

This chapter will address this dimension of failed states caught in ethnic, religious and social strife. More precisely, it will look at current problems, the lessons learned, and perspectives regarding the key instrument the international community has developed over the last decades to handle violent conflict: peace operations, including peacebuilding. Finally, this chapter will question the extent to which the Americans and the Europeans, in their endeavour to stabilize post-Taliban Afghanistan, have implemented the lessons learned in the light of President Bush's forceful warning not to repeat past errors in war-torn Afghanistan.

FROM FIRST GENERATION PEACEKEEPING TO MULTIDIMENSIONAL, ROBUST THIRD GENERATION PEACE OPERATIONS

In his report *We, the People* for the Millennium General Assembly in the autumn of 2000, Secretary-General Kofi Annan was very explicit about the need for a profound rethinking of traditional peacekeeping: 'While traditional peacekeeping had focused mainly on monitoring cease-fires, today's complex operations are very different.'[1] Indeed, the character, dynamics and principles of peace operations have dramatically changed since the deployment of the first military observers of UN Truce Supervision Operation in the late 1940s and the first blue helmets (the UN Emergency Force) in the Sinai in the mid-1950s or UNFICYP (the UN Peacekeeping Force in Cyprus) in the mid-1960s. Today's operations in East Timor, Bosnia and Herzegovina, Kosovo, Sierra Leone and other places bear little resemblance to those early operations.

Conceptional clarity was a major advantage of this first generation of peace-keeping. Consent, neutrality and the non-use of force, except in cases of personal self-defence, were and are the well-known doctrinal pillars of this generation. Yet it suffered from one major disadvantage: in terms of conflict resolution, this first generation was static. Operations like UNEF and UNFICYP had no built-in mechanism for conflict resolution. During the cold war, the two blocks and their superpowers could only agree on halting violence to prevent the escalation of regional conflict into a global, possibly nuclear, confrontation. Agreeing on how to solve conflict was ruled out. Profound ideological antagonism and a zero-sum understanding of global strategic competition were insurmountable obstacles. The blue helmets were true children of the cold war and its specific dynamics. Many of the operations deployed in that period are still in theatre. A few years ago, efforts to withdraw UNFICYP from Cyprus failed dismally. UNEF on the Sinai had to be withdrawn, not because of success, but because of another bloody cycle of fighting between Arab states and Israel. In May 1967, Egypt ended its consent to the presence of UNEF troops and demanded their immediate withdrawal.

It was the end of the cold war in the late 1980s and the unlocking of the Security Council which paved the way for a second generation of operations. Suddenly, long-standing conflicts became solvable. This profoundly changed the character of peacekeeping operations. They became multidimensional and dynamic in terms of conflict resolution. The UN Transitional Assistance Group (UNTAG) in Namibia (1989–1990), UN Observer Mission in El Salvador (UNOSAL, 1991–95), UN Transitional Authority in Cambodia (UNTAC, 1992–93) and UN Operation in Mozambique (UNOMOZ, 1992–94) are further examples of this new, broadened type of peacekeeping. In contrast to the first generation, their mandates were no longer limited to the monitoring of ceasefires. Emergency aid, ensuring basic public security, infrastructure and administration as well as the rule of law, repatriation of refugees, disarmament, demobilization and reintegration (DDR) of armed groups, preparing and conducting elections on local and national levels as well as economic reconstruction and other non-military issues were added to the list of tasks. In his *An Agenda for Peace* in 1992, UN Secretary-General Boutros Boutros-Ghali coined the term 'post-conflict peacebuilding' for this complex and ambitious undertaking. It has become of strategic importance for the success of modern peace operations. Indeed, these missions aim beyond peacebuilding. Their ultimate purpose is nation-building and to re-establish governance, that is, to enable the local population to govern itself peacefully and democratically.

This development of peacekeeping into multidimensional peacebuilding and governance operations had two major implications. First, operations developed into an enormous complexity and diversity. Planning, organizing and conducting such missions became much more demanding. The chance of failure or of committing serious blunders grew considerably. Second, military forces were joined by a rising number of police and hundreds of civilian actors to accomplish the task of peacebuilding. Civil-military co-ordination, more precisely civilian, police and military coordination, became of prime importance.

In Namibia, Central America and Mozambique, these second generation operations achieved quick and remarkable successes in bringing peace and re-establishing governance. Unfortunately, this led to highly unrealistic expectations regarding the UN future role in ensuring international peace and security. Other operations, particularly the UN Operation in Somalia

(UNOSOM), the UN Assistance Mission in Rwanda (UNAMIR) and the UN Protection Force (UNPROFOR) in Bosnia and Herzegovina, ran into serious difficulties with tragic outcomes. The genocides in Rwanda and in Srebrenica inflicted an almost mortal blow to the UN's reputation as the world's supreme guardian of peace and human rights. In cases of civil war, ethnic-religious strife and state fragmentation, the solemn signing of peace or ceasefire agreements no longer meant an end to violence. In Somalia, Rwanda, Liberia, Bosnia and other places, hundreds of such agreements were broken. Local leaders had understood the new, post-Somalia game: please the world, in particular the west, by negotiating and signing such agreements, but do not care to honour them.

The peacekeepers, as well as their civilian counterparts, were confronted with all kinds of violence, perpetrated mainly by local leaders, warlords, militias and armed gangs. An abundance of small arms and light weapons left behind by the cold war and hordes of unemployed, hungry youths provided fertile ground for ongoing violence. There was no way to continue peacebuilding under these conditions. Increasing numbers of local and international civilian agency staff were killed. In the late 1990s, Secretary-General Kofi Annan warned the international public that the number of civilian casualties in peace operations had risen beyond that of soldiers.

Establishing and upholding a secure environment for humanitarian aid and socio-economic as well as political reconstruction became a primary demand on the soldiers and on the police. The old doctrine of non-use of force became untenable. Therefore, in Somalia, the Security Council felt compelled to provide UNOSOM II with a so-called robust mandate based on Chapter VII of the UN Charter, allowing for the limited use of force. UNPROFOR in the former Yugoslavia, the UN Mission in Haiti (UNMIH), the Implementation Force (IFOR) and Stabilization Force (SFOR) in Bosnia, the UN Transitional Administration in Eastern Slavonia (UNTAES) as well as the French Operation Turquoise in Rwanda, the Multinational Force in Haiti and an Inter-African Monitoring Force (MISAB) in the Central African Republic received similar authorization. The third generation of peacekeeping, now mostly called multidimensional (robust) peace support operations, had come into being.[2]

This form became the dominant mode of peace operations in the 1990s, despite the dramatic failure of UNOSOM II in Somalia in 1993. Predictions from inside the UN, including the then head of the Department of Peacekeeping Operations (DPKO) and future UN Secretary-General Kofi Annan, and from outside experts that robust peacekeeping had no future, were proven wrong. Rwanda, Angola as well as UNPROFOR in Bosnia and Herzegovina demonstrated that without robustness, there is hardly any chance of success.

Worse, the danger that the international community may contribute to mass killing and even genocide by deploying weak, half-hearted operations, became tragically apparent in these cases. In August 2000, a panel of eminent experts, chaired by Lakhdar Brahimi, drew a key conclusion in its report to the Secretary-General on improving UN peace operations: 'Robust rules of engagement, against those who renege on their commitments to a peace accord or otherwise seek to undermine it by violence'[3] are a precondition for conducting a peace operation successfully.

Despite this clear statement in favour of robust operations, there is no reason to completely abandon traditional peacekeeping. Indeed, whenever possible, it still is the preferable model. The UN Mission in Ethiopia and Eritrea (UNMEE) is a good example of the continued need for traditional peacekeeping, not the least because it is less risky and costly. The correct choice, that is, finding the appropriate model, has to be made on the basis of a sober analysis of the character, dynamics, actors and so on, of the conflict in question. A thorough assessment of possible worst case scenarios is of particular importance. The lack of adequate contingency planning proved fatal for some missions, like in Angola in the autumn of 1992, when the National Union for Total Independence of Angola (UNITA) leader Jonas Savimbi refused to accept the result of the internationally sponsored elections. Regretfully, the Special Committee on Peacekeeping Operations did not follow the recommendation of the Brahimi Panel to allow the UN to create an Information and Strategic Analysis Secretariat (ISAS).[4] Such a unit would be indispensable for the proper planning and conduct of complex operations and for continuously providing worst case analysis and other kinds of strategic information. The present Best Practices Unit seems too weak for performing such a demanding task. Some nations from the south, as well as leading members in the Security Council, obviously felt unhappy about such a proposal.[5]

KOSOVO AND EAST TIMOR: A FOURTH GENERATION OF PEACE AND GOVERNANCE OPERATIONS ON THE RISE?

Since the mandates for the UN Transitional Administration in East Timor (UNTAET) and the UN Mission in Kosovo/Kosovo Force (UNMIK/KFOR), there is good reason to speak of a fourth generation of peace operations.[6] In contrast to the operations of the second and third generation, these go a significant step further regarding international involvement. Those in charge of the mission are authorized to exercise 'executive powers', that is, they take over government as a kind of international trusteeship in the respective territories. They can directly order local leaders and people to do or not to do certain things; they can order the detention of criminals, decide when elections are to be held and who is allowed to participate; they can remove politicians and public servants from office and so on. In other words, they are in charge of government, whereas in the operations of the first three generations, the international personnel is limited to monitoring, reporting, advising and supporting the local authorities. Whether they are called Transitional Administrators, Special Representatives of the Secretary-General or High Representative (as in Bosnia and Herzegovina), those in charge of the operations have exercised this executive power quite frequently and with resolve. UNTAET in East Timor, UNMIK/KFOR in Kosovo, earlier UNTAES in Eastern Slavonia and, to a lesser degree, the Office of the High Representative and UN Mission in Bosnia and Herzegovina (OHR/UNMIBH) and UNTAC in Cambodia, belong to this type of operation. Obviously, they are quite similar to the trusteeship mandates foreseen in Chapter XIII of the UN Charter. There is however one significant difference: the trusteeship is directly administered by the international community itself via the UN, whereas in Chapter XIII, selected states are entrusted with the trusteeship.[7]

The term fourth generation operation has yet to find a place in academic writing. It is also absent from the Brahimi Report, though the Panel's work was very much influenced by the lessons learned in the Balkans. In Chapter II, paragraph 19, the Panel briefly mentions executive mandates: 'In two extreme situations, United Nations operations were given executive law enforcement and administrative authority where local authority did not exist or was not able to function.'[8] The Panel, not quite accurately, states that there have been only two operations with executive mandates, UNTAET in East Timor and UNMIK/KFOR in Kosovo. As mentioned before, UNTAES in Eastern Slavonia was also vested with an executive mandate, implemented with great success. In Bosnia and Herzegovina, the OHR was also given some executive power, albeit less comprehensive than for the principal administrators in Kosovo and East Timor.

UNTAC in Cambodia is often quoted as having been a kind of temporary international trusteeship. Under the Paris Agreement of October 1991, the Supreme National Council of Cambodia (SNC) was 'the unique legitimate body and source of authority in which, throughout the transitional period, the sovereignty, independence and unity of Cambodia are enshrined'. However, it also stipulated that the SNC, which was made up of the four Cambodian factions, delegated to the UN 'all powers necessary' to ensure the implementation of the Agreement. The authority thereby given to UNTAC included aspects relating to human and military questions, civil administration, the maintenance of law and order, the repatriation and resettlement of the Cambodian refugees and displaced persons, the rehabilitation of essential Cambodian infrastructure during the transitional period as well as the organization and conduct of free and fair general elections. In sum, UNTAC's powers were very similar to the powers exercised by UNTAES, UNTAET and UNMIK/KFOR.

In view of the operations in East Timor and Kosovo, one might argue that their executive mandates are based on the unclear or transient legal status of these territories. But this formal, legalistic answer is probably insufficient. It does not explain other mandates with executive elements, like those mentioned above. The Brahimi Report indicates a more convincing, systematic answer for the need of executive mandates when it states that 'executive law enforcement and administrative authority were given where local authority did not exist or was not able to function'.[9] In other words, in a globalized world, it may be very difficult or even impossible to bring peace, stability and governance to countries which are suffering from the 'failed state syndrome', whatever the origins of this syndrome may be.

Therefore the term *peace and governance operations* seems to be particularly appropriate for this fourth generation of operations – in a twofold sense. Not only do these operations reflect the desire of local communities for better governance, with its key elements of democracy, rule of law and human rights, they also demonstrate the increasing pressure on the international community and its leading powers to assume more responsibility in this regard as part of improving global governance.

KEY LESSONS LEARNED

By and large, fourth generation, executive operations address the same issues of peacebuilding as third generation operations. At the same time however, they are a step into a new dimension. Executive mandates are not only more demanding in degree, but also in principle. By vesting itself with governmental powers, the international community assumes full responsibility for the welfare of the local population. Its expectations regarding the quality of international leadership, professionalism of the international staff and resources made available for a sustained period, will rise accordingly. When these expectations are not met and the operation fails, the population will not only be disappointed, but also angered. This anger could easily become a threat for the peace operation and its personnel.

In Somalia, the first robust operation conducted by the UN revealed how perilous multidimensional and robust operations can be. The Brahimi

Report is refreshingly explicit in its assessment of these missions: 'Risks and costs for operations that must function in such circumstances are much greater than for traditional peacekeeping. Moreover, the complexity of the tasks assigned to these missions and the volatility of the situation on the ground tend to increase together.'[10]

Despite the publicity of the Brahimi Report, only a few politicians have fully grasped the difficulty of modern peace operations, their demands in terms of capabilities, planning, skills, sustained political will and so on. The international media and public opinion display an even more severe lack of understanding. Yet both groups are crucial for supporting operations with a sustained and coherent political will. The volatility of the international media and public constitutes a major problem for those who are in the field.

Since the mid-1990s, galvanized by the dramatic setbacks in Somalia and in the former Yugoslavia, national defence ministries, but also NATO and UN headquarters, have become very active in the field of lessons learned. In 1995, Kofi Annan, at that time still head of the Department of Peacekeeping Operations (DPKO), initiated a Lessons Learned Unit which conducted a series of seminars and studies. In a report published in December 1996, it gave a first overview of important lessons from past experience: the need for a clear and realistic mandate; early and integrated planning as well as thorough pre-mission training for quick deployment of sufficient capabilities; careful preliminary selection of the political leadership for the operation; a mission-based media unit, radio or TV, to inform the local population about the policy of the international presence and so on.[11] Most of these lessons are also to be found, in a more elaborated form, in the Brahimi Report. Like no previous document, this report summarized the current discussion among practitioners and experts regarding lessons learned and unsolved problems of modern peace operations. The final part of this article therefore will be limited to pointing out a few key lessons for successfully conducting robust, and particularly fourth generation, operations.

Consent, Impartiality and Credibility

Despite the authority to use limited force, consent and impartiality remain strategic pillars of peace operations. US politicians and military commanders who ordered the hunt for General Aideed in Somalia in the summer of 1993 were not aware of this necessity, with fatal consequences for UNOSOM II. In first and second generation peacekeeping, consent is indispensable for a simple legal reason: without consent, the international community has no right to intervene. In third and fourth generation operations, the legal argument is less relevant because these operations are normally based on Chapter VII of the UN Charter. Yet, consent and impartiality remain vital for practical reasons. Without the consent of the local population and the relevant parties to the conflict, effective peacebuilding will not be possible. Military force cannot enforce peacebuilding, it can only protect peace-building against the activities of 'spoilers'.

In modern complex emergencies, however, consent and impartiality are very difficult to apply. The lines of conflict as well as the numbers of com-batant parties are fragmented and in flux. Already in 1995, the *UN General Guidelines for Peacekeeping Operations* proposed a more dynamic definition of impartiality:

> The effort to maintain impartiality must not promote inaction. On the contrary, peacekeepers must discharge their tasks firmly and objectively, without fear or favour. Impartiality should not be interpreted as equidistant between the mandate and the party's newly revised position. It is the Security Council mandate which manifests the legitimate will of the international community.[12]

The fragmented, fluid nature of most modern conflicts poses difficult questions for those leading and working in the field. To which parties to the conflict should consent and impartiality apply? Which parties are relevant and which are not or even have to be considered as 'spoilers'? Peacekeepers have a hard time deciding which actors' consent is relevant. In Somalia, Bosnia, Liberia and other places, this became an almost impossible task. Violent groups acquired a great deal of leverage over the peacekeepers by denying consent.

The fact that the use of force is per se incompatible with impartiality and consent is also a false assumption among some journalists and academics. The very moment peacekeepers use force beyond the purpose of self-defence, they are accused of 'taking sides'. This is a flawed understanding. The decisive question is whether the actions taken conform to the mandate and are undertaken in an even-handed way. Impartiality is not equal to neutrality or passivity. The UN Charter – demanding respect for certain basic values and norms[13] – is not neutral, nor are the mandates given by the Security Council. Charter infringements and massive human rights viola-tions such as mass murder, rape, ethnic cleansing and genocide have become a frequent pattern of socio-ethnic and similar conflict. These crimes are not accidental. They have become a systematic pattern of the military-political strategy of most warring factions in failed states. Any action by the peace-keepers and their civilian counterparts to prevent such crimes is therefore bound to pit them against one side or the other. The accusation of partiality inevitably follows. Old concepts of 'neutrality' or 'static impartiality' are obviously dysfunctional when dealing with such perpetrations.

It is not easy to execute impartiality in a coherent, systematic way. One major reason is to be found in the fact that operations often lack the necessary military and police capability for coherent and consistent implementation. UNPROFOR's credibility was eroded due to this weakness. Credibility in terms of the number, equipment and quality of units available is therefore of overriding importance for third and fourth generation operations. Troops must be able to deter 'spoilers'. Past experience shows that it is highly dangerous to do so without sufficient capabilities, that is, without unambiguous escalation dominance. The Brahimi Report is quite explicit about this requirement.[14]

The hope of politicians responsible to taxpayers, that costs can be saved by deploying understaffed operations has turned out to be an illusion in most cases (for instance in Angola, Rwanda, Srebrenica, Sierra Leone). Indeed, operations become much more expensive in the longer run because of the need to strengthen them after considerable human damage as well as material costs. There is a better rule of thumb: deploy a strong force and then, when the peace process is consolidating, thin out forces step by step. SFOR in Bosnia and KFOR in Kosovo are successfully applying this rule. It is more effective and ultimately also cheaper.

Good military-police-civilian cooperation

The rise of civilian actors is one of the remarkable phenomena of the move from first to fourth generation peace operations. Today, in contrast to the operation in the Sinai (UNEF) in the mid–1950s for instance, civilian actors are essential for a successful operation. That peace operations have become militarized, as occasionally stated in the press, is not quite correct. Due to this fact, civil–military coordination has become a key issue in planning and conducting operations that not only have to deal with an insecure environment and numerous local parties, but also with a multitude of international actors. The military, the police as well as the civilian personnel of the UN, of humanitarian agencies and of hundreds of big and small NGOs have to work together. Good coordination and management of all these actors is of strategic importance. The lesson learned is indisputable: an integrated approach is needed and must be planned from the very beginning.

This is easier said than done or, as one popular saying among practitioners goes: 'everybody wants coordination but nobody wants to be coordinated'. Soldiers and NGOs have very different, sometimes downright antagonistic, 'operational cultures'. The military are used to following orders without much questioning. Not so in NGOs, particularly those working on a voluntary basis. The police, for that matter, also have an operational culture which is clearly distinct from that of the military or the NGOs. In contrast to UN terminology, police and other civilian actors should be distinguished when it comes to coordination. It makes no sense to lump the disparate civilian actors together.

To complicate matters still further, the international NGO community itself is extremely heterogeneous (see Nicholas Stockton's chapter in this volume). All organizations have their own *raison d'être*, their own agendas and peculiarities, even vanities. Still, many of the NGOs are valuable for rendering humanitarian assistance and contributing to peacebuilding. They can perform tasks which the military has difficulty with, particularly regarding complicated socio-economic and socio-cultural peacebuilding tasks. Although effective, the humanitarian work done by the military tends to be more costly.

In summary, the operations since the early 1990s have shown that soldiers, police and civilian actors learn and have learned to act together in an effective and constructive way, if certain prejudices and psychological barriers are overcome.

Integrated mission and unified command

The analysis of the robust, multidimensional operations since the early 1990s teaches one indisputable lesson: these operations need an integrated structure to be effective. Military, police and civilian components have to be brought under one roof, with a unified command and communication structure. The overall organizational structure of an operation plays an important role in the smooth development of its cooperation. The necessary skills and professions as well as the number of states participating in modern peace operations are enormous. Participation of more than 30 nationalities in the military or police components is the rule, not the exception. The number of states participating in the civilian sector tends to be even higher.

Unity not only of purpose, but also of strategy and action are a *sine qua non* for successful peace operations. Joint structures for distributing and sharing information, joint analysis and planning, as well as joint implementation mechanisms have shown their effectiveness for improving civil-military cooperation. Joint pre-mission training and regular executive meetings to monitor developments are also proven tools. At all stages, the relevant actors (especially the World Bank, UNDP, UNICEF, UNHCR, the donor community and NGOs) should be closely involved in the decision-making process, led by the UN or a regional organization. A lead agency should be earmarked to take over coordination in the early stages. To enhance and clarify the role and authority of the Special Representative of the Secretary-General (SRSG) or similar leaders of peace operations and peace-building as the 'head of the family and team leader' is of prime importance.

Unfortunately, only in some organizations have the lessons regarding integrated structure been followed. UNTAES in Eastern Slavonia as well as UNTAET in East Timor were exemplary missions in terms of an integrated structure encompassing all actors. The missions in Cambodia, Haiti or in Sierra Leone (UNAMSIL) come next in line. They achieved quite a good level of integrated organization and unity of command. The two-pillar UNMIK/KFOR structure in Kosovo can only be considered second best. Indeed, it was not even a genuine two-pillar operation. The OSCE and the European Union, in charge of two of the four pillars of UNMIK, are still reluctant to conform to the lead-authority of the UN. There is often more rivalry and bureaucratic turf war than coordination and integrated strategy. It is therefore more accurate to speak of a four-pillar structure in Kosovo.

In Bosnia and Herzegovina, the model is even worse than in Kosovo. It is, as most observers acknowledge, a model to be avoided. Very often, SFOR goes its own way, as do the OSCE, the EU, UNMIBH or the UNHCR. In theory, the Office of the High Representative (OHR) is supposed to be the overarching coordinator. *De facto* and *de jure,* however, it does not have the authority and competence for this role. The local parties, particularly the 'spoilers', are well aware of this 'balkanization' of the international presence and have quickly learned to abuse it to their own advantage.

The need for an integrated, unified structure is undisputed among practitioners and experts. Unfortunately, this is not so when it comes to high politics and in particular to the UN Security Council. Its capability and willingness to follow lessons learned seems to be quite limited. Governments are often motivated by considerations which have little reference to the lessons learned about organizing a peace operation most effectively. Their delegates in New York act accordingly, often against their better knowledge. Indeed, most lessons learned end at the Security Council.

*Basic public security and rule of law: western standards
to dominate?*

It has been said that the need to establish and uphold a secure environment for humanitarian aid and socio-economic as well as political reconstruction has been the trigger for developing robust third and fourth generation peace operations. Establishing basic public security and rule of law has moved centre stage in modern peace operations. The level of consent about this necessity among all actors in peace operations is remarkable. In a study on *US and Allied Commanders' Views of the Military's Role in Peace Operations*, even US generals agree 'that problem number one now facing peace operations is the "rule of law" issue'.[15] The commanders even go one step further and concede 'that in the early phase of operation, the military must take the lead role in establishing law and order', though the long-term solution of this problem is not a military one.[16] Past, rigid views, particularly in the US military about the danger of mission creep have given way to a more flexible view about the role of the military.

Yet, the military and the police are not the sole actors when it comes to establishing public security and the rule of law. Neither can operate successfully without a civilian component. The operations in Bosnia, East Timor and Kosovo have demonstrated the importance of having criminal courts as well as a proper prosecution and prison systems in place as soon as possible. Without them, the military and police are in danger of becoming discredited as an arbitrary, occupational power. The experience suggests that this becomes a very sensitive issue for the local population once the euphoria, if any, about the arrival of the international force has faded. There is little doubt that this will also be the case in Afghanistan with a population accustomed to the rules of shariah.

The case of Afghanistan points to one of the basic problems in the area of public security and rule of law. It is easy to postulate these principles in general, but to what extent can these principles realistically be applied in modern peace operations? Most western countries have quite a concrete and common understanding of their practical implications. The standards which they have developed regarding institutions, the training and quality of personnel as well as the resources available are quite high. But these are the standards of rich and functioning countries.

It is their understanding of these standards which has overwhelmingly shaped the relevant UN and other international documents in this field. This begs the question of the possibility of applying these standards to poor, war-torn countries without functioning state structures and more often than not without a tradition of this specific understanding of public security and rule of law. How rigidly can they be applied in Sierra Leone, the Congo, Angola or Afghanistan? Are there ways to design public security and rule of law standards and institutions – with regards to their costs – in a way that they are also sustainable in poor countries?

In summary, there is an urgent need to explore the practical aspects of applying the principles of public security and rule of law in peace operations in a much more thorough and concrete way than has been done so far – based on the lessons learned in Bosnia, East Timor, Kosovo and other recent operations.[17] These operations have also highlighted further issues, such as organized crime and the uncontrolled proliferation of small arms and light weapons. Both are major obstacles for establishing public security and rule of law in the mid and long term.

Fighting organized crime

The operations in the Balkans in particular have shown that fighting organized crime and successful peacebuilding – in terms of good governance, rule of law, democratization – are closely intertwined (see Jacques Klein's chapter in this volume). This is due to the particular social, economic and political dynamics in war-torn countries. Conflict in these countries cannot be understood in terms of conventional warfare. To a considerable extent, but to varying degrees depending on each case, violence is a very profitable way of doing business. This is clearly true for most conflicts, not only in the Balkans, but also in Africa, Central Asia and elsewhere. Failing state structures, protracted ethnic or similar type of conflict, a poverty stricken population in conjunction with a resource rich land-base (be it valuable minerals, timber or drugs), provide fertile ground for war economies and mafia-type socio-economic structures.[18]

Fighting organized crime is, in itself, an extremely time-consuming, sophisticated and tough endeavour. In war-torn societies, these aspects are amplified, for a number of reasons: the lack of functioning state structures and therefore of effective law enforcement agencies; the proliferation of small arms and light weapons; and an abundance of unemployed men, particularly youths, ripe for recruitment to violent and criminal ways of earning their livelihood. Especially troubling for the success of peace operations is that those involved in organized crime and those who present themselves as the relevant political elite to guide the country to peace are often closely intertwined or even identical. This is true for the three main parties in Bosnia and Herzegovina, it is true for Kosovo and also for a number of leaders in Afghanistan.

Due to this connection, organized criminals in war-torn countries exercise additional leverage to pursue their business. They jeopardize the outcome of a peace operation because organized crime can mobilize its political followers, mostly by playing on ethnic or religious sentiments, against the international presence. Threats against mission staff, targeted killing of local people who cooperate with the international presence, incitements to mass unrest or even direct violence against the international presence are common methods and have occurred in Somalia and in the Balkans among other places.

The international community, and organizations like the UN, NATO and the EU, are only beginning to understand the threat which organized crime constitutes for successful peacebuilding and good governance in peace operations. They have not yet developed the necessary means and techniques to tackle this problem in a meaningful manner.

Disarmament, demobilization and reintegration

Tension and violence do not suddenly disappear as soon as a peace agreement or ceasefire is signed. Indeed, they may even increase for a number of reasons. This is one of the bitter lessons since the operation in Somalia. Progress in the field of disarmament, demobilization and reintegration (DDR), and progress with regard to public security and rule of law are highly inter-dependent. DDR is one of the most demanding elements of peacebuilding. In affluent western societies there is a notion that 'violence does not pay'. However, in ethnic and similar types of conflict, well-considered economic interest is, more often than not, the dominant reason for rampant and continued violence. It is therefore extremely important to understand the 'economics of violence' and the 'economics of war'. Warlords represent a sinister combination of military commander, gang leader, businessman and political leader. They tend to be the key 'spoilers' of peace processes. As already indicated, unemployment, particularly among the young, provides a fertile ground for recruiting militias. The wide availability of small arms and light weapons in most conflict regions makes it cheap to arm these 'youngsters'.

DDR is an area which has been widely explored by the UN and other actors. Some of the important lessons learned are the following:

- Coercive disarmament in the context of peacebuilding carries considerable risk. An overwhelming, determined force and credible leadership is neces-sary. In most cases, however, political as well as military leaders have shied away from enforced disarmament. Consent-based strategies therefore are preferable but, depending on local conditions, tend to achieve quite limited results. There has hardly been any disarmament enterprise which has achieved the results it was mandated to achieve; yet this may not hinder their positive political role.

- Weapon buy-back programmes may play an important role in dis-armament and demobilization, as in El Salvador and Eastern Slavonia. But their record, too, is mixed. Especially if money is offered as compensation, buy-back programmes can create streams of weapons flowing from one region to another. It may be better to spend these funds on improving the police and judiciary to foster the security conditions in the country concerned.

• Weapons destruction programmes are the most effective way to reduce arms flows and to get rid of collected weapons. If done in public with a ceremony and in the presence of the media, it sends a strong political signal to combatants and to the society. The case of Mali and its public burning of collected weapons was powerful evidence of this. The *'flamme de paix'* has become a symbol for a society at peace.

But disarmament and demobilization without well-planned and sufficiently funded programmes of reintegration will fail. Much attention has therefore to be given to the social and economic impact of externally sponsored demobilization programmes. Success also depends heavily on the extent to which the former warring parties and individuals believe that their physical and economic security will be assured after relinquishing their arms and abandoning what has become a way of life and means of economic survival. In other words, DDR is an enormously complex enterprise. If done successfully, it can pave the way for a successful peace process.

Beware early elections

Elections and constitution-drafting have been a strategic objective in UN peace missions since the end of the cold war. Internationally monitored elections were the concluding activity in a number of cases. Elections are conceived to be the best mechanism to guarantee an orderly, peaceful, participatory and transparent succession of governments and to make executive power more accountable to the people.

These manifest advantages may be the reason why elections have often been held too soon in conflict-ridden societies, but were unable to terminate the conflicts in the way anticipated. Indeed, elections in fragmented societies may result in further fragmentation, as *inter alia*, in the cases of Angola and Sierra Leone. In Liberia, premature elections elevated the warlord, Charles Taylor, into government. His role in destabilizing neighbouring countries is internationally known. Now Liberia itself has slid back into violence.

The evaluation of a number of peacekeeping operations by the Lessons Learned Unit of the DPKO has helped to better understand the problems of elections in peace operations. The right timing is a central issue. Elections, like other elements of peacebuilding, must also be planned well in advance, ideally two or three years before they are conducted. Sufficient demobilization and integration of combatants into the new army, police force or civil society and a satisfactory restoration of the judicial system and of public administration are necessary preconditions. Credibility and integrity of the electoral process help to prevent disputes over the outcome and forestall a relapse into violence. International monitoring should continue throughout the electoral process and even beyond. This is important because of the lasting distrust of the formerly conflicting parties. Elections in war-torn countries are in danger of simply being a continuation of war by other means, particularly in the case of 'winner takes all' elections. In extreme cases of fragmentation and violence, interim power-sharing could be the preferable solution in the general transition from war to peace and democracy. Western-style democracy will not work, at least in the short run; governments of national unity may be the only way to forestall reverting to combat. In such cases, the international community should at least try to establish a mechanism to monitor minimum standards of human rights.

Finally, one lesson of past democratization processes, inside and outside of peace operations, is crystal clear: elections are only a starting point for democratization, not a successful conclusion. Past peace operations have been therefore rightly criticized for having abused elections as a quick exit option from difficult peace processes.

Fortunately, this lesson seems to have been learned by political decision-makers, unlike some of the other lessons extolled here. In the Bosnia and Kosovo missions, elections were not abused as a quick exit for the international presence. They have become one element of a complex, long-term process of stabilization and democratization. The UN leadership in particular must be praised for the readiness to accept lessons. It has adopted a new policy and made the Security Council agree to post-conflict peace-building missions after elections had been successfully held in a number of cases, particularly in Guatemala, the Central African Republic and Liberia.

The UN Mission of Support in East Timor (UNMISET) is the most recent and interesting development within this strategy of post-conflict peacebuilding missions. The carefully timed and well-planned withdrawal from East Timor after the elections provides a 'milestone-based approach', as Kofi Annan has written, proposing interesting and innovative elements for practical implementation.[19] As a follow-up to UNTAET, the UNMISET mandate pledges to support East Timor's new government in three key areas: stability, democracy and justice; internal security and law enforcement; and external security and border control.

LESSONS LEARNED AND 11 SEPTEMBER

This brief overview of some of the major lessons learned regarding modern peace operations arrives at two basic conclusions. First, robust and executive operations are very demanding in terms of planning, capabilities, training, coordination, quality of leadership and sustained political will.[20] Second, operations that are not robust have a high probability of failure, at least when it comes to restoring peace and security in failed states. The number of operations which did or do not meet these standards and therefore ran into considerable difficulties or even failed dramatically, is quite high.[21]

In other words, if lessons learned are not heeded, international intervention could wreak more havoc and induce more bloodshed than suffered prior to the mission. Angola (1992), Somalia (1993), Rwanda (1994) and Srebrenica (1995) are dramatic examples of this truth.

Has 11 September, often labelled as the beginning of a new era of international policing for peace and security, improved the likelihood that past errors regarding peace operations will not be repeated? And what about President Bush's promise not to repeat past errors in war-torn Afghanistan? Unfortunately, to date, the answer is negative. The International Security Assistance Force (ISAF) and UN Assistance Mission in Afghanistan (UNAMA) are test cases. The basic lessons pointed out in this chapter have not been followed. Indeed, past lessons learned have been pushed aside to an amazing degree. A few examples may suffice to substantiate this statement.

First, ISAF's mandate is limited to Kabul and cannot properly be called a robust operation although, in formal legal terms, it is based on Chapter VII of the UN Charter. Annex 1 to the Petersberg Accord from December 2001 explicitly states that the responsibility for 'providing security and law and order throughout the country resides with the Afghans themselves'. Accordingly, ISAF has no authority of its own to act. Its units are limited to 'assisting' the Afghan Interim Authority.[22] In terms of capabilities, ISAF also cannot be labelled as a robust force, as it has at its disposal fewer than 5,000 soldiers. In case of serious security problems, for instance an attack by one of the warlords who commands thousands of armed men, ISAF would be too weak for a forceful reaction. Military planners are even worried that in a worst case scenario, they may not be able to exit safely. The security of the civilian personnel of UNAMA and other international actors outside of Kabul is in even greater danger. They may end up at the mercy of local warlords or bandits if special units of the US-led coalition-force pursuing Al Qaeda and bin Laden would not be able to extract them in time.

Second, the state of anarchy and fragmentation in Afghanistan, much worse than in East Timor or in Kosovo, would have warranted an 'executive' mandate. For a number of reasons, such a mandate was ruled out from the very beginning (see Thierry Tardy's chapter in this volume). Indeed, in view of the size of the country, its difficult terrain and the backward, almost completely destroyed administrative and support infrastructure, such a mandate would have been extremely difficult to implement. The capabilities needed would have been enormous. A brief comparison with the capabilities deployed in Kosovo and East Timor is enlightening. UNTAET had a military strength of about 9,000 when it started, although the population of East Timor is about 30 times less than that of Afghanistan. Based on a per capita calculation, an equivalent force for Afghanistan therefore would have amounted to 270,000. About 50,000 soldiers were sent into Kosovo as of June 1999. Afghanistan has about 13 times the population of Kosovo; an equivalent force would therefore have been about 650,000. A calculation based on the size of the terrain to be covered by the peacekeeping forces leads to even more fantastic numbers. Afghanistan is about 600 times as large as Kosovo, so the force needed would be more than five million – a figure beyond any realistic achievement.

Third, there is also no integrated command and communication structure. On the contrary, the structure is fragmented. ISAF has its own command, like UNAMA. Outside Kabul, US and coalition troops that pursue Al Qaeda and ex-Taliban fighters are under the exclusive command of Central Command (CENCOM) in Tampa, Florida. In the case of an emergency, CENCOM could also take over the command of ISAF. Staff members of UNAMA complain that they are neither sufficiently informed nor consulted by the US generals, although the actions taken by the coalition troops have or may have direct repercussions on UNAMA's endeavour to recover and to reconstruct the different provinces of Afghanistan. The building of a new Afghan police and army is also outside an integrated structure. Germany is the lead-nation to rebuild the police. UNAMA seems to be content with the level of coordination and consultation. The training of a new Afghan army, by contrast, is controlled by the Americans. Coordination with UNAMA is minimal.

Fourth, disarmament and fighting organized crime, decisive for long-term stabilization, have not yet started in any serious way. In view of the high level of armament and other factors particular to Afghanistan, it may be an illusion even to try. The lesson learned that both are vital for successful peacebuilding, nevertheless, holds.

Does this neglect of past lessons mean that ISAF and UNAMA will fail? It is too early to give a final answer to this question. Yet, the probability that they will get into serious trouble or may even fail is high. If they do, it will not be a simple repetition of the disaster in Somalia. Due to Afghanistan's regional importance, it may be much more dramatic.

CONCLUSION

Does the successful completion of the Loya Jirga in June 2002 contradict this prediction? Not really. At a closer look, the results of the Jirga are ambivalent. On the one hand, a new interim administration with Mr Karzai as its leader was approved. On the other, there is a number of worrying facts. The new administration is not well balanced in ethnic terms. The marginalization of the Uzbeks and other minorities has created bitter feelings. In particular, the continuing dominance of Tajik leaders, like Defence Minister Fahim, coming from the Panjshir Valley, is deeply resented. The Tajiks not only run the defence ministry but also control the powerful intelligence service and the office of administration. The killing of Vice-President H. Abdul Qadir shortly after the completion of the Loya Jirga has eliminated any doubts that the struggle for power in Afghanistan will continue to be ruthless and bloody. President Karzai has asked for US body guards to protect him, distrusting the guards provided to him by Fahim. In several parts of the country, the security situation is deteriorating.

Indeed, with regard to creating a secure environment for successful peace-building, Afghanistan displays one of the worst combination of negative factors one can imagine. The mix of poor peasants, dependent on growing opium, and of heavily armed warlords, is particularly explosive. The latter are prepared to play on ethno-regional diversities in order to further their criminal interests. Afghanistan is the world's biggest producer of raw opium. Seventy per cent of the heroin sold in Europe is smuggled from Afghanistan.

Two factors explain the relative calm which has governed in Afghanistan after the Petersberg Agreement (December 2001) despite this dangerous mix. First, the war weariness of the Afghan population after about 20 years of war and violence is immense. Second, the omnipresence of US war planes deters warlords from massive, sustained acts of violence. However, war weariness is a decreasing factor, as is probably the deterrence of US bombers. An international intervention, received enthusiastically in the beginning, may look very different to the local population one year later, particularly if hopes linked to this intervention have not been fulfilled to some extent. In 2002, emotions were already starting to run high in Afghanistan against the fatal errors of US bombers in killing a considerable number of civilians. The fact that US-led coalition troops seem to be more interested in cooperating with criminal warlords to pursue Al Qaeda than in providing security for the local population and more humanitarian aid is exacerbating this resentment.

For a considerable time to come, neither the American-trained Afghan army nor the German-trained police will be able to handle major outbreaks of violence in Afghanistan. Both training programmes are very much at the beginning stage. Even when they are more advanced, it remains doubtful as to the extent that new units can be trusted to handle serious crime and violence in which regional warlords or even politicians of the central government are involved. The lessons from the Balkan peace operations are not encouraging. It takes years to create a functioning police and army that respects the rule of law. In Kabul, some cynics even hold that these training programmes will help to strengthen the warlords and their followers rather than to create a law abiding national army and police.

The calls for extending ISAF beyond Kabul to fill the security vacuum have therefore been numerous. Kofi Annan and his SRSG in Afghanistan, Lakhdar Brahimi, as well as international humanitarian organizations and Interim President Karzai have repeatedly made this demand publicly.[23] Indeed, most Afghans seem to favour such an extension, hoping that it would help to curb the insecurity infringing on their daily lives. About 25,000–30,000 additional troops are estimated to be required to do the job, assuming their task were limited to securing major cities and lines of communication.[24] The Bush government and the governments in Berlin, London, Paris and Istanbul, continue to oppose such an extension of ISAF. If the United States changes course, the other governments would probably follow. Yet, there are no indications to date that the Bush government is prepared to alter its position.

The refusal to do so cannot really be explained by the events of 11 September, for the following reasons. Failed states have been identified as a major reason for the increased threat of international terrorism. It would be logical therefore to make their stabilization a strategic element of the fight against international terrorism. Following this logic, US legislators from both parties urged the Bush Administration to support the extension of the international security force in Afghanistan.[25] A different US position regarding the role of peace operations in fighting international terrorism has also been proposed by several American generals. In the report on *US and Allied Commanders' Views of the Military's Role in Peace Operations and the Impact on Terrorism of States in Conflict*, they state that 'Senior military leaders believe that engagement in multilateral peace operations is in our national interests and will be a key ingredient in the war against terrorism.'[26]

The unwillingness of the Bush Administration to heed these calls is to a large extent due to the way in which three of its principal security advisors, Secretary of Defence Donald Rumsfeld, Deputy Secretary of Defence Paul Wolfowitz and the National Security Advisor, Condoleeza Rice, perceive contemporary international foreign and security policy. All three resent direct US involvement in peace operations and nation-building. This resentment was already a popular attitude in Bush's election campaign. Such an involvement does not seem to be appropriate for the dominant global power. Some, like Secretary of Defence Rumsfeld, even label peace operations as a 'wimpish' business which should be left to weak nations, like the Europeans and others. Rumsfeld and Wolfowitz see the American vocation rather in combat scenarios, eradicating elements of the 'evil', like the Taliban in Afghanistan or Saddam Hussein in Iraq. Here, they feel, America can bring its awesome global military dominance to bear. Involvement in peace operations, by contrast, they fear, might undermine the combat capability of US units. Furthermore, the three advisors are also highly suspicious of multilateral approaches and institutions which may curtail and forbid unrestricted use of American power. The United States may use such institutions when opportune, as in the case of the anti-terrorism resolution of the Security Council after 11 September,[27] but it should never be subjected to them.

The Bush Administration's crude unilateralist, hegemonic vision on how to conduct global politics collides with the multilateral vision of the Europeans and other states. The conflict in the UN Security Council in late June 2002 about the immunity of US personnel in peace operations leaves little doubt that a deep divide has opened in the transatlantic relationship on how to organize international security and global governance. As one unnamed official wrote, when they triggered the controversy in the Security Council, Rice, Rumsfeld and others hoped 'to kill peacekeeping and the International Criminal Court (ICC) with one stone'.[28] Fortunately, the Europeans managed to negotiate an acceptable compromise.[29]

There is no doubt that this basic controversy about the role of multilateralism in general, and of peace operations and peacebuilding in particular, is blocking any meaningful development of peace operations as an instrument of global governance. The systematic improvement of peace operations by taking past lessons seriously cannot be achieved against the aggressive opposition of US policy. It needs at least benign tolerance.

It may be that Afghanistan forces the Bush Administration to rethink its approach. If there is a further deterioration of security and stability, one of its strategic goals in the war against terrorism, the stabilization of Afghanistan, is in danger. The Bush Administration already had to give up one of its tenets, never to be involved in nation-building, when assuming the responsibility of building a new, ethnically balanced and law abiding Afghan army.[30] Building such an army is a centrepiece of modern nation-building, like building up a police force. Leading American officers are no longer sure whether bombing raids against Al Qaeda fighters is a suitable job for them either. These raids are becoming increasingly counterproductive and may lead to a Vietnam-type situation: the fighters are seldom hit; civilians, however, quite often are. Supporting ISAF and UNAMA in their endeavour to stabilize and build up the country may be a more rewarding job for the US army.

The perspective for an improvement of international peace operations is not hopeful at this point in time, but it may become brighter in the mid and long term. At the time of writing, the effect of the Iraq war on the development of peace operations is difficult to predict.

NOTES

1. Kofi Annan, *We, the People, The Role of the United Nations in the 21st Century*, New York: United Nations, 2000.
2. In the early phase of peacekeeping, an operation which had all the elements of a modern multidimensional, robust operation, was deployed in the Congo *Opération des Nations unies au Congo* (ONUC) after 1961.
3. 'Report of the Panel on United Nations Peace Operations' (Brahimi Report), A/55/305, 21 Aug. 2000, para. 55.
4. 'Report of the Special Committee on Peacekeeping Operations, Comprehensive review of the whole question of peacekeeping operations in all their aspects', A/55/1024, 31 July 2001.
5. See Winrich Kühne, in cooperation with Jochen Prantl, *The Brahimi Report. Overcoming the North–South Divide*, Report of the 6th International Workshop, Berlin, 29–30 June 2001.
6. This term cannot be found either in the relevant literature or in UN documents.
7. One famous, although abusive, example was the trusteeship of South Africa over the former German colony of Southwest Africa, today Namibia.
8. See Brahimi Report, para. 19.
9. Ibid.
10. Ibid.
11. *Multidisciplinary Peacekeeping: Lessons Learned from Recent Experience*, Lessons Learned Unit, DPKO, United Nations, Dec. 1996.
12. *General Guidelines for Peacekeeping Operations*, DPKO, United Nations, 1995, paras 31–2.
13. See for instance Articles 1 and 2.
14. See Brahimi Report, para. 64.
15. *A Force for Peace and Security. US and Allied Commanders' Views of the Military's Role in Peace Operations and the Impact on Terrorism of States in Conflict*, Washington DC: Peace Through Law Education Fund, 2002, p. 9.
16. Ibid., p. 10.
17. A good study is provided by Tor Tanke Holm and Espen Barth Eide (eds), *Peacebuilding and Police Reform*, London: Frank Cass, 1999.
18. See Mats Berdal and David Malone (eds), *Greed and Grievance: Economic Agendas in Civil Wars*, Boulder, CO: Lynne Rienner, 2000.
19. See 'Report of the Secretary-General on the UN Transitional Administration in East Timor', United Nations, S/2002/432, 17 April 2002, paras 63–4.
20. Only a handful of operations have fully met these standards: UNTAET in East Timor,

UNMIK/KFOR in Kosovo and, to a lesser degree, UNTAC in Cambodia and UNAMSIL in Sierra Leone (in its present configuration). OHR/SFOR/UNMIBH in Bosnia do not really fit into this category. Although well staffed, these operations are deficient because they lack an integrated structure and coordination. The UN Transitional Mission in Haiti was also well planned, staffed and organized. Yet, it was not concluded successfully. The particularly corroded political culture in Haiti is a major factor for this lack of success.

21. Most significant in this regard are UNOSOM I and II in Somalia, UNAMIR in Rwanda, UNAVEM II and III in Angola, UNPROFOR in former Yugoslavia, ECOMOG/ UNOMIL in Liberia, UNMIH in Haiti, UNOMSIL (first phase) in Sierra Leone, and MONUC in the Democratic Republic of Congo.

22. See UN Security Council res. 1386, 20 Dec. 2001.

23. Before and during the time of the Petersberg negotiations, the SRSG Lakhdar Brahimi was very outspoken against an extended international presence.

24. In a short study prepared for the German parliament and government in November 2001, I estimated that about 40,000–50,000 were needed to implement such a limited mandate. Winrich Kühne, *UNO-Friedenseinsatz in Afghanistan* [A UN peace operation in Afghanistan], SWP-Aktuell, No. 24, 2001.

25. *The New York Times*, 27 June 2002.

26. *A Force for Peace and Security*, p. 8.

27. UN Security Council res. 1368 of 12 Sept. 2001 and res. 1373 of 28 Sept. 2001.

28. 'US Takes Chance to Target Peacekeeping', *Financial Times*, 2 July 2002.

29. The compromise is based on Art. 16 of the ICC's Rome Statute.

30. James Dao, 'Bush Sets Role for the US in Afghan Rebuilding', *The New York Times*, 18 April 2002.

SIX

UNMIBH: Combating Organized Crime and Terrorism Through Law Enforcement Capacity Building

Jacques Paul Klein

In the post-11 September world, countries immediately began to recalibrate the lenses of their international relations; defining friends and foes and setting the strategic agenda for the foreseeable future. As the needs and requirements of the international community shifted in kaleidoscopic fashion, so too did the mechanisms that provide for international peace and security. This impact was particularly dramatic in several nations hosting United Nations peace operations.

Peacekeeping practitioners have long reported that instability within states and on their borders has made for breeding grounds – where a nexus is formed between organized crime syndicates and terrorist networks. In the absence of the rule of law, organized crime becomes entrenched. Criminal activities, both economic and paramilitary, support terrorists, extremists and indicted war criminals – allowing them not only to survive, but also to thrive. This situation is evident in the Balkans, where 'terrorists' have employed organized criminal distribution networks, and in return have provided armed protection and other in-kind forms of payment. The ultimate result is the further degradation of societies, with criminal elements living off the profits from arms smuggling, drugs and human trafficking, prostitution, illegal migration and other criminal ventures.

These are precisely the situations that the international community simply cannot and should not ignore. More than ever, those involved in peace operations must support and assist their legitimate partners in local governments to build professional law enforcement capacities that will eliminate hotbeds of support for organized crime and terrorism. There is consensus that, to achieve this, establishing the rule of law is the first priority. The rationale is straightforward: until human rights are established, and until local police maintain law and order, prosecutors file suits against criminals, and judges jail offenders, criminality will remain pervasive and UN peace-keeping forces and resources will be stuck in place. Therefore, embedding the rule of law is not only the means to win the peace, it is also the exit strategy and a post-conflict nation's recovery and acceptance in the international community.

Bosnia and Herzegovina (BiH) provides an in-depth case study of UN involvement in this endeavour through building national, regional and inter-national law enforcement capacities. This chapter provides an overview of the United Nations Mission in Bosnia and Herzegovina (UNMIBH) mandate implementation to provide the skills, equipment and mechanisms to fight organized crime and international terrorism in BiH and the Balkans region.

UNMIBH

UNMIBH was established by Security Council Resolution 1035 of 13 December 1995 at the request of the parties to the General Framework Agreement for Peace (GFAP) in BiH,[1] to assist them in the implementation of their obligations to 'provide a safe and secure environment for all persons by ensuring that civilian law enforcement agencies operate in accordance with internationally recognized standards and with respect for inter-nationally recognized human rights and fundamental freedoms'.[2] Annex 11 of the GFAP enumerates the International Police Task Force (IPTF) agreed programme of assistance and, in article VII, states that 'Annex 11 applies throughout BiH to [all] law enforcement, criminal investigations, public and state security, or detention or judicial activities.'

UNMIBH's mandate has evolved since 1995 through successive Security Council resolutions, which have corresponded to the dictates of peace imple-mentation. In straightforward terms, UNMIBH's mandate comprises the following tasks:

- monitoring, observing and inspecting law enforcement activities and facil-ities including associated judicial organizations, structures and proceedings;
- advising law enforcement personnel and forces;
- training law enforcement personnel;
- facilitating, within the IPTF's mission of assistance, the parties' law enforcement activities;
- assessing threats to public order and advising on the capability of law enforcement agencies to deal with such threats;

- advising governmental authorities in BiH on the organization of effective civilian law enforcement agencies; and assisting by accompanying the parties' law enforcement personnel as they carry out their responsibilities, as the IPTF deems appropriate.

It is important to emphasize that UNMIBH does not exercise police authority. The local police are not under UNMIBH's command and control. Executive authority lies within the competency of the Entity Ministries of Interior and the BiH State Border Service (SBS). While on the one hand this limitation has hindered the possibilities for robust peacekeeping, on the other hand, UNMIBH has engendered sustainable local ownership of law and order, and has successfully filled the void between unarmed members of the IPTF and armed NATO-led Stabilization Force (SFOR) combat troops with professional local police.

A sample analysis of UNMIBH's mandate implementation between December 1995 and April 2002 would likely note fundamental changes in BiH policing culture due to the following initiatives in three core areas: police personnel reform; police organizational restructuring; and institution building and inter-police force cooperation.[3]

Police personnel reform

In the field of Police Personnel Reform, the following measures were taken:

- reduction of regular police forces from 40,000 wartime personnel in 1996 to under 18,000 provisionally authorized police officers serving in BiH;

- establishment of a Law Enforcement Personnel Registry to conduct checks on background, housing status and educational qualifications. Provisional authorization has been withdrawn from 142 police for offences, including wartime acts (29), dereliction of duty, violation of laws or unbecoming conduct. They are not eligible to serve again in any police force in BiH;

- administration of compulsory basic training courses in human dignity, transitional training, community policing and traffic awareness for every currently serving police officer and a management course for supervisors. Other specialized training courses were completed and some are ongoing, on drug control, organized crime, crowd control, firearms, computers and senior management;

- training (or in the process of training) of more than 1,163 cadets, including 409 females, at the two police academies in Sarajevo and Banja Luka that UNMIBH helped establish;

- establishment of a fully multiethnic police service in Brcko District;
- investigation or assistance with local investigations of over 13,000 cases of alleged human rights abuses by law enforcement personnel, of which 11,000 cases have been resolved. Endemic institutional deficiencies through 'special audits' and remedial plans were also addressed;
- establishment, in close cooperation with SFOR, of joint training for specialized local police units in crowd control and major incident management;
- enhancement of anti-trafficking efforts of local police through the UNMIBH Special Trafficking Operations Programme (STOP).

Police organizational restructuring

In partnership with local police forces, implementation of the Systems Analysis project, designed to assess and accredit those law enforcement agencies that meet clear criteria for democratic police institutions, was commenced. Local police 'Change Management Teams' to guide the restructuring process have been established and on-site assessments have been conducted in seven out of 12 law enforcement agencies in the Federation, majority areas of the Republika Srpska and the State Border Service. The Brcko District police has instituted all necessary changes and has been accredited as the first police institution in BiH to meet democratic law enforcement standards.

The establishment of non-political Police Commissioner positions to ensure that career professionals lead police forces was also initiated. Ad-interim Commissioners have been appointed in eight cantons and ad-interim Directors of Police have been appointed in each entity Ministry of Interior.

Finally, through the academies, some 702 minority police were trained and deployed. Refresher training courses have produced 76 graduates; many of whom have been assigned to middle and senior management ranks. A total of 164 officers were voluntarily re-deployed to their pre-war locations, including the first senior Serb as Chief of Police in Drvar and a Bosniac as Deputy Chief in Srebrenica.

INSTITUTION BUILDING AND INTER-POLICE FORCE COOPERATION

Institution building and inter-police force cooperation also led to some important measures:

- negotiation of the Presidential Decisions in February 2000 for the establishment of the multiethnic BiH State Border Service, with deployments of the first units in June 2000. The State Border Service (SBS) now controls 88 per cent of the state's borders through 17 Border Service units and four out of six regional Field Offices (1,750 SBS officers have been deployed), including at three international airports in Sarajevo, Banja Luka and Mostar;

- the Service now has its own professional training centre in Suhodol, near Sarajevo, which has conducted 42 specialization courses with 534 participants. Another 529 officers have undergone transition training. In April 2002, 50 cadets commenced training at Suhodol;

- the effective operation of the SBS has contributed to an estimated 20 per cent increase in customs revenue. Together with the introduction of a partial visa regime and an airport landing card, the establishment of the SBS has resulted in a 66 per cent decrease in illegal migration through Sarajevo airport in 2001 (from 24,000 to 8,000), with further decreases (92 per cent) at airports in the first four months of 2002 compared to the same period in 2001;

- establishment of the Ministerial Consultative Meeting on Police Matters (MCMPM) and the Joint Entity Task Force (JETF) for inter-entity police cooperation. Three operations have been conducted targeting illegal migration, trafficking in human beings, and stolen vehicles;

- brokering of the Regional Cooperative Law Enforcement Arrangement (Croatia, BiH, FRY-Serbia/Montenegro) that established a Committee of Ministers and a Regional Task Force (RTF) to combat on a regional basis organized crime, illegal migration and, post-11 September, international terrorism. An agreement was negotiated with Hungary in June 2002 to become a member of these bodies. Furthermore, regional operation 'Common Purpose' against organized crime, including surveillance of known/suspected terrorism affiliated groups, is ongoing;

- facilitation of consensus on the establishment of a State Information and Protection Agency (SIPA). The draft SIPA legislation has passed through initial BiH parliamentary processes;

- promotion and support of the establishment of the National Bureau of Interpol in Sarajevo;

- support of a Court Police programme to secure judicial personnel and property and to set up a witness protection programme. Court police are deployed in 75 per cent of the Federation.

SETTING THE AGENDA TO COMBAT ORGANIZED CRIME
AND TERRORISM

To combat terrorism and organized crime, UNMIBH identified inter-entity cooperation within a regional framework as the most expedient approach. Transnational criminal activities cannot be fought from any one state. A common strategic approach by all effected nations is required – for crime knows no boundary and is not hindered by ethnicity or religion. Towards this end, UNMIBH's initiatives have focused on the following five principal areas:

- inter-entity police cooperation;

- police operations undertaken at the BiH national level;

- Special Trafficking Operations Programme (STOP);

- regional law enforcement cooperative efforts;

- operation 'Common Purpose' to combat organized crime and terrorism.

Inter-entity police cooperation

In March 2000, UNMIBH established the BiH Ministerial Consultative Meeting on Police Matters (MCMPM) for inter-entity police cooperation. The MCMPM is the only forum by which the ten Cantonal Ministries of Interior and the Republika Srpska Public Security Centres meet on a monthly basis to cooperate and coordinate law enforcement activities.[4]

The MCMPM is made up of the minister of Interior of the Federation (FMUP), the minister of Interior of the Republika Srpska (RS MUP), and the Director of the SBS.

In August 2000, the MCMPM signed a Cooperative Law Enforcement Arrangement,[5] which established a Joint Entity Task Force (JETF) specifically charged to: cooperate, coordinate and carry out police activities against illegal migration and organized criminal activities, including trafficking in human beings, throughout BiH.

Members of JETF include representatives of the Republika Srpska MUP; Federation MUP; Brcko District Police; the SBS; and a member of the BiH Interpol National Coordination Bureau. JETF meets on a monthly basis and has a rotating chair between the Entity Ministries of Interior. Following 11 September the work of both the MCMPM and JETF expanded to encompass anti-terrorism measures.[6]

Police operations undertaken at the BiH national level

With the approval of the MCMPM, the JETF has carried out three combined operations in BiH against: illegal migration (Operation EBB Tide in December 2000); trafficking in women (Operation Macro in March 2001); and organized vehicle theft rings (Operation Auto Alarm in July 2001). Additionally, UNMIBH has facilitated dialogue among state institutions, the Republika Srpska MUP and the Federation MUP to establish a State Information and Protection Agency, tasked with providing security to VIPs, state institution buildings and combat national and international crime. The Council of Europe Venice Commission has provided its opinion on the Agency's legality under the BiH Constitution and the draft law is before Parliament.

Special Trafficking Operations Programme (STOP)

UNMIBH has undertaken robust action against trafficking in human beings in accordance with the development of local police capacity building. Since 1999, in close cooperation with other international organizations, UNMIBH has implemented a multi-pronged approach comprising of:

- protection and repatriation of trafficking victims;
- monitoring and improving local police capacity and willingness to combat trafficking and organized crime;
- applying severe measures against local police complicity in trafficking;
- urging and assisting in the criminal prosecution of perpetrators;
- undertaking systemic administrative measures to close legal loopholes and lax administrative procedures that assist traffickers; and
- maintaining a zero tolerance policy against any involvement in trafficking or prostitution by UNMIBH international personnel.[7]

    Trafficking routes have become well-established between BiH and other eastern European countries. The legacy of weak state-level institutions once unable to coordinate responses to the problem and porous national borders, entrenched and facilitated the work of traffickers. The trade in human beings is run by well-established local and international organized crime rings, which have flourished because local law enforcement and political officials are either involved in trafficking themselves, or they are unable or unwilling to fight crime rings. The supply of women forced into the prostitution has been fuelled by poor social and economic conditions in several eastern European countries. To date, over 80 per cent of assisted trafficking victims originate in Moldova and Romania.

The primary systemic basis of the trafficking problem lies in the relationship between organized crime, local law enforcement officials and local politicians. UNMIBH has focused extensive efforts on addressing this volatile relationship. Under the auspices of the UNMIBH Joint Task Force, UNMIBH gathers intelligence on recruiters, traffickers, smuggling routes and night-club owners. The BiH SBS further assists in controlling porous borders and gathering intelligence.

Since early 1999, the UNMIBH Human Rights Office was designated as having the lead role within UNMIBH to address the serious human rights violations of trafficked human beings. UNMIBH's tasks in this regard were defined as:

- monitoring local police raids of night-clubs and interviewing women present to ascertain if any of them were victims of trafficking;
- providing protection to trafficked victims (which includes ensuring that victims are safely repatriated); and
- monitoring investigations, pressing for prosecutions and gathering intelligence on organized crime.

UNMIBH has identified nearly 300 night-clubs in BiH suspected of involvement in prostitution and has monitored hundreds of raids conducted by local police since 1999. In March 2001, UNMIBH initiated the largest-ever BiH anti-trafficking police operation (Operation Macro), in which Entity, cantonal, Brcko police and the SBS, under the JETF, simultaneously raided 38 night clubs and interviewed 178 women and girls, of whom 13 admitted to have been trafficked and sought repatriation assistance.

The number and scope of such raids has since increased dramatically, and in July 2001 the Special Trafficking Operations Proramme (STOP) was created to streamline an increased number of IPTF monitors involved in anti-trafficking efforts. Since the creation of STOP, police forces have also appointed local police to combat trafficking and conduct raids on night-clubs. To date, STOP teams have monitored 446 raids on suspected brothels and interviewed 1,561 women. Of this number, 186 have been assisted with repatriation to their home countries. Unfortunately, due to lack of evidence or women refusing to provide evidence, only 102 charges have been laid with only 6 convictions resulting while the others are before the courts.[8]

The STOP programme also incorporates the work of the joint UNMIBH/ International Organization for Migration (IOM) Counter-Trafficking Project established in March 1999 to rescue and repatriate trafficking victims to their countries of origin. Three shelters have been set up where victims remain until IOM arranges repatriation. UNMIBH has ensured 24-hour local police security, and STOP team members escort victims to court, medical appointments and the airport upon repatriation.

The UNMIBH/IOM project has assisted over 410 trafficked victims since 1999. It is important to note that the figure includes most, but not all, trafficked victims since less than 5 per cent of identified victims do not seek IOM assistance. Furthermore, it is not clear whether the growing number of identified victims since 1999 is the result of greater incidence of trafficking or the beginning of effective police operations or both.

UNMIBH has further initiated independent investigations into the involvement of local police authorities in trafficking. In the context of the UNMIBH/IPTF local police registration process, UNMIBH ensures that local law enforcement officials are de-authorized when independent evidence of involvement in trafficking is found and presses local authorities to initiate criminal proceedings against such individuals.

After an investigation in Bijeljina, Republika Srpska, UNMIBH pressed for and followed an internal investigation of local police officers that had been identified by trafficking victims as being involved in trafficking. UNMIBH found evidence that the Bijeljina Ministry of Interior Department of Foreigners has systematically facilitated trafficking, and an internal investigation is ongoing into the level of involvement of Bijeljina police officials. To date, six local police officers have been de-authorized as a result of an investigation conducted by the UNMIBH Human Rights Office. Similar investigations and audits of the Department of Foreigners are also being undertaken in other key areas in BiH. In addition, UNMIBH is screening and counselling women who are brought to the Department of Foreign Nationals to register for work permits by checking for false passports and conducting interviews of the women to determine whether they are potential trafficking victims.

UNMIBH has likewise advised, coordinated and facilitated joint operations, including with the Ministries of Interior, Health, Trade and Employment and Social Welfare for combined inspections of the night clubs to verify and prosecute possible violations of local laws with a view to shut down the night clubs when there is evidence of violation of law and administrative regulations. This approach has been extremely successful in Brcko, where cooperation between UNMIBH and the Departments of Labour, Finance and Commerce resulted in the successful closing of all bars and motels determined to be engaged in organized trafficking and prostitution on the basis of violations of labour, taxation, zoning or residence laws. However, night club owners may re-open once they have complied with the laws, and

UNMIBH continues to examine more permanent ways of shutting down the clubs. This includes examining ways to prevent the issue of work permits to foreign 'dancers' and 'waitresses'.

Clearly a concerted approach between all elements of the legal system is warranted to end this sordid trade. However, long-term success will only be possible when the same degree of international support and assistance provided to local police, is extended to the reform and restructuring of the judicial system.

Regional law enforcement cooperative efforts

In May 2001, UNMIBH brokered a Cooperative Law Enforcement Arrange-ment between the Ministries of Interior of the Federal Republic of Yugo-slavia, the Republic of Croatia and BiH. The arrangement sought to combat organized crime and international terrorism. A Committee of ministers representing the three parties, and chaired by UNMIBH, meets bi-monthly. Membership comprises the minister of Interior of the Republic of Croatia, the minister of Interior of the FRY, the minister of Interior of the Republika Srpska, and the minister of Interior of the Federation.[9]

As a result of the arrangement, a Regional Task Force was established to exchange information and to coordinate police activities. On 12 September 2001, the Committee of ministers approved a regional strategy to combat criminal activities that was proposed by the Regional Task Force. This included an operational plan to fight international terrorism. The following is a summary of security measures planned, or carried out, in BiH by the respective Ministries of Interior of the Republika Srpska and the Federation.

Ministry of Interior-Republika Srpska (RS)
On 12 September 2001, the RS MUP initiated the following measures:

- reinforcement of physical and operational security measures to protect diplomatic and consular premises and international organizations;
- tasked their organizational units to carry out appropriate checks of registries of all foreign citizens residing in or visiting the RS;
- identification of foreigners who have obtained citizenship and passports and are resident in the RS;
- conduct of checks and surveillance on all persons and organizations that may be affiliated or connected to terrorist activities; and
- increase of control over border crossings not yet handed over to the SBS including the Banja Luka airport.

The RS MUP further stepped up action in identifying and detaining illegal migrants and exchanging information through the Regional Task Force with appropriate law enforcement agencies including Interpol. Finally, the RS MUP has established close cooperation with the RS Ministry of Finance to control and identify postal and bank accounts that may be linked to terrorist activities or organizations.[10]

Ministry of Interior-Federation of Bosnia and Herzegovina
In the aftermath of 11 September the Federation MUP initiated the following actions:

- intensification of physical and operational security of diplomatic/consular offices with special emphasis on security for the US embassy in Sarajevo and appropriate residences;
- establishment of data bases on individuals with suspected links to terrorist organizations; and
- increase of exchange of information with local, state and regional law enforcement agencies including Interpol.

The Federation Ministry of Interior further adopted a strategy to combat international terrorism defined by:

- hastening the passage of appropriate laws (Law on Fighting Terrorism, '*lex specialis*'), amendments to the Law on Criminal Procedure and the Law on Internal Affairs, and the introduction of measures (with approval of the Office of the High Representative and UNMIBH) to overcome deficiencies in present laws;
- training, equipping and deployment of personnel in anti-terrorist units;
- enhancing information linkages with Cantonal Ministries of Interior, the RS MUP, SBS, Brcko District Police Services, Interpol and regional law enforcement agencies;
- close cooperation with judicial organs within the Federation; and
- establishment of an appropriate arrangement for cooperation between intelligence services in BiH for information sharing under the auspices of a third party.[11]

Operation Common Purpose

On 12 September 2001 the Committee of ministers endorsed a regional operational strategy to combat organized criminal activities and terrorism. The plan Operation Common Purpose began on 1 December 2001 with concurrent operations in the FRY, the Republic of Croatia and in BiH to ensure:

- tighter security at borders to detect weapons smuggling and illegal migration;
- surveillance operations against known or suspected terrorists and affiliated organizations; and
- combating drug trafficking.[12]

Operation Common Purpose immediately proved effective. In the FRY, Belgrade police detained 32 Afghanis and 2 Iranians in connection to possible illegal activities and carried out a wide operation against trafficking in women resulting in 150 charges against criminal elements. Information was passed to Republika Srpska police and criminals in Bijeljina were arrested on charges of trafficking. In the area of weapons smuggling, numerous illegal weapons, including assault rifles, grenade launchers and large amounts of ammunition have been confiscated along with illicit drugs.

In BiH, the combined forces of the SBS and other law enforcement agencies have carried out operations, which include:

- the search of 61,000 vehicles at the BiH border resulting in over 400 charges laid and 131 arrests; and
- entry-refusal to 135 persons at 13 BiH land border crossings for improper documentation.

With regard to operations against known or suspected terrorist and affiliated organizations operating within BiH, there are further encouraging results. After the terrorist attacks on 11 September, the BiH Presidency, Council of ministers, presidents and premiers of entities agreed to establish a Joint Coordination Team to Fight Terrorism. Currently, the team is comprised of 24 members that include representatives of Entity governments, UNMIBH, other international organizations and several embassies.

The Joint Coordination Team has undertaken a review of BiH citizenship obtained by foreigners and has pushed for the adoption of deportation legislation in order to identify known or suspected terrorists and their activities. Two commissions have reviewed the records of all BiH citizenship granted to some 900 foreigners between April 1992 and April 2002. To date 94 persons have had their citizenship revoked for obtaining documentation by illegal means and another 741 are under review. UNMIBH is ensuring that new or amended deportation legislation is within European and international standards of justice.

The Joint Coordination Team is further awaiting the results of investigations undertaken by the BiH Federation Ministries of Trade, Social Care and Financial Police into the activities of six international aid organizations that are suspected of having links with terrorist groups.

CONCLUSION

If we have learned anything from the complex peace operations of the past decade, it is that the greatest threat to stability in BiH and the Balkans comes from the institutional weaknesses of the states themselves, from the inability of new democracies to control borders, to fight organized crime, terrorism and promote the rule of law.

Building law enforcement capacities is a long-term process requiring patience, professional personnel, resources and political will. The UN experience in BiH since 1996 has shown that through pragmatic approaches with realistic goals and objectives, local law enforcement agencies will perform to a level consistent with European policing standards. Law enforcement officers will cooperate professionally across ethnic, political and state boundaries with their counterparts to great effect. However, it is absolutely clear that to meet the security challenges in BiH, the trust and cooperation fostered by UNMIBH must increasingly be strengthened and expanded through criminal information exchanges and continued joint policing operations. For only then, will organized crime and terrorists have no places of chaos in which to hide, and the people of BiH and the broader region will have the opportunity to live in societies that function free of fear under the rule of law.

NOTES

1. The General Framework Agreement for Peace in Bosnia and Herzegovina, Annex 11, article III 1.
2. GFAP, Annex 4, article III 2 (c).
3. United Nations Mission in Bosnia and Herzegovina, Mandate Implementation Plan, Jan. 2000.
4. Ministerial Meeting on Police Matters (MCMPM) established on 11 Mar. 2000.
5. Cooperative Law Enforcement Arrangement between Republika Srpska Ministry of Interior and Federation of Bosnia and Herzegovina Ministry of Interior, 12 Aug. 2000.
6. Joint Entity Task Force established under the MCMPM.
7. UNMIBH Special Trafficking Operations Project initiated in July 2001.
8. Figures for Regional IPTF-STOP teams, 25 July 2001–24 May 2002.

9. Regional Cooperative Law Enforcement Arrangement between the Federal Republic of Yugoslavia, the Republic of Croatia and Bosnia and Herzegovina, 4 May 2001.
10. Republika Srpska Anti-terrorist Strategy, 1 Oct. 2002.
11. Federation of BiH Strategy to Combat Terrorism, 5 Oct. 2002.
12. Operation Common Purpose established by the Regional Task Force on 17 November 2001. The operation began on 1 December 2001 and will run for an indefinite period.

—◄◦►—

SEVEN

NGOs and Peace Operations in the post-11 September Context

Nicholas Stockton

To address the question, 'whither non-governmental organizations (NGOs) in peace operations after 11 September 2001?', it is useful to first outline the role of NGOs in peace operations before 11 September. This is not however a straightforward task, since it first requires some clarity about which organizations should be classified as 'non-governmental'. Nevertheless it is still necessary, as the complexity of the NGO universe has a direct bearing upon the highly diverse nature of the roles undertaken by them in peace operations. Their involvement, in what are often also referred to as 'complex emergencies', eludes easy generalization: ranging from logistically dominated material relief operations, to community-based or 'track-two' peace-building, post-traumatic stress counselling, human rights monitoring and reporting, advocacy and campaigning, to name just a few. The NGO appellation covers multinational humanitarian agencies with annual turnover in excess of US$100 million, small village or neighbourhood based self-help groups, and more (or less) radical advocacy organizations focusing variously upon such matters as the environment and the rights of women, children, refugees, disabled persons and ethnic or religious minorities. Some NGOs are 'faith-based', while others are secular. As well as their diversity of origin, purpose and scale, NGOs have very varied relationships with governments. Some maintain a strict separation to ensure their independence, while others work in close collaboration with official agencies and are highly income-dependent upon government aid budgets. This diversity in terms of size, objectives and degree of independence makes any generalization about NGOs a risky and sometimes pointless undertaking, one compounded by their sheer numbers in some situations.[1]

With regard to the post-11 September future, as much as to the pre-11 September past, one thing is quite certain: the roles of NGOs in peace operations will continue to be highly varied; for some people in coordinating functions, perhaps, bewilderingly or even frustratingly so. However, it is important to stress that NGOs are not, by and large, just voluntary or low paid service deliverers funded by governments. Most human rights NGOs, for example, attempt to bring about change almost exclusively through advocacy and campaigning work, rather than through welfare provision, operational development or humanitarian action. Some NGOs combine all of these approaches. Historically, NGOs, such as the Anti-Slavery Society and the Save the Children Fund, have been society's 'whistle-blowers', exposing the human impact of unfettered and irresponsible commercial, military or political interests. Their charitable service delivery functions are sometimes necessary, and exemplars of what can be achieved through material assistance. But some see these as secondary functions, which have only minimal impact upon the great mass of poverty and suffering. Exposing injustice and poverty, and advocating appropriate policy responses, is the primary *raison d'être* of many NGOs. To fully gauge the impact of 11 September and its aftermath upon NGOs, it is therefore necessary to review how it has affected their advocacy and campaigning work as well as their humanitarian and development 'operational' work.

INTERNATIONAL AID AND 'STRATEGIC DISENGAGEMENT' PRIOR TO 11 SEPTEMBER 2001

The world, on 10 September 2001, was being 'shaped' on the basis of the 'Washington Consensus', rooted in the belief that a liberal free-market democracy is the best, most natural and proper order for organizing human affairs. The role of the state should be limited to a minimal regulatory function, with 'good governance' seen to be the product of a dynamic relationship between a democratically elected government, the private sector and 'civil society'. In the evolution of a new global order based upon these characteristics, NGOs were expected to play an important role: helping to break government service provision monopolies, acting as monitor and whistle-blower, and helping to safeguard young and fragile democracies. NGOs occupied the rather unique position of being both the means and the end of the development process.

However, while a consensus of sorts existed about some elements of this new vision of the world, the efficacy of international aid in helping to bring this to fruition was subject to growing doubts. During the latter part of the 1990s, international aid was in a steep, apparently inexorable, decline, both in absolute terms and as a proportion of GDP. By 2000 it had fallen by 12 per cent from its 1992 zenith.[2] The international development system was seen to have failed by growing numbers of commentators outside the aid system and by many within it too.[3] UN peace operations, especially those outside Europe, were also considered as ineffective, expensive and unacceptably dangerous, particularly after the debacle of Operation Restore Hope in Somalia. In addition, the international humanitarian system was widely and repeatedly condemned for making bad situations worse.[4] With the quality of international aid subject to growing disquiet, the quantity of resources put into aid budgets by the Organization for Economic Cooperation and Development (OECD) countries had fallen into recession. Perhaps associated with this loss of confidence in, or lack of commitment to development aid, humanitarian assistance and UN peacekeeping, there was growing evidence of US disengagement from 'non-strategic' countries. Its international aid expenditure in failed and failing states declined accordingly. Africa was particularly affected, although the reduction in international aid for the continent, rather conveniently, coincided with a chorus of calls for 'African solutions for African problems', thereby shifting the spotlight away from the continent's falling aid receipts. Although the UK government actually stepped up international aid spending in the late 1990s, it became apparent during this period that the domestic and international political opportunity costs associated with the reduction in aid budgets were negligible in most OECD countries and the broad trend of declining aid flows continued.

From the perspective of NGOs, the retrenchment of aid budgets during the 1990s had been more than compensated for by the growing proportion of official aid channelled through them, especially in humanitarian emergencies. This helps to explain why many of the larger international NGOs, which had been the major beneficiaries of 'aid privatization' in the 1980s and 1990s, were rather muted in their response to dwindling official aid budgets. Paradoxically, while international aid was shrinking, an emerging consensus about the relative efficiency and effectiveness of NGOs, compared to their government counterparts, combined with the notion that good governance was dependent upon the development of 'civil society', led to rapid 'supply-side', official aid-sponsored growth in the NGO sector.

It was not just the significant fiscal expansion fuelled by official funds that perhaps made the early 1990s a heyday for NGOs. The political space in many 'third world' countries created by the reduction of western involvement at the end of the cold war produced a vacuum within which NGOs expanded their mandates and, at least with regard to weaker or fragmented 'southern' governments, their influence too. While the rapid growth of NGOs invited some accusations of their incorporation by donor governments, the ideological objections to receiving funds from official sources had, for many agencies, receded after the end of the cold war. Furthermore, in the early days of western government induced NGO expansion, there were remarkably few strings attached, only limited monitoring and fairly modest reporting requirements. In these respects NGOs were enjoying the benefit of being an end as well as the means of development. For donor governments, an added benefit was that many major NGOs were gradually brought 'inside the tent' of the aid establishment, and advocacy became more often a matter of cosy chats with ministers than the more troublesome device of noisy protest on the streets.

However, by the mid 1990s, the NGO gloss was beginning to dull. While the 'Goma' episode was perhaps the humanitarian agencies' Nemesis, with extensive media reports of dysfunctional agency competition, clumsy efforts at media manipulation and 'feeding the killers in the camps',[5] many NGOs in the mid-1990s rather deftly re-aligned themselves with new varieties of 'humanitarianism' and 'peacebuilding'. Macrae and Leader have documented how these approaches placed a new emphasis upon the achievement of desirable political outcomes in conflict situations.[6] This period was characterized by some quite extravagant claims about what aid in general, and NGOs in particular, could potentially achieve in peace operations.[7] Based upon the attractive premise that prevention is better, and cheaper, than cure, the latter part of the 1990s was heavily influenced by Mary Anderson's proposition that aid could be used for 'building local capacities for peace'.[8] In many respects, the growth of NGO involvement in peacebuilding and 'track 2' diplomacy, represented the posterior logic of official major power political disengagement in a number of 'failed' or so-called 'rogue' states in the south. Although there remained a residual major-power political monitoring and representational function embedded in official aid bodies such as the UK's Department for International Development (DFID), government funding and encouragement for NGO expansion into conflict-related diplomacy probably implied official buck-passing rather than burden-sharing with civil society. By taking on these new political roles in peace operations, the NGOs also raised expectations of what they might be able to achieve, where conventional diplomacy and official peacebuilding had failed.[9] However, by the first year of the new century, the seemingly intractable nature of the conflicts in Sudan, Somalia, Burundi, Uganda, Democratic Republic of the Congo, Colombia and Afghanistan, and the apparent failure of the new humanitarian and peacebuilding paradigms to live up to their promises, was causing yet further introspection in the peace operations business. This was reflected in the Brahimi Report and its call for a more authoritarian approach to conflict management and aid coordination.[10] In part, at least, this was in response to a growing hubbub of allegations expressed by senior officials of the UN about the problems of NGO proliferation and unruliness in the peace-building context.[11]

The contraction of aid, peacekeeping and diplomatic involvement in southern conflicts, unease about the efficacy of international aid, the concomitant promotion of 'budget-lite', 'local solutions for local problems', and a growing concern about the quality of globalization, therefore, more or less summarizes the pre-occupations of a great many NGOs involved in peace operations on the eve of 11 September 2001.

THE POST-11 SEPTEMBER 'PAX-AMERICANA'

At a stroke, the events of 11 September transformed the 'south' from being an object of general western strategic disinterest, to the subject of urgent and principal political priority for the US-led coalition against terrorism. US national security had been breached by a group of people whose leader resided in Afghanistan and whose membership was apparently distributed globally. Suddenly, the failing parts or 'rogue' elements of the south became important again, but primarily in recognition of their potential to host an anti-western movement that had struck so audaciously at two domestic icons of US military and economic power.

In response, the UN Security Council charged member states 'to root out terrorism by all means',[12] and tasked the UN system to facilitate the creation of a post-Taliban political dispensation in Afghanistan.[13] While compromising the neutrality of the UN system and associated NGOs in Afghanistan, resolutions 1373 and 1378 also prepared the way for the military re-mobilization of the United States in the south, with US forces becoming active in the greatest array of countries since the Second World War.[14] While Afghanistan received the greatest news coverage, the operations in the Philippines, Pakistan, Colombia, Georgia, Uzbekistan, Yemen and Tajikistan have all been established or significantly strengthened since 11 September in a radical turnaround in US military policy. Thus the era of considerable NGO autonomy in a US policy vacuum in many southern and 'transitional' countries has now been overtaken by a new era of US diplomatic and military activism. However, this new US-led western political and military activism has yet to reach Somalia, Sudan, the Democratic Republic of Congo (DRC) and many other 'failed' or 'weak' states, thus, in effect, creating a complex patchwork of robust US engagement in some countries and a more disengaged 'business as usual' stance in many others. Whether the newly enhanced threat of potential US intervention is sufficient to alter the political context in countries with only a limited US presence is not yet clear.

While western public commentary about the 'war against terrorism' has largely focused upon its military dimension in Afghanistan, a new post-11 September strategy has also been developed for US foreign aid, with considerable potential importance for the role of NGOs in peace operations. In a speech of great significance for the aid establishment, President Bush announced on 14 March 2002 that his Administration would reverse the long decline in the United States' aid budget. He explained that:

> the growing divide between wealth and poverty, between opportunity and misery, is both a challenge to our compassion and a source of instability. ... The advance of development is a central commitment of American foreign policy. We work for prosperity and opportunity because they're right. We also work for prosperity and opportunity because they help defeat terror.[15]

In concluding this speech, President Bush reversed this order of purpose when he said:

> As the civilized world mobilizes against the forces of terror, we must also embrace the forces of good. By offering hope where there is none, by relieving suffering and hunger where there is too much, *we will make the world not only safer, but better.*[16] [author's italics]

Exactly what President Bush meant by 'too much' suffering and hunger is not clear, but his proposed criteria for the disbursement of the new funds relate less to conventional humanitarian principles of resource allocation than they do to old-fashioned political 'realism': '(C)ountries that live by ... three broad standards – ruling justly, investing in their people, and encouraging economic freedom – will receive more aid from America'.[17]

In spite of the best efforts of some leading NGOs to put a positive gloss on this, it was obviously not a vote in favour of humanitarian impartiality in the aid resource allocation process: giving more where need is greatest.[18] It was instead the promise of a reward scheme for friends of the coalition against terrorism. President Bush's speech thus provides early evidence of a new determination to recast the development aid system as an instrument for the enhancement of US domestic security. Arguably, the impact of the wars in the Balkans had already generated similar pressures from European governments for international aid budgets to deliver domestic political relief by stemming the flow of asylum seekers fleeing the former Yugoslavia. The willingness of many humanitarian NGOs to operate within the political space created by NATO forces in Kosovo had already demonstrated the pliability and manipulability of almost all components of the humanitarian aid system for the pursuit of purposes concerned primarily with domestic European politics. In Afghanistan, the incorporation of the entire assistance effort into the US-led pacification strategy was just another logical step in the same direction.

For NGOs, the once rather empty debating rooms considering humanitarian and peacebuilding policy now feel increasingly crowded, as those working in Kabul in the leading laboratory of this new policy environment could attest. The diverse, often contradictory, but above all NGO implemented, aid programme of 'peacebuilding' in mid-2001 in Afghanistan has now been overtaken by a dramatically more ambitious strategic goal for international assistance in 2002. But this is a new reality in which the 'regulatory regime'[19] of foreign aid is no longer labouring under the handicap of American disinterest, but is instead now operating close to, if not directly under, a recast and newly energized American foreign policy. It is also a context in which less familiar 'humanitarian' and 'peacebuilding' actors from the military and private sectors are challenging the once undisputed monopoly of NGO project implementation.

However, with UN Security Council backing,[20] the west has taken a gamble of considerable historic significance, with the almost complete integration of the humanitarian system, NGOs included, into an explicitly partisan, integrated military/political project. The engineering of a post-Taliban regime through the combined efforts of the Coalition military intervention, the International Security Assistance Force (ISAF, created by resolution 1386 of 20 December 2001), and the wholesale integration of all UN-coordinated international assistance to Afghanistan, for purposes principally concerning the security of western states, is a hitherto untried projection into the south of the robust political intercession methods, dubbed by UK Prime Minister Tony Blair as 'humanitarian intervention', that had been pioneered in the Balkans.

THE PROSPECTS FOR NGOS IN PEACE OPERATIONS

There are two significant ways in which the war against terrorism is likely to affect NGOs involved in peace operations. First, humanitarian organizations are likely to come under increased pressure to comply with the political strategies pursued by the coalition against terrorism and to demonstrate their actual contribution to political objectives in priority theatres of war. This pressure is most likely to be experienced in an indirect manner, through greater competition for government aid funds coming from the military and the private sector, although it is also likely to be felt through closer political monitoring and greater intelligence surveillance of NGOs. The fact that the broad spectrum of civil society organizations encompasses a range of radical, populist, direct-action anti-globalization and anti-war groups will ensure the latter. Second, in countries or regions which are subject to conflict but which are not believed to host active terrorist networks, the weakness of US (and allied) strategic engagement is likely to continue, or possibly wane still further as official aid resources are re-deployed to priority theatres.[21] The enhanced political instrumentalization of official aid budgets will create new challenges for the provision of humanitarian assistance on an impartial and equitable basis both within priority theatres and between priority and non-priority theatres.

For humanitarian NGOs these are not entirely new problems. Many of the OECD countries have pursued a policy of coherence between their political and aid programmes for some years. As the Development Assistance Committee of the OECD opines: 'development co-operation is only one instrument of foreign policy: mechanisms for coordination between policy instruments available to donor states (military, political, development and trade) must be strengthened'.[22] The UN 'strategic framework' initiative is another attempt to promote coherence between assistance and political instruments through a process which has the basic objective of adapting international assistance to better 'inform and be informed by' the UN political programme.[23] The Brahimi Report proposed even more integration (or rather subordination) of international assistance in the service of the political programme of the UN, an approach which has placed new pressures upon NGOs in Afghanistan to demonstrate their political utility and to down-play their humanitarian identities.[24]

Although 'coherence' with some rather unobtrusive and often vague 'conflict management' policies may have alarmed some NGOs in the past, the agencies have in general been somewhat quietly divided about the problems posed by, for example, the 'new humanitarian' policy of DFID.[25] While this seems to impose political conditionalities upon the provision of humanitarian aid, DFID justified its new policy on the basis of the claim that it would achieve better political, economic and humanitarian outcomes in the longer term. Few NGOs would find any reason to be against that objective in principle. The new humanitarian policy did not in that respect represent a substantial shift in strategic direction, but rather it was an adaptation of conflict management tactics founded upon empirical arguments, however questionable these may be.[26] However, the emerging agenda, especially for US-funded aid programmes, does represent a radical extension of this logic, by seeking to link the outcome of local aid projects with remote effects in the domestic domain of the donor nation. For example, a development programme might now be deemed to be a failure where it raises local living standards by a significant margin, but fails to prevent newly generated household income from being donated to the nearby *madrassa* (Islamic School) as a contribution to the 'jihad' against US 'imperialism'. Thus, from a US perspective, otherwise 'successful' development could equate to increased capacity of militant Islamists to wage war against the United States and further undermine US domestic security.[27] The burdens of expectation and responsibility placed upon aid agencies are therefore increasing as the political priority for international assistance switches from alleviating poverty and suffering in the recipient country to leveraging greater domestic security in the donor country. Receiving government funds tied to these objectives will test the basic purpose of many NGOs, although in reality the challenge appears to be targeted at the level of the system rather than at the individual agency project contract.

In other words, for the time being at least, the NGOs may be able to act as if nothing much has changed since 11 September. By and large, this is what the great majority of the larger international 'humanitarian' NGOs appear to be doing. However, President Bush's 14 March speech also served notice that within the Republican Party the scepticism about the efficacy of international aid has only been suspended temporarily. Without clear evidence of effective results, it would seem likely that the private sector and the military may well turn out to be the major institutional beneficiaries of the new aid policy. In Afghanistan, the planned opening of an office in every province of the country by the Coalition Joint Civil-Military Task Force (CJCMTF) to undertake 'humanitarian' projects on a nationwide basis is perhaps an early indication of what might happen to the new US Agency for International Development (USAID) money. For the time being, the NGOs seem to be transfixed, apparently unable to comprehend what is happening, and thus unable to either endorse or reject the new US aid dispensation. But in Afghanistan at least, it is no longer business as usual. The political stake invested in achieving a peaceful and terrorist-free outcome in Afghanistan demands unprecedented levels of achievement from the aid agencies and probably signals an unfamiliar degree of political monitoring of their performance. Those agencies which choose, either on principle or by default, to carry on as before are likely to find themselves witnessing a more politically compliant military, or private sector counterpart, getting on with the job instead.

In contrast, in countries where there is (currently) no evidence of the presence of international terrorist cells, the absence of robust US and other western powers engagement seems likely to continue, not least due to the current human-resource draining military focus upon Afghanistan and Iraq. In the Democratic Republic of Congo (DRC) for example, where it is estimated that over three million people may have died from the effects of war since 1999,[28] the contrasting nature of the international response could hardly be greater. Local war-lords continue to wreak havoc with complete impunity and the aid agencies remain for much of the time confined to their bases in a few major cities. There is no 'B–52' factor available now, nor even in distant prospect, and the level of financing for the, already very modest, UN consolidated appeal continues to be very weak. No troop contributor can be found to provide a single combat-ready soldier for the UN peace-keeping operation, rendering the UN Mission in the DRC (MONUC) practically toothless, as acknowledged by the Secretary-General.[29] The NGOs face no new competition from either the military or the private sector, largely because there are barely any resources to compete over. In spite of the fact that the humanitarian case for providing assistance in the DRC is far stronger than the case for Afghanistan, it appears the DRC's misfortune may, rather bizarrely, rest in it having so far not played host to Al Qaeda.

THE CHALLENGE OF THE WAR AGAINST TERRORISM FOR NGOS

For many NGOs, the association recently discovered by President Bush between poverty, political disempowerment and terrorism will have come as no surprise. What is less likely to generate a robust consensus is the nature of the US-led response. While the proposed increase in US development aid is politically significant, the additional funds are clearly inadequate for the purpose of fulfilling the economic and political aspirations of all those 'at risk' of becoming terrorists. Furthermore, the balance of expenditure between the military stick and the developmental carrot is so heavily weighted in favour of the retributive arm, that the distributive justice that might be achieved through increased development assistance will be barely noticed by those whose sense of grievance against the current sole superpower constitutes the reservoir of potential terrorists. That 'swamp' is only likely to expand and deepen if the retributive elements of the war against terrorism are taken further into Pakistan and into Iraq.

For the time being at least, such anxieties remain largely unvoiced by the NGOs. Among American NGOs especially, the reluctance to be publicly equivocal about the US response to the events of 11 September is based upon the fear of being denounced as unpatriotic, un-American and 'against us'.

For the time being, perhaps, this might work. But the real challenge for NGOs resides less in the operational adaptations to the war against terrorism, difficult as some of these will be, than it does in developing an informed opinion about the likely longer-term impact upon poverty and suffering that the war against terrorism, in all of its manifestations, is likely to produce.

While it was largely absent from the most fragile states in the south, the United States could be properly chided for sins of omission. This new era of US foreign activism will inevitably produce circumstances where NGOs witness the impact of ill-judged or mismanaged military and political sins of commission, and where sharp differences of opinion are almost bound to occur over matters of policy at a tactical level. This has the potential for generating far greater discomfort in government–NGO relations. Salman Rushdie, in an article that is generally highly supportive of the US position, asks:

> how can you present yourselves as defending the great values of freedom and justice, if that defence promotes unfreedom [sic] and injustice? ... People may judge that Americans care only about their own security and are once again prepared in the name of that security, to sacrifice the freedoms of others. If that judgement is made, America's cause will be lost. America's national interest can only lie in the advancement of the cause of freedom and justice.[30]

The challenge for NGOs notionally committed to social and economic justice is therefore not really about 'are you with us or against us?', as President Bush originally framed it, but rather whether the *means* or *tactics* employed in the war against terrorism are consistent with its ends, and whether these are acceptable in legal and ethical terms. For NGOs, a conflict of interests might well arise when their actions are driven in one direction by their mandated commitment to policies consistent with the independent and impartial pursuit of justice and equity, and in another direction by the offer of large sums of official money to act as instruments of potentially flawed donor strategies designed first and foremost to enhance western domestic security.

In a study of attempts in the UK and the Netherlands to achieve greater coherence between international aid and foreign policies, Macrae and Leader chose to focus their analysis solely on government agencies.[31] They presumed a lack of NGO independence, simply upon the basis of the old materialist adage, 'he who pays the piper calls the tune'. On this basis, as the major humanitarian NGOs are highly dependent upon government funding, they can thus be assumed to follow the funds rather than abide by some awkward humanitarian principles. International NGO responses to the new policy challenges in Afghanistan would appear, initially at least, to bear out the Macrae and Leader analysis. If the proposition is correct, the outlook for the larger 'humanitarian' NGOs that depend heavily upon government funding will, in the post-11 September world, presumably therefore presage further incorporation into the strategies developed to engineer the new global Pax-Americana. However, this analysis does not take any account of the considerable privately-donated financial resources mobilized by some large NGOs such as Save the Children, OXFAM and *Médecins sans Frontières* (MSF). Furthermore, such organizations have large constituencies of public support and, on certain occasions, have demonstrated their capacity and willingness to run the gauntlet of government disapproval.[32] Both private funds and public support, in different but complementary ways, continue to hold out the prospect of a certain independence of thought and action, provided that these NGOs adhere to their founding principles rather than to the seductive dynamic of organizational growth and the political patronage of western leaders.

Potentially, therefore, for such NGOs there remains some possibility of acting independently, but can independent thought and action have any impact on government policy? Neil Macfarlane argues that:

> perceived state interest is the product of a complex interaction between external and domestic pressures on governments. On issues for which there is a serious perceived external threat, the opposite is likely to be the case, and the classical understanding of 'interest' therefore seems to be inadequate as a basis for explaining state behaviour.[33]

This analysis envisages some window of opportunity for NGOs to influence the agenda of their governments through vigorous domestic political action, although in the post-11 September context where a serious perceived external threat most certainly exists, the space for influence is probably more constrained than ever. Macfarlane's argument would imply that it is likely to be especially difficult for humanitarian organizations to bend official foreign policy towards humanitarian principles where the strategic interests of states are involved. Exaggerated assumptions about the influence of NGOs derive from a bygone era of great powers' strategic disinterest, when the NGOs were relatively free to act in accordance with humanitarian principles while simultaneously taking government funds. But in situations redolent with big-power strategic engagement, the key issue will be less with the question about how far the NGOs can influence the states concerned, and more with searching tests of the courage and integrity of NGOs to stand up to and resist their wholesale incorporation into the new domestic security dominated foreign policies of western governments. On the basis of Macfarlane's hypothesis, one might predict that where humanitarian objectives and strategic interests do not coincide, as for example in Afghanistan in the autumn of 2001, only the most determined and truly independent humanitarian agencies will be able to operate in a genuinely impartial and neutral manner. So far the evidence bears out this proposition.

This would suggest that the prognosis for the NGOs will be a clear split between those heavily financed by their governments, such as CARE and OXFAM, and more determinedly independent humanitarian NGOs, perhaps led by MSF, who are intent upon retaining some critical distance to observe and challenge the manner in which the war against terrorism is prosecuted. What might then be at risk for MSF is its membership of the international humanitarian oligopoly: the small club of aid donors and NGOs which together fund and implement the great majority of international humanitarian assistance. Many donors in Afghanistan privately expressed the view that MSF will come under increasing pressure to 'toe the line', while MSF in response, continues to argue that its private financial support is sufficient to enable it to refuse funding from Coalition force governments.[34] While this might be sustainable as a funding strategy for one or two countries, it may be more problematic for MSF if the war against terrorism is carried into many more theatres.

From a fairly cursory examination of NGO websites, a very interesting and perhaps indicative pattern of the split between the large government backed humanitarian agencies and the more financially independent NGOs does seem evident.[35] Using the agencies' own website search facilities, several variations on the theme of the 'war against terrorism' produced no results on the sites of OXFAM, Save the Children, the International Federation of Red Cross and Red Crescent Societies (IFRC), the International Committee of the Red Cross (ICRC), CARE, World Vision and MSF. In contrast, the websites of Greenpeace and Amnesty International generated 571 and 13 'hits' respectively, in the former case reflecting a vibrant debate about the subject and in the latter, some heavy criticism of the US and Coalition tactics. In a more detailed search in the Afghanistan web-pages of OXFAM, Save the Children and CARE, not a single critical comment was offered about the coalition operation in Afghanistan, beyond that is, the rather peculiar common refrain that the military should stay out of relief work.[36] For agencies that all claim to be contributing to public education on the great issues of our time, the big NGOs are remarkably silent on the manner in which the most fundamental principles of humanitarianism have been set conveniently aside. There is no 'obituary' marking the burial in every one of Afghanistan's neighbours of the principle of non-refoulement in October 2001, nor any comments about the humanitarian impact upon civilians of the continuing actions of Coalition forces in Afghanistan. Even the characteristically strident tones of MSF are muted on the subject, limiting their comments to a somewhat limp expression of concern over the 'unacceptably high number of Afghan civilian casualties from the military operations (in Afghanistan)'.[37]

From the websites of the larger humanitarian NGOs, one is thus left with the impression that Afghanistan is a country at ease with itself after the country's liberation from the Taliban and the destruction of Al Qaeda. Contrast this with the human rights agencies and the sense they give of a country self-destructively engaged in retributive ethnic cleaning of Pashtun populations in the north, while suffering extensive 'collateral damage', villages being razed for example, by the Coalition forces in the south. Their reports of gross human rights abuses are clearly inconsistent with the stated objectives of the war against injustice and terrorism, but so far it would seem that the major humanitarian NGOs are either unaware of, or unwilling to speak out about, these matters.

This is not the case for the activists within Human Rights Watch, Greenpeace and Amnesty International. The very direct nature of Amnesty's commentary upon the conduct of the war against terrorism is encapsulated in the title of its position paper setting out how those responsible for the 11 September crimes should be dealt with. It is called 'Pursuing Justice, Not Revenge'.[38] MSF, caught half-way between the humanitarian establishment and the more independently minded human rights NGOs, offers some comment, but it is fairly muted and limited to somewhat formulaic expressions about the non-political nature of humanitarian assistance: 'It is our responsibility to demand that warring parties use proportional force, respect the impartial nature of humanitarian assistance, and avoid co-opting humanitarian actions for their own political and military aims.'[39] By contrast, the sole concern of one major NGO seems to be with the safety of its own staff, arguing that: 'to minimize the risk to aid workers of blurred distinctions, it is vital that transparency be maintained in any military involvement in civil affairs operations. ... The humanitarian community objects in the strongest possible terms to armed soldiers dressing in civilian clothes in order to engage in civil assistance programs.'[40] By implication, it would appear that this NGO has no view about a belligerent military force being involved in 'humanitarian' operations while *wearing* uniforms, or about the civilian casualties which so exercise the human rights agencies.

And it is not as if in all of these cases that the large international NGOs can claim that the security of their staff would be at stake if they did speak out. The argument that they are not human-rights agencies wears rather thin when many analysts believe that the success of the whole assistance enterprise in Afghanistan depends heavily upon the willingness of Pashtuns to be courted through UN-led reconstruction efforts, while being simultaneously bombed into submission by Coalition B-52s. Being a part of this integrated military/political/assistance carrot and stick strategy makes the international NGOs particularly vulnerable to reprisals should they be seen to turn a blind eye to ethnic revanchism against Pashtun communities in the north of Afghanistan. If the international peacebuilding strategy fails, or even just falters, and, for example, parts of Afghanistan experience another conflict driven humanitarian crisis that involves the Taliban or their ideological successors, it is highly unlikely that these same agencies will be allowed to return to the situation *ex ante*, with their impartial and independent humanitarian status intact. This may be the price to be paid for their lack of critical distance from the war against terrorism. Even now, who would be able to gain local consent for humanitarian intervention should substantial human suffering occur in Pashtun areas of Afghanistan is not at all clear. The larger international NGOs have very likely forfeited or at least impaired their credibility as independent and impartial actors in these areas. It remains to be seen how far-reaching and corrosive this politicization of the humanitarian system will be. While it may be too early to tell, the prospects of networked global response from Taliban 'fellow-travellers' against the soft targets of international NGOs must surely be a real possibility.

Rather ironically, Macfarlane, writing a couple of years before 11 September, warned humanitarian NGOs that 'the positioning of humanitarian agencies outside or above politics may prove self-defeating'.[41] While attempting to occupy a position 'above' politics would invite charges of arrogance and conceited moral grand-standing under any circumstances, choosing to operate 'inside' the new politics of aid instrumentalization may prove to be equally self-defeating. The problem in the post-11 September context is that by not positioning themselves outside politics, the NGOs are likely to be seen to have been fully incorporated into the new security strategies of the west. From a purely pragmatic point of view, this might be a perfectly reasonable approach to take provided that the Coalition forces provide adequate security for the protection of the NGOs when working in other politically hostile environments. However, given the dire warnings about military overstretch caused by Operation Enduring Freedom and the claim that Coalition force protection capacity is now at its very limits, the notion that Coalition forces might provide security and evacuation guarantees in, for example, Sudan, Somalia, the DRC, Colombia and other theatres of complex humanitarian intervention, is highly implausible. Thus, for the NGOs whose impartiality has been compromised in Afghanistan, the security of their operations elsewhere will depend upon their new political alignment having no exportable implications. In the networked world of global movements, this may yet turn out to be a forlorn hope.

After more than a decade of the post-cold war 'Washington consensus', some observers, especially in the south, had already begun to conclude that the 'end of history'[42] is more concerned with the coercive policing of an unfair international system which preserves a small club of rich states and powerful corporations determined to protect their affluence and privileges at all costs, and less interested in the promotion of an international meritocracy founded on equity, justice and genuinely free trade. In the new environment, NGOs may now need to decide in which direction their humanitarian principles point, if the choice has to be made between these two models of international relations.

CONCLUSION

In post-11 September peace operations, the great diversity of roles played by NGOs is likely to continue, but the institutional and political environments within which peace operations are conducted are now more clearly demarcated between those theatres within which the war against terrorism is actively pursued and those in which it is latent. It is likely that the 'rules of the game' will be somewhat different in each type of environment.

In the 'Afghanistan' type environment, where hot military operations are mounted in the war against terrorism, the following characteristics are more likely to apply:

- NGOs will encounter a hardening of official donor attitudes in favour of the 'new humanitarian' policies, placing primary emphasis upon achieving a particular political outcome. NGOs, and other humanitarian organizations which attempt to maintain their operational neutrality and to uphold the principles of impartiality and universality in planning and implementing emergency relief programmes, are quite likely to experience increased funding difficulties.

- Competition with private-sector and military humanitarian service providers is likely to increase. The 'market-share' enjoyed by NGOs is therefore likely to decline. Those NGOs that are willing to operate in specific areas and in particular ways favoured by the major donors are most likely to retain their income from government aid budgets. Assistance is more likely to be provided as a political emollient to target groups based upon ethnic, religious or political affiliation. However, there are also likely to be much higher expectations resting upon development agencies to deliver 'public goods' and to close the 'grievance' gap.

- Local consent for humanitarian access in contested areas is likely to be withheld from those agencies closely associated with the United States, the UK and other members of the Coalition against terrorism. In practice, this is likely to mean an increase in attacks directed at NGOs. Greater insecurity may also lead to an increase in the use of protected humanitarian convoys. In turn, greater use of protected convoys will reinforce the perception that participating agencies are politically aligned and are thus legitimate military targets.

- Much closer political monitoring and scrutiny by intelligence services is likely to occur. Whether a post-11 September version of 'Macarthyism' in US dealings with NGOs will emerge, probably depends upon the duration of the war against terrorism and the extent to which the covert means of warfare employed are legal and ethical. Should the war be protracted and the means employed extend to arbitrary and illegal methods, and, as many fear, have the effect of increasing the capacity of the terrorist networks to recruit new members, the chances of repressive and paranoid official behaviour will probably increase.

In the 'DRC' type environment, in which robust US and coalition political and military intervention is excluded, the operational context is more likely to take the following form for NGOs:

- Low cost policy 'solutions' will be preferred. NGOs will probably have to fund an increasing proportion of their operations from their own resources, whether for conventional relief or for peacebuilding work. 'Track 2' diplomacy and 'building local capacities for peace' are likely to be preferred official aid options as these are 'budget-light' and conveniently shift the political burden from states to non-state actors. If such approaches fail, NGOs will find themselves shouldering the blame.

- NGO project implementation dominance in the aid market, albeit based upon diminishing official financial support, is likely to continue. NGO comparative advantage, the deployment of private resources and a relatively low waged work-force, is unlikely to be significantly challenged by private sector contractors. By definition, the 'DRC' type context will be a US/coalition military free zone.

- Conventional humanitarian principles of neutrality and impartiality will continue to be the most important security assets for operational humanitarian agencies. Whether NGOs can convincingly sustain their humanitarian identities in 'DRC' type contexts while simultaneously abandoning them in 'Afghanistan' type contexts is unclear. If not, the larger operational NGOs may experience attacks against any of their operations anywhere where terrorist cells operate.

- While more intensive political monitoring and surveillance by intelligence services of NGOs will probably focus upon agency headquarters and field operations in high priority theatres of war, there is likely to be an increased level of 'watch' wherever the capacity exists for this.

As the passage of time allows for a more empirically-based analysis of the implications for NGOs involved in peace operations, it is likely to become clear that 11 September changed little with regard to the conceptual issues confronting the international peace support system, but much in terms of the actual practice of global pacification. For NGOs, the world has become a much more uncertain, dangerous and testing place.

NOTES

1. NGO 'proliferation' is probably over-stated. Of the 'hundreds' of agencies reported to be in Goma in 1994, or the 'thousands' registered by the Ministry of Planning in Afghanistan in 2002, a significant number represent 'speculative' enterprise or bureaucratic artefacts.
2. Judith Randel and Tony German, 'Trends in Financing of Humanitarian Assistance', in Joanna Macrae (ed.), *The New Humanitarianisms: a Review of Trends in Global Humanitarian Action*, London: Overseas Development Institute (ODI), HPG Report 11, April 2002.
3. Peter Uvin, *The Influence of Aid in Situations of Violent Conflict*, Paris: OECD/Development Assistance Committee, Informal Task Force on Conflict, Peace and Development Cooperation, Sept. 1999.
4. See for example Alex de Waal, *Famine Crimes: Politics and the Disaster Relief Industry in Africa*, Indiana University Press, 1998; Michael Bryans, Bruce Jones, and Janice Stein, *Mean Times: Humanitarian Action in Complex Political Emergencies – Stark Choices, Cruel Dilemmas*, Toronto: Center for International Studies, University of Toronto, 1999.
5. There are several distinct elements of the 'Goma' story. The arrival in July 1994 of a million refugees provoked a chaotic and belated relief response which exemplified for some the problem of 'NGO proliferation'. During the next two years, UNHCR and implementing NGOs were often accused of 'feeding the killers' in the camps, although UNHCR actually made many attempts to seek assistance from the UN Security Council and many individual member states to assist in the demilitarization of the camps. In November 1996 the closure of the camps in Goma by the Rwanda Patriotic Front

prompted MSF to state that 'millions are dying' in Zaire. Many journalists covering the story were convinced that the agencies were exaggerating the problem and when hundreds of thousands of refugees returned 'in good health', this seemed to be sufficient proof. In fact, over 100,000 did subsequently die in their flight deeper into Zaire.

6. Joanna Macrae and Nicholas Leader, *Shifting Sands: The Search for 'Coherence' between Political and Humanitarian Responses to Complex Emergencies*, London: ODI, HPG Report 8, 2000, and Macrae, *New Humanitarianisms*.

7. For example, in a pre-11 September review of the UN's Strategic Framework for Afghanistan (SFA), it was noted that 'The SFA is one example of a wider trend that uses aid as a local peacebuilding and political mollification tool. The use of aid as a means of local peacebuilding/elite encouragement also establishes the possibility of an inter-national regulatory regime that, through the aid programme, can modulate behaviour by rewarding positive characteristics while penalizing or ignoring the negative.' See Mark Duffield, Patricia Grossman and Nicholas Leader, *Review of the Strategic Framework for Afghanistan* (draft), Strategic Monitoring Unit, Afghanistan, Oct. 2001.

8. Mary Anderson, *Do No Harm: Supporting Local Capacities for Peace Through Aid*, Cambridge, MA: Collaborative for Development Action, Local Capacities for Peace Project, 1996.

9. As a corollary, NGOs may have unwittingly set themselves up as convenient scapegoats in the event that the new peacebuilding paradigm bears no fruit.

10. 'Report of the Panel on United Nations Peace Operations', United Nations, A/55/305, S/2000/809, 21 Aug. 2000.

11. See *Command from the Saddle: Managing United Nations Peacebuilding Missions*, Fafo, Peace Implementation Network, 1999; and *Shaping the UN's Role in Peace Implementation*, Recommendation Report of the Forum on the Role of the Special Representative of the Secretary-General, Fafo, Programme for International Cooperation and Conflict Reduction, New York, 1998.

12. UN Security Council Res. 1373, 28 Sept. 2001.

13. UN Security Council Res. 1378, 14 Nov. 2001.

14. 'From Suez to Pacific, US Expands its Presence across the Globe', *The Guardian*, 8 Mar. 2002.

15. President Bush Speech, 14 Mar. 2002, accessed at www.whitehouse.gov/news/releases/2002/03/20020314-7.html.

16. Ibid.

17. Ibid.

18. Rather oddly, Peter Bell, President of CARE-US, responded to President Bush's speech as follows: 'We look forward to working with the Administration to channel new resources into programs where the need is greatest and where the most victories over poverty can be won,' *Care Press release*, Atlanta, Georgia, 14 Mar. 2002

19. Duffield et al., *Review of the Strategic Framework*.

20. UN Security Council Res. 1401, 28 Mar. 2002.

21. The 'Afghanistan' effect has already resulted in the redeployment of some USAID funds from Africa. Current speculation suggests that the regime change scenario for Iraq would require a considerably greater concentration of aid resources over a sustained period of time.

22. *Conflict, Peace and Development Cooperation on the Threshold of the 21st Century*, Development Assistance Committee, Development Cooperation Guidelines Series, Organization for Economic Cooperation and Development, Paris, 1998, p. 28.

23. Macrae and Leader, *Shifting Sands*.
24. Nicholas Stockton, *Strategic Coordination in Afghanistan*, Afghanistan Research and Evaluation Unit, Kabul, 2002.
25. In the rather notorious case of Sierra Leone, where humanitarian aid was withheld for fear that it would fuel the conflict and confer some legitimacy upon the RUF, it was perhaps only Action-Aid in the UK which took a strong public stance that was critical of this particular expression of coherence.
26. Macrae and Leader, *Shifting Sands*.
27. While this might sound far-fetched, the case of the seizure of Somalia's Al Barakaat bank's assets undoubtedly adversely affected many development projects. To date, no linkage between Al Barakaat and Al Qaeda has been established.
28. Final report of the Panel of Experts on the Illegal Exploitation of Natural Resources and Other Forms of Wealth of DR Congo, UN doc., S/2002/1146, 2002.
29. 'A major problem facing MONUC as it prepares for the main task of phase III, which is the facilitation of voluntary disarmament, demobilization, repatriation, resettlement and reintegration in the eastern part of the Democratic Republic of the Congo, is the lack of a capable force for this challenging task. The Mission's strategy depends on the creation of a climate of confidence and security in the east, for which the deployment of a robust contingent is essential. In the continuing absence of a country willing to provide a force with the necessary capacity, phase III of the Mission's deployment remains, for the present, delayed.' *Eleventh report of the Secretary-General on the UN Organization Mission in DR Congo*, UN Doc., S/2002/62, para. 27, 2002.
30. Salman Rushdie, 'How to Fight and Lose the Moral High Ground', *The Guardian*, 23 Mar. 2002.
31. Macrae and Leader, *Shifting Sands*.
32. See for example Maggie Black, *A Cause for Our Times: Oxfam, the First 50 Years*, Oxford: OXFAM, 1992.
33. S. Neil Macfarlane, *Politics and Humanitarian Action*, Providence: Thomas J. Watson Jr. Institute for International Studies, occasional paper No. 41, 2000.
34. Interviews carried out by the author in Kabul during April 2002.
35. Examination conducted on 13 and 14 Mar. 2002.
36. Nicholas Stockton, 'The Failure of International Humanitarian Action in Afghanistan', *Global Governance*, Vol. 8, No. 3, 2002, pp. 265–71.
37. 'MSF Calls Upon Warring Parties to Spare Afghan Civilians', *MSF Press Release*, 5 Dec. 2001.
38. *Pursuing Justice Not Revenge*, Amnesty International, AI Index, ACT, 30 June 2001.
39. Austen Davis, MSF Holland, as reported in *Christian Science Monitor*, 11 Oct. 2001.
40. *The Need for a Clear Distinction between Humanitarian Program and Military Activities in Afghanistan*, CARE-US, 23 Feb. 2002, accessed at www.careusa.org/newsroom/specialreports/afghanistan/03202002_distinction.asp.
41. Macfarlane, *Politics and Humanitarian Aid*.
42. Francis Fukayama, *The End of History and the Last Man*, London: Penguin, 1993.

——◄◦►——

EIGHT

Opposing Insurgents, during and beyond Peace Operations

John Mackinlay

It is sometimes irritating to be told, usually by historians citing Chinese Communist dogma about the French revolution, that in the perspective of the next hundred years, today's massive changes will seem insignificant. This is not a useful message for those who grapple with distant emergencies that interfere with our lives in a very immediate manner. International military commanders and the humanitarian agencies executives find the pace of change is real enough and they must respond to it. In the past decade, its harbingers have been extremely visible. Few western adults can reasonably claim not to have seen television footage of the destruction of the inner German border obstacle, the Soviet forces leaving Europe in their east-bound trains and the multiple images of genocide and humanitarian disaster. However, our ability to respond has not matched the speed of events. Our international leaders have not adapted themselves with much facility or vision to a new strategic era and our military forces and the humanitarian agencies have been beset with the baggage of the cold war for too long. It has taken western armed forces a decade to disentangle themselves from the mental straitjacket of peacekeeping and fundamentalist writers who insisted on its rigid separation from other military operations.[1] Similarly, humanitarians have spent much of the 1990s recovering from a crisis of identity when their self-image as occupying a separate moral position in the conflict area collided with the realities of civil war.[2] These stresses were already visible in the international operations during the early 1990s, from Sudan to Cambodia.

Nevertheless the international response has moved, if ponderously, from the mantras of the cold war period. Change came from the ground level: under pressure from their young field executives at the front lines of an altered conflict environment, the 'Barons of the Poor' in New York and Geneva,[3] as well as the rear guard of conventional warriors in NATO, Whitehall and Washington, gradually turned away from the influences of the cold war period. Although the international intervention into Kosovo could not be regarded as a trouble-free operation, it demonstrated a degree of acceptance of the use of military force that would have been unimaginable at the beginning of the decade. After the Kosovo intervention, the international response was beginning to have an identity, a way of coping with stabilization and a tacit framework for civil-military cooperation.[4]

Collectively the 'international community' achieved a containment. The word was not used explicitly, nevertheless the modus vivendi and the level of commitment that emerged, in many cases served to contain problems rather than to solve them. An operational structure began to emerge; the comparatively short stabilization phase of interventions was followed by the scaling down of the campaign-capable elements and the arrival of burden-sharing international structures began to create a long-term bureaucracy, which could last for several decades in the manner of a traditional peace-keeping garrison. Just as military doctrine writers began to sharpen their pens in anticipation of a new version of 'Peace Support Operations',[5] no doubt formalizing the institutional lessons of the Kosovo campaign, Usama bin Laden's attacks on the United States pushed them across the page to another chapter of events. By demonstrating that an internationally organized insurgent force could reach out from a distant place and strike at the heart of the richest and most powerfully protected cities, bin Laden also torpedoed containment as a universally acceptable response. It was no longer enough to contain the problems of a conflict zone that sheltered a globally organized insurgent force, there was now an imperative to defeat and dismantle an adversarial structure that could survive and foster anarchy in weakened states. This turn of events was set to cause operational change and to move institutional thinking much more swiftly than the ten years it took – doctrinally speaking – to get from Cambodia[6] to Kosovo.

This chapter argues that 11 September has compelled us to notice and react to developments, which had been gradually altering our security for some time. Global change has expanded the definition of insurgency, encouraging the more commercially adroit and internationally structured insurgent organizations to challenge powerful states with greater impunity. In the 1990s rebel forces had threatened and derailed peace processes in every region, but international forces had been reluctant, or unable, to deal with them effectively. Local insurgents were treated indulgently, despite the evidence in many cases that they were reneging on agreements and stood to gain from the failure of the mission. The 2001–2 operations in Afghanistan saw these inhibitions removed. Action against Al Qaeda heralded a new relationship between the leading civil agencies in the conflict area and the western governments, a relationship that was increasingly underwritten and controlled by donor-government funding.

DEFINING THE ADVERSARY

During the cold war, NATO armies created models of the enemy forces which opposed them. These described in some detail the enemy's organization, weapon systems and tactics, and provided an essential stage in NATO's planning and preparations for war. Before a military unit could design a training programme, it had to understand the characteristics of the enemy; before weapons manufacturers could build a new system, they needed to know the limitations and strengths of the opposing systems. In the case of the British, these models were nicknamed the Fantasian and Vandal forces order of battle.[7]

After the end of the cold war, NATO armies found themselves serving alongside the same Russian and eastern European forces on which the models were based; the Fantasians and Vandals became history, but nothing replaced them. In the early 1990s, doctrine writers were conspicuously vague about the nature of the adversary. In 'Wider Peacekeeping'[8] the authors suggested that there could be 'local armed opposition' and that this could be organized as 'numerous parties' which thrived in a general 'absence of law and order'.[9] However, in case these vague descriptions were used as a basis for training, the reader was also warned that 'guarding consent' was the key to success and that a force which took sides, used an overly muscular approach or acted in a confrontational manner was likely to find itself on the wrong side of the 'consent divide',[10] an awful predicament that was reinforced by dark references to Mogadishu[11] and the Rubicon, from where recovery would be impossible. As recently as 1996 military doctrine writers and academics were continuing to insist on the importance of separating peacekeeping from other military operations.[12] The significance of this familiar and frequently rehearsed discussion[13] here, is that in the 1990s traditional peacekeeping baggage also prevented international forces on the ground from seeing that they had a defined military task. In the circumstances of a complex emergency they could not succeed if they continued to regard themselves as placatory umpires,[14] acting at the benign interface of disciplined military forces. Their role required them to stabilize a violent area and restore a monopoly of power into the hands of an approved or elected government. In carrying out this task they faced an adversary, but the inhibitions of the peacekeeping ethic denied them the opportunity to study or define this adversary for the purposes of planning or training.[15]

The failure to recognize this situation led to an imprecise definition of their real tasks that was reinforced by the continued use of 'peace-doing' labels to describe a military activity that had less and less to do with traditional peacekeeping. In military staff colleges post-cold war contingencies were explained as peace-enforcement, peacebuilding, peacemaking and so forth. But in reality the military task of restoring a monopoly of violence in the crisis zone had more in common with the deeply unfashionable principles of counter-insurgency.[16] The military community was looking in the wrong direction for its sources of past experience.

This problem was additionally complicated by confusions of definition. In 1995 the British army defined insurgency as the 'actions of a minority group within a state who are intent on forcing political change by means of a mixture of subversion, propaganda and military pressure, aiming to persuade or intimidate the broad mass of people to accept such a change'.[17] This recognized the systemic nature of an insurgent movement, which required a similarly systemic counter-strategy. But in some failing states, this definition was already blurred by elements of the host government which acted in the manner of insurgents, pillaging state resources and terrorizing particular communities within the population. A greater problem arose from the confusion with terrorism. In the media, the word 'terrorism' was being used synonymously with insurgency. However in UK doctrine there was an important distinction: terrorism was the military tactic of the insurgent. 'Terrorism' therefore referred to the 'use of indiscriminate violence to intimidate the general majority of people in a state to accept the political changes advocated by the insurgents'.[18] Terrorism was merely the weapon or the tool of the insurgent. It was not a viable modus operandi on its own and could not be the sole sustaining energy of a long-term campaign or the reason for the support of a population. Behind a successful terrorist there had to be an intelligence gathering system, funding, a logistic organization and above all, political cells that were derived from a much wider supporting constituency within a population. Isolated extremist groups without a genuine political manifesto did not usually survive for long, but terrorist cells that could move and operate from within a larger insurgent organization generally could, and therefore were extremely dangerous. By the mid-1990s, the effect of global change in the conflict areas was putting the existing definition of terrorism and insurgency under pressure. Although the world did not suddenly change on 11 September, bin Laden forced us to see that the definition of insurgency had been widening for some time.

THE GLOBALIZATION OF INSURGENCY

Globalization was spreading its linkages across the social, political, cultural, military and economic activities of the world, creating greater interdependence between regions, states and individual communities.[19] In particular, four developmental strands of this multiform activity influenced the nature of insurgent forces, particularly in weak states that were in many cases also post-colonial states, where local forces challenged feeble governments. Far away in rich, safe countries transport, communications, commercial transactions and the flow of ideas and information had been proliferating for more than a hundred years.[20] But in poorer states these facilities were sparsely developed and since the preceding colonial regimes, this condition had allowed governments to exercise control through monopoly. Only large and powerful organizations, usually authorized by the government, could reach the wilderness areas,[21] move bulk cargoes, communicate internationally and transact large sums of money, allowing governments, which were otherwise weak and undemocratic, to control the population.

Global change upset this monopoly. Dispersed rural populations were by now concentrating into the urban areas.[22] Improvements in transport technology had produced cheaper '4x4' vehicles, the Toyota minibus and the Tata series of cargo lorries, which began to arrive through the retail market in the developing regions.[23] Aid programmes reinforced their impact as instruments of change by building new road systems. A similar proliferation of options in communications, the transfer of information, ideas and commercial activities effectively removed a weak government's controlling monopoly.[24]

The concept of 'portable wealth' expanded from its narrower definition as gold, gemstones and drugs, to include large cargoes. The small entrepreneur could now reach the wilderness areas with the same facility as the government, remove these resources and trade them illegally onto markets that avoided international trading regulations.[25]

The small entrepreneur was in many cases acting for the local war leader who now held the territory that enclosed these vulnerable resources. Global change had altered the balance between weak governments and local forces which sought to overthrow them; weak governments became weaker and local insurgents stronger. In richer and more developed states, different kinds of techniques and tactics emerged by which the insurgent could take advantage of a new proliferation of communications; the image of a movement and the visibility of its actions became almost more important than its military impact. The propaganda value of the deed had become more significant than the deed itself. Millions of potential supporters could now recognize an insurgent leader and listen to his speeches without actually meeting him. Simultaneously migration had spread poor and displaced communities into rich, safe states where employment and living conditions were more favourable. Using a proliferation of global systems, it was now possible to harness the insurgent energy of a population that was dispersed across several states. Within migrant communities, their frustrations, their sense of exclusion and feelings of outrage could be exploited, using the same communications that the host state enjoyed.

DIFFERENT CATEGORIES OF INSURGENCY

These developments expanded the definition of insurgency; it was no longer possible to see the widening variety of insurgent movements as variations of the same theme. There were now several kinds of insurgent forces, their distinctions were not so much a matter of their apparent intent as anarchists, egalitarians, traditionalists, pluralists, separatists and preservationists[26] but in their practical manifestation. Their declared intents were easily altered by day-to-day political expedients but their command structures, political organs, recruiting systems and logistic infrastructure had taken years to develop and were a much surer measure of their real purpose. Four distinct categories of insurgent forces had by now emerged.[27]

1. *Lumpen* forces, which were a response to a weak state environment, were horizontally organized and the command linkages between fighting units were fragile, encouraging disloyalty and opportunism among junior commanders. In a *lumpen* force, individual fighters tended to be selfishly motivated and the units were militarily weak with a local operating range.

2. *Clan* forces were in some respects similar to *lumpen* forces, with the important distinction that their organization was based on family groups that were related to a particular clan or tribe. This gave them a significant, long-term survivability that dictated a different counter-strategy approach.

3. *Popular* forces were a response to a stronger state in which the insurgent had less freedom of movement and thus were required to be better organized. *Popular* forces had vertical structures and more developed international elements as well as an effective organ for mobilizing political support. Individual followers were comparatively educated, motivated and formally trained as fighters.

4. A fourth category, the *global* force was supported by a very narrow sample of one case, Al Qaeda. However, its significance was that the passions and techniques it exploited could also be aroused and copied by other

internationally dispersed communities. The *global* force was a virus that could flourish in a very modern culture; although in some respects it was similar to the *popular* force, its revolutionary objectives were much wider than the overthrow of the regime of a particular state. *Global* insurgents were organized to survive in an international environment using supporting cells and communities in different countries. Militarily, the *global* insurgent had demonstrated an international reach and was emphasizing a different tactic of insurgency that relied on the visibility of a deed rather than its practical consequences.

Therefore, by the end of the 1990s, the emergence of more potent forms of insurgency was set to challenge our acceptance of the ad hoc nature of containment operations and peace operations that were exemplified in the Balkans and sub-Saharan Africa.

DEFINING CONTAINMENT

Meanwhile, during the same period, but particularly in the 1990s, military forces were periodically refining their doctrinal literature, and in common with the UN and humanitarian agencies, individually conducting their lessons-learned procedures. By the time Kosovo had been stabilized, an increasingly familiar operational process (described below) drew together the principle actors of an emerging culture of military intervention. This process had not yet been articulated officially as a concept; nevertheless it could be identified as having two or three operational phases that occurred between the arrival of a military intervention force and its reaching a plateau of activity that indicated the start of a garrison phase. The following events or conditions distinguished each phase, although by no means were all manifested in every one of the contingencies that arose in the 1990s.

PHASE 1: INTERVENTION

Prior to the deployment of ground forces

- Steering group or contact group of nations puts pressure on warring parties in a potential or active conflict zone by instituting sanctions and threatening action.
- International forces achieve military superiority in the conflict area by use of conventional forces including warships and combat aircraft.

- Warring parties make outward show of accepting the concept of a peace process at a signing ceremony.

On deployment of ground forces

- International military forces move tactically into the conflict area.
- Immediate tasks: establish security, restore law and order, assist humanitarian survival, restore basic civil amenities.
- Operational area at this stage is under military control.

PHASE 2: STABILIZATION

- Initially there is not an effective nucleus or presence of humanitarian agencies or a viable level of development funding.
- The international military force makes efforts to restore shelter and amenities for the civil community using short-term funds supplied directly by individual governments to their respective national contingents.[28]
- The international forces move to suppress overt armed resistance to peace process; consequently armed resistance reorganizes to a covert structure.
- Results of consolidated appeal by humanitarian agencies and bilateral funds begin to reach the conflict area.
- Effective humanitarian presence increases.
- Military scale back presence from humanitarian sphere of responsibility.
- The international military forces reduce their campaign-capable element.

PHASE 3: GARRISONING THE CONFLICT ZONE

- Arrival and establishment of UN and regional organizations which organize and supervise: trustee governance, law and order, development, economic recovery, etc.
- Military commander relinquishes all previous influence over and control of non-military activities.
- Establishment of the High Representative of the authorizing power.
- Civil agencies carry out peacebuilding and nation-building programmes.
- Some military units focus on what amount to counter-insurgency tasks.

This approximate model, constructed from a distillation of experiences in the 1990s, does not set out to depict the circumstances of a particular operation, it merely serves as a basis from which to illustrate the nature of the containment strategy that emerged from that period. The sectoral capabilities, represented by the actors involved in each emergency, were a recurring characteristic of the response. However their relationship to each other varied from one contingency to another. The coordinating structures were driven by individual relationships and could not be translated from one contingency to another.

Despite evidence of the widening of insurgency into distinct categories, a monolithic view of the adversary was represented doctrinally. But at a tactical level, the military approach was nuanced to account for the variations of each crisis. However, although commanders were adapting locally to change, at a higher political level, a one-fix approach emerged as the common factor of agreement. This was less the result of a failure to define an adversary and more the crude manifestation of a fairly low level of coordinating ability. Although it was never officially acknowledged to be a containment policy, that is all it could achieve in real terms. Even in contingencies that were hailed as successes such as Mozambique, Cambodia and in the post-Dayton Balkans, the process of restoring a monopoly of legitimate violence and power to state level was seldom completed. In each of these theatres there remained serious political obstacles or a rump of local resistance that continued to threaten individual security and degrade the power and authority of a legal government. Ostensibly the massive international presence in the Balkans had the intent of restoring a monopoly of power and sovereignty but, for reasons explained below, the best they could do was to contain the problems of displacement and internal security on a long-term basis. In the majority of less successful cases, for example Angola, Liberia, Zaire, Afghanistan and Somalia, the restoration of the host government's authority was not attempted, or in some cases attempted with very little conviction. This failure was not just a problem of the faltering commitment of rich, powerful states whose practical and political support was the sine qua non of success. Even under the most favourable circumstances, moving beyond the nominal security that was implied by containment, to crush all the elements that challenged the peace process and restore a complete monopoly of power and violence within a state, was an extremely complex and long-term undertaking. In the case of the British in Northern Ireland, by 2002 it had taken 34 years to reach a level of personal security which was by no means evenly enjoyed throughout the Province of Ulster. The British had achieved this moderate result at great financial cost, with an experienced counter-insurgency army and a well established coordinating structure that joined a one-nation police force, a one-nation army and compliant government departments to a common security policy. By comparison, the intervention forces and agencies involved in a complex emergency comprised an unstructured constituency of individual institutions which moved through the operational space on different paths, with different interests, sometimes in unison and sometimes in collision. Each agency, particularly in the humanitarian sectors, had a distinct interest. There was no overriding pressure or incentive for them to be integrated or even coordinated even when several agencies were working within the same sector. In this form the international response could not be fashioned into an instrument for counter-insurgency and therefore achieve the degree of individual protection that is the precondition of a viable civil society.

In addition to the problems within the conflict zone, the international structures for successful action against insurgent forces were missing. The ill-defined version of the adversary failed, even in its most developed forms within western defence intelligence organizations, to show that there were now several distinct categories of insurgent forces, which in turn urged for different approaches to intervention. In the case of a crisis zone that was disturbed and threatened by *lumpen* or *clan* forces, an *ad hoc* policy of containment could be a viable response, which more or less appeared to restore the situation sufficiently for some form of development to take place. But now in the Middle East, in Afghanistan and the adjacent sub-region, where *popular* or *global* forces threatened the crisis zones, there was an important international dimension to the adversary that sustained the violence and allowed the insurgent forces greater space in which to move and retaliate. At the strategic level, a one-fix approach did not go far enough, there was another dimension to the counter-strategy that required an additional range of capabilities to be deployed globally beyond the operational area.

The response to the UN's Brahimi Report on Peace Operations[29] emphasized the reluctance of the international community to move beyond the limitations of a containment style operation. Although Brahimi's recommendations were well received and generally regarded as a sound remedy to improve the effectiveness of international peace forces, they also condoned a one-fix mentality. Brahimi's panel reproduced recommendations that in many cases had arisen from previous lessons-learned exercises. At its most innovative, the Report invoked a Kosovo model of containment as its goal for a future UN operational capability and failed to anticipate an international dimension of operations that a more precise definition of insurgent forces, even prior to 11 September 2001, would have anticipated.[30] More important than the limitations of the Report, was the likelihood that, despite their visible enthusiasm, neither the most powerful military nations represented in the Security Council, nor the majority in the General Assembly, had a strong desire to empower the UN in a way that would confer on its peace forces a genuine campaign-capable element. Speaking off record, Secretariat officials indicated that the scope of the high-level panel had been limited prior to its assembly and that the Report could be delayed and diluted by the institutional procedures of the General Assembly.[31] Within the UN Department for Peacekeeping Operations (DPKO), the absence of a genuine planning capability was reinforced by politically-dictated staff selection procedures, which ensured that the majority of the planning staff were from military forces which had no competence in campaigning. The Brahimi Report was an admission that the UN on its own could not conduct a containment mission and was unlikely to improve this state of affairs.

AFTER 11 SEPTEMBER 2001

The attacks on the United States on 11 September 2001 diminished the significance of Kosovo as a milestone in doctrinal development. In their response, the US efforts went beyond containment and moved the intervention community, if such a thing existed, across the threshold to a new level of operation. The 11 September attacks served to reduce, or remove altogether, the comfort of distance and the perception of a safety curtain between the rich, safe countries, which habitually responded to complex emergencies, and the hostile forces at their epicentre. The emerging operational model that represented the success of the Kosovo genre, was jeopardized by the capability of an insurgent force based outside the United States, to mount a devastating attack on its most protected cities. Western nations, their financial centres, facility to travel, culture and institutions were directly threatened; this increased their resolve to contribute armed forces in a more committed and interventionist way towards a collective solution.

To be fair, it was unlikely that faced with the suddenly altered template represented by Afghanistan, the allied leaders and their forces would immediately arrive at the correct long-term solution. Understandably, the intervention developed in an *ad hoc* manner. Initially the sequence of events followed the familiar routines of a one-fix approach: political pressures, bombing campaign and a tactical build-up, which led to military efforts to dominate the area. A large and apparently inexperienced international media contingent enthusiastically reported the bombing and then the tactical arrival into Kabul. Nevertheless Taliban and Al Qaeda were not effectively crushed and the list of wanted figures was not significantly reduced.

However, in the first few months after the arrival of the military forces, several events and characteristics distinguished what has happened in Afghanistan from the 1990s or Kosovo model of containment. Two differently constituted military forces, with separate tactical missions, coexisted in the same space; the International Security Assistance Force (ISAF) maintaining security in the Kabul urban areas, and under a separate commanding authority and as a separate entity, the mainly US/UK troops campaigning to destroy Taliban and Al Qaeda in a wider area of interest that extended over the north west frontier provinces of Pakistan and northward into Kashmir. The major element of the latter force was directed at a higher level from a national HQ in the United States. In the stabilizing phase, its main aim was not just to contain the opposing forces, but to destroy them and dismantle their organization. To achieve this, the campaigning element comprised a greater proportion of combat troops and special forces, who were more powerfully supported by combat aircraft, mortars and artillery. There were also developed structures for gathering intelligence including the uninhibited, but not always effective, use of human intelligence, deep patrolling and elaborate arrangements for prisoner screening and long-term interrogation.

It is hard to predict the long-term outcome of the campaign in Afghanistan; nevertheless some short-term problems are visible. The operational disappointments in May 2002 were significant, arising from a lack of awareness by both the press and UK defence public relations officials on the real nature of the military task.[32] The constant references to 'terrorism' and the 'war on terrorism' had focused public expectations on an unlikely outcome. 'Terrorism' implied a narrowly-defined military counter-activity, but Al Qaeda is more than a terrorist organization.

CONCEPTUAL FAILURE

By continuously using the wrong definition, both the military and their commentators had failed to see or acknowledge bin Laden's real strengths and the nature of his organization. Since the late 1980s, he had created an insurgent movement and a cellular structure that extended over 63 different countries.[33] The cells were supported by an array of dispersed, dispossessed, displaced and migrant populations that numbered in the millions. The visible Al Qaeda units in Afghanistan were the lesser part of the problem. It was the invisible cells across the world which immediately threatened western lifestyles. Al Qaeda was more than a superficial network of terrorist squads, they were a globally dispersed insurgent movement with well-developed commercial, logistic, intelligence gathering, public relations, political as well as ideological elements.[34] They could not be removed by a military expedition or the narrowly forceful techniques implied by counter-terrorism or a 'war on terrorism'. Stamping out Al Qaeda required a more systemic approach that would have to be politically led and driven by something more sophisticated than a desire for military retribution. In the rush to claim, explain and re-label the Al Qaeda event, commentators and even the military staff itself had abandoned some hard-won lessons. Nevertheless, despite the novelty of Al Qaeda's international dimension, the western (but not so much the American[35]) tenets of counter-insurgency were still valid. Contrary to the expectation of the British Ministry of Defence's public relations machinery, a counter-insurgency campaign would be a very slow moving affair, which might require many thousands of man hours of patrolling and intelligence gathering for one short contact with the enemy. But, more than that, it required a sophisticated political policy at the highest level that could separate the insurgents from their supporting constituency. It was useless just to offer vast financial rewards for information leading to the capture or death of wanted Al Qaeda men if the populations that sheltered them were resolutely opposed to the culture that stood for a 'war on terror-ism'. The main effort could not be invested in a military manhunt across the Afghanistan foothills, it had to be a bigger political campaign to secure the support, the hearts and minds, of the Al Qaeda diaspora. Bin Laden's supporters could be reached and possibly even subverted by a coordinated campaign which drew together all the elements of the international response; politically they might respond to better living conditions and having the self-esteem that arose from possessing a place in the world. If this was also part of bin Laden's manifesto, the political counter-strategy would be to wrest these banners from the insurgent and adopt them in a different form.

Despite the imperative to do more than contain the situation, the civil agencies deployed in an *ad hoc* manner to the Afghanistan crisis zone. Among the civil agencies, cooperation was enhanced by the Joint Logistics Centre; but beyond these cooperating structures which essentially organize the civil element of the response, they have not integrated their efforts in a significant way either with the military operations in the same area or with the inter-national dimension further afield. Nevertheless, in Afghanistan, more than ever before, there has been an opportunity for donor governments to exercise more control over the humanitarian agencies. On this occasion, the indepen-dence that arises from the ability of each agency to raise its own funds from public subscription has been greatly diminished. Much of the funding has been from government sources and there is a greater degree of government control exercised as a result.

Beyond the Afghan crisis zone, there was also an identifiable effort led by the US to address the wider global dimension of Al Qaeda's organization. The scrutiny of illegal traffic in weapons, drugs and human beings intensified. Military assistance missions were despatched to several states that were potential refuges for Al Qaeda including Sudan, Yemen, the Philippines and Indonesia. Around the world the movement of shipping and private aircraft was monitored more closely and satellite-imagery was re-monopolized for a while by the United States.[36] Electronic communications were screened and intercepted, and where possible, transfers of money tracked and audited. Migration was more carefully watched and the unregulated or unlawful movement of individuals, communities and populations across borders became a higher priority for intelligence units. The organization and deployment of these efforts have given the United States, as the framework-providing nation, an unusually powerful influence over the management of intervention into Afghanistan.

Although 11 September had energized the speed and military intensity of the US/western response to this particular contingency, no distinguishable pattern has yet emerged that could become a model for future operations. The international dimension of the western response had an incremental, ad hoc character; it was a reactive array of isolated activities, not a coherent political offensive. There was nevertheless an irresistible motive for making every effort to defeat Al Qaeda. In Beirut (1983) and in Somalia (1993), the United States had been deterred from further campaigning by casualties. In face of a local setback, withdrawal had been a politically popular choice of action. Now, further attacks by Al Qaeda would have the opposite effect. The more effective and damaging Al Qaeda's attacks became, the more it might steel the determination of the intervention forces to deal with the problem.

IMPROVING THE INTERVENTION MODEL

The success of international reactions to Al Qaeda has been patchy, this is a reasonable expectation given the suddenness of the need to find a new approach and the previously low level of international cooperation from which a response had to be developed. But the imperative to improve the lack of international cooperation in emergencies is now stronger and on this occasion will be further strengthened, not diminished, by each new outrage against the west. Therefore, in the possibility that 11 September proves to be a significant milestone in the improvement of the international response, what important elements of success may emerge in a new regime of intensive commitment?

The response to a complex emergency, in which the crisis area is threatened by a popular or global insurgency, will require three defined elements: the military intervention forces; the civil agencies in the crisis zone; and the civil and military elements acting against the insurgent movement's wider international dimension. A successful campaign to restore the crisis area and completely disarm and dismantle the insurgent units, which lie at the heart of the problem, will require the following:

A better definition of the adversary

A complex emergency arises from several different strands of degeneration that coalesce over a long period to transform a state or sub-region into a humanitarian disaster area. The insurgent movement which may be established at the epicentre of the crisis zone is just one of these degenerative strands but is also likely to be a key to the long-term solution. For without first of all achieving a degree of personal security, the local population may not benefit from development or governmental reform. The process of defining the security problem and in particular the nature of the opposition to the peace process or restoration of a monopoly of violence to the government, also defines the nature of the response. It may be necessary to confront and even destroy the opposing insurgent movement; conversely the insurgents may become the nucleus of a future government after the election. In both cases it is important to identify the constituents of the insurgent movement, the degree of their popularity and the extent to which they are internationally established. The clear identification of these factors will precede and shape a successful international response.

A politically driven counter-strategy

No insurgent movement has ever been defeated solely by the military techniques that are implied by 'counter-terrorist' operations. A military counter-strategy must be preceded and led by a coherent political campaign plan. One of its key objectives is to isolate the active cells of the insurgent movement from their supporting constituency.

Reducing the number of moving parts in the operational area

The international response to a complex emergency is inherently unmanageable because it has too many independently moving parts that are controlled from beyond the crisis area by different interests. After 11 September, it is in the hand of a single nation, or small group of nations to control and reduce the number of individual participants. This may achieve:

- military forces that are more integrated and coherent with much greater command delegation to the leading military formation in the field and the imposition of very stringent rules about the use of opt-out procedures by national defence ministries;
- each humanitarian sector (or a distinct group of tasks) to be dealt with by only one agency. Any specialist sub-contractors will have to relinquish their institutional identity and become part of a sectoral agency for the duration of a campaign or emergency. NGOs are to operate as part of this one agency to one sector system and not as before in an array of individual interests;
- foreign movement into and through the crisis zone to be strictly controlled by intervention forces, in addition to the host country authorities, at air, sea and land entry points as well as by military check points on key routes throughout the area. The purpose is to eliminate the presence of unauthorized organizations which refuse to accept the above authority.

A strategic directorate

At the highest coordinating level, possibly in a single location beyond the region of the crisis, a strategic directorate is required to integrate the efforts of the three elements of the response:

- at a global level: the civil and military elements to counter the international dimension of the insurgent movement;
- at an operational level: the military intervention forces; and
- at operational and local levels: the civil agencies.

Bilateral donors, the contingent contributor nations and the contact group of nations will be represented at operational level.

A director of operations

The director of operations in the operational area will control both the international military force and the civil agencies. The reason why this appointee will have more power than any similar previous appointment (such as a Special Representative of the UN Secretary-General or Higher Representative), is that he or she represents the authority of both the cash-donors and the military contingent providers. With this authority it will at last be possible to overcome the distant influence of the UN officials in Geneva and New York as well as the nationally motivated defence ministry officials and create a unity of purpose that is the pre-requisite for success.

Integrated international dimension

Where the opposing insurgent forces have a developed international supporting structure, the responding nations will require a commensurately organized international dimension to their operations. This will include the control, monitoring and sharing of: domestic intelligence; migration of communities; movement of cargoes, personnel, ships and private aircraft; currency, commercial transactions and banking information; electronic communications as well as the ongoing countermeasures for drugs, weapons, and so on. These diverse activities need to be integrated at every level and centrally controlled by a single strategic directorate.

Finally, in the current climate of poor international and interagency cooperation, these suggestions will seem optimistic, overly centralized and over-controlling. But it is worth pointing out that they contain very little that is essentially new. The concept of a director of operations to control the military, the police and the civil elements in a campaign to restore internal security was developed and successfully used in Malaya in the 1950s. Embryonic versions of strategic and operational level directorates and the desire to have fewer actors in the operational area are already in the public domain. In the past, what has been lacking is the international commitment to put it all together, and for better or for worse, 11 September may now provide us with the missing ingredient.

NOTES

1. See for example Alan James, 'Internal Peacekeeping', in David Charters (ed.), *Peacekeeping and the Challenges of Civil Conflict Resolution*, Federicton, New Brunswick: Centre for Conflict Studies, University of New Brunswick, 1994; Allen Mallinson, 'No Middle Ground for United Nations', *Jane's Defence Weekly*, Vol. XXI, 14 May 1994 (Colonel Mallinson, as he was at the time, was a British staff officer closely involved in the development of a doctrinal response to the post-cold war contingencies); Charles Dobbie, 'A Concept for Post-Cold War Peacekeeping', *Survival*, Vol. 36, No. 3, Autumn 1996, p. 123.
2. Mary Anderson, *Do No Harm: Supporting Local Capacities for Peace Through Aid*, Local Capacities for Peace Project, 1996.
3. An expression popularized by Michael Ignatieff, *The Warriors' Honor: Ethic War and the Modern Conscience*, London: Vintage, 1999.
4. This growing sense of a community is well represented in the record of the 2000 Copenhagen CIMIC Conference: Peter Viggo Jakobsen (ed.), 'CIMIC – Civil-military

Co-operation. Lessons Learned and Models for the Future', *DUPI Report* No. 9, Copenhagen: Danish Institute of International Affairs, 2000.

5. British Ministry of Defence, 'Peace Support Operations', Joint Warfare Publication 3-50, HMSO, 1996.

6. Referring to the structures of the UN Transitional Authority in Cambodia (UNTAC); see *Blue Helmets: A review of UN Peacekeeping*, 3rd edn, UN Department of Public Information, New York, 1996.

7. British Ministry of Defence, 'Notes on the Fantasian Army', Army Code No. 70737, HMSO, 1972.

8. British Ministry of Defence, 'Wider Peacekeeping', HMSO, 1994.

9. Ibid., see pp. 1–7 under 'Characteristics'.

10. Ibid., see pp. 2–12 under 'The Consequences of Crossing the Consent Divide'.

11. The 'Mogadishu line' refers to the same concept as above but is attributed to Lieutenant General Sir Michael Rose as commander of UNPROFOR in 1994–95.

12. After 1996, the publication of 'Peace Support Operations' began to acknowledge a more flexible response to 'grey area' operations.

13. A clash of views took place between authors who represented the 'Wider Peacekeeping' version of doctrine development (see n.1 above and Charles Dobbie – the principle writer of 'Wider Peacekeeping') and authors such as Richard Connaughton, 'Time to Clear the Doctrinal Dilemma', *Jane's Defence Weekly* 21, 9 April 1994, pp. 19–20. For a contemporary account, see also Christopher Bellamy, *Knights in White Armour*, London: Pimlico, 1996, pp. 150–70 ('A Clash of Doctrines').

14. The image of the peacekeeper as a referee was reinforced in official doctrine, see 'Wider Peacekeeping', pp. 2–8, para. 15 ('The Importance of Impartiality').

15. 'Peace Support Operations' also failed to recognize the presence of an adversary acting against the peace process, p. 2-2, para. 205 ('Complex Emergencies'), which uses a similar terminology to 'Wider Peacekeeping' to describe the conflict environment.

16. Chief of General Staff, 'Counter Insurgency Operations', in Army Field Manual, Vol. 5, 'Operations Other than War', Army Code 71596, British Ministry of Defence, 1995, chapter 3 ('Principles').

17. Ibid., p. 1-1.

18. Ibid., p. 3-4.

19. For this definition see David Held, Anthony McGrew, with David Goldblatt and Jonathan Perraton, 'Globalization', *Global Governance*, Vol. 5, No. 4, 1999, pp. 483–96.

20. David Harvey shows that improving the speed of ships and land transport had been compressing the world since 1850; David Harvey, *Conditions of Post-Modernity*, Oxford: Blackwell, 1989, cited in Ankie Hoogvelt, *Globalization and the Postcolonial World*, 2nd edn, Baltimore: Johns Hopkins University Press, 2001.

21. In a Maoist insurgency, the wilderness areas referred to an extensive refuge where an insurgent could survive in a space so wild, that the technical and numerical advantages of the government forces were greatly reduced and combat would therefore be on the insurgent's terms.

22. For example see an account in 'Somalia, Human Development Report 2001', UNDP, p. 58 ('Urban Migration').

23. From information supplied by Paul Molinaro, Department of Defence Management and Security Analysis, Cranfield University, 6 Aug. 2001.

24. Frances Cairncross, *The Death of Distance 2.0: How the Communications Revolution will Change our Lives*, London: Texere Publishing Limited, 2001.

25. The genre of literature which explains this process is represented by David Keen, 'The Economic Functions of Civil Wars', *Adelphi Paper*, No. 320, 1998; and the authors who contributed to Mats Berdal and David Malone (eds), *Greed and Grievance: Economic Agendas in Civil Wars*, Boulder, CO: Lynne Rienner, 2000.

26. Christopher Clapham, 'Analysing African Insurgencies', in C. Clapham (ed.), *African Guerillas*, Oxford: James Currey, 1998, pp. 6–7; and Chief of General Staff, 'Counter Insurgency Operations', in Army Field Manual, Vol. 5 ('Operations Other than War'), Army Code 71596, British Ministry of Defence, 1995, pp. 1-4 and 1-5.

27. The information on the four categories of insurgent forces is derived from John Mackinlay, 'Globalization and Insurgency', *Adelphi Paper*, No. 352, 2002.

28. In an unpublished study by the Centre for Defence Studies (for the British Ministry of Defence, 2000), it was found that government funds were used to finance the initial restoring efforts of their incoming military contingents on their arrival in Bosnia and Kosovo (US, UK and Netherlands for example).

29. 'Report of the Panel on UN Peace Operations' ('Brahimi Report'), United Nations, A/55/305-S/2000/809, 21 Aug. 2000.

30. Ibid., p. 4. The Brahimi Report fails to take into account the changing nature of the adversary in the conflict area except for a few words on 'non-state actors' and 'spoilers, who renege on their commitments'.

31. The following information was provided off-record by international civil servants working in the UN Secretariat in 2000: 'Ambassador Brahimi is a talented and energetic diplomat who cares about the outcome of his efforts and, at the time of writing, remains in New York to shepherd his report through the UN committee process. So why did he appear to focus the general thrust of his recommendations into the UN's comfort zone, where many of these issues have already been generically explored as previous lessons learned? And was it a UN comfort zone as much as a US comfort zone? It is possible that after the Secretary-General's confrontational address on humanitarian intervention to the September 1999 General Assembly some nations, which habitually oppose the development of a greater problem solving capability in the UN, reacted badly. It is also possible that in his informal instructions concerning the scope of his report he may have been warned away from taking radical approaches in the same vein as the General Assembly address.' John Mackinlay, 'UN Peacekeeping Report: Mission Failure', *World Today*, Nov. 2000, p. 11.

32. UK Royal Marines initial search and destroy operations in May 2002 failed to make any significant finds as might have been anticipated by an elementary knowledge of counter-insurgency operations. However, an inexperienced and impatient press corps was wrongly led to expect more exciting results by equally inept Whitehall briefers. The result was a rancorous denunciation of the operational plan and the Royal Marine ethos.

33. When the Afghan campaign ended, Al Qaeda's recruiting and manpower organizing machinery went into reverse cycle to disperse up to 22,000 surviving mujahidin veterans back to their countries of origin. The destinations of the majority of the fighters were: Saudi Arabia – 5,000; Yemen – 3,000; Egypt – 2,000; Algeria – 2,800; Tunisia – 400; Iraq – 370; Libya – 200; and a balance dispersed to Jordan, UAE, Sudan, Lebanon, Syria and to western countries. The estimated total is between 15,000 and 22,000. Adam Robinson, *Bin Laden: Behind the Mask of the Terrorist*, Edinburgh: Mainstream Publishing, 2001, pp. 113–14; cited in John Mackinlay, 'Globalization and Insurgency'.

34. Until 2001 Bin Laden controlled his forces in the manner of a corporate chief executive. His command system worked best when it was concentrated in one safe base. His

management technique was to delegate into functional areas. These operated individually and could also be separated in space, but their most successful manifestations have been in Jeddah, Sudan and Afghanistan, when he could locate them together and move easily between them in a coordinating role. His chief functional areas were: financial operations, military operations, media and information policy, legal/religious policy and political policy. He also had a highly effective travel and movements department. See *Oxford Analytica*, 16 Jan. 2002, pp. 1–3 and Adam Robinson, *Bin Laden*, p. 203, cited in John Mackinlay, 'Globalization and Insurgency'.

35. Junior officials of the Blair Administration describe their despair at the US's 'march-in shooting' tactics in 'Blair's Aides Denounce US "blundering" in Afghan War', *Sunday Telegraph*, 30 June 2002, p. 1.

36. Bhupendra Jasani, 'Orbiting Spies – Opportunities and Challenges', *Space Policy*, No. 18, 2002, pp. 9–13, cited in John Mackinlay, 'Globalization and Insurgency'.

—————◄○►—————

NINE

Conclusion: Change, Continuity and Conceptions of World Order

Donald C. F. Daniel and Michael Pugh*

The collapsing World Trade Center towers and the smoke rising from the Pentagon triggered in many observers an uneasy sense that 'everything had changed' – that the path of global politics was turning swiftly and sharply in a new direction. Fuelling disquiet was uncertainty about where this road would lead and what stops would be encountered along the way. The passage of time has allowed for considered judgements – some still preliminary, some more definitive – about the effects of 11 September. Asked to address the impact on peace operations, the authors of this book offer conclusions that apply to specific national and institutional actors and to the conduct of operations themselves.

This chapter ties together some of their conclusions and observations and modestly goes beyond them. The task of drawing the threads together has been facilitated by the fact that the authors for the most part seem to agree broadly on major trends, and many of their specific conclusions mirror or are compatible with one another. It must be stressed, however, that this chapter is not a comprehensive summary of each author's contribution. No author was consulted on how their material was to be presented, nor should each be expected to concur with the arguments made.

Jolyon Howorth's chapter offers three possibilities about how much 11 September transformed global politics. One is that, notwithstanding the spectacular nature of the attacks, very little had changed. A second is that everything had indeed changed. A third is that 11 September was not imme- diately transformational, but it accelerated trends which might be so in the indefinite future. Howorth himself believes that 'reality is located somewhere between the second and third' possibilities. He also argues, however, that the subject of his concern, the EU, will need time to tackle the many questions thrown up in the wake of 11 September: 'about threat assessment, about the range and types of instruments required to deal with those threats, about relations with most regions and major countries around the world, and above all with the USA, about cooperation between ESDP [European Security and Defense Policy] and NATO, and about institutional reform'. Along the same lines, Dick Leurdijk and Winrich Kühne may be very prescient when they draw attention to the implications of launching a war against Iraq. For Leurdijk, NATO's future is 'overshadowed by the perspective of the transition from the first phase of the war on terrorism (Afghanistan) to the second and politically most sensitive phase, the attack against Iraq'. For Kühne, 'it is impossible to predict what kind of effect [an attack against Iraq] would have on the development of peace operations'. Thus, Howorth, Leurdijk and Kühne in effect suggest a fourth possibility: that major change could be in the offing, depending on how circumstances develop.

All these possibilities are not consistently applicable across the board. For some actors or features of operations, the first possibility might be most applicable. For others, the second, the third, the fourth or a combination. The fourth possibility, furthermore, cautions against making premature definitive judgements; the best or worst may be yet to come.

Certainly the most immediate effects of the events of 11 September were a dramatic heightening of vulnerability to domestic attack felt by Americans and Europeans and the parallel rise in their concern for states that breed or abet terrorists. These changes support most of the conclusions offered in this volume. For discussion purposes, the chapter is divided into three sets of conclusions: those indicative more of continuity – at least in the short term – than of change; those indicative more of change than of continuity; and those that suggest that significant change could be in the offing depending upon yet-to-occur developments. As will become evident, the placing of a conclusion into one or another set reflects judgements about the degree, rate and persistence of change embodied in each conclusion. Complicating such decisions was the subsequent 'loss of momentum', as Thierry Tardy puts it, in the international sense of urgency to respond collectively to the terrorist threat represented by 11 September. That this loss was more marked in Europe than in the United States further complicated our judgements about rate and persistence.

MORE CONTINUITY THAN CHANGE

Writing about the United Nations, Tardy concludes that 'the events of 11 September have had no fundamental and observable consequences on [its] role in maintaining peace and security in general, and in peace operations in particular'. Rather, they reinforced a pattern that had become well-established since the mid-1990s. Specifically, for potentially coercive operations that engage the national interests of the major members (particularly the United States and its allies), the UN's role is to provide the universal forum, the Security Council, for legitimizing what these members want to do. On the administrative side, the UN's role is to conduct three types of missions: those occurring in Africa and other areas where the major members are not directly engaged and are happy to have the UN take charge; those that are consent-based and thus presumably non-coercive; and those that involve the coordination of civilian entities and personnel in nation-building. When this last type of activity occurs in conjunction with, or following upon, a coercive operation carried out by the major powers, the latter undertake to provide military security to the nation-building personnel. That the 11 September events did not change this model of the UN's 'place' in peace operations was evident when the Security Council approved several anti-terrorist initiatives put forward by the United States. These included assigning the UN responsibility for the civilian Assistance Mission to Afghanistan (UNAMA); mandating a coalition of states to form the International Security Assistance Force (ISAF) with Chapter VII coercive authority; and endorsing the proposition that US combat operations in Afghanistan are consistent with Charter provisions on self-defence. Further confirming the UN's place was that there was no acceleration in implementation of an ongoing programme to reform the UN's capabilities to conduct peace operations.

The EU also was reforming on 11 September, Howorth remarking that the events of that day 'were particularly ill-timed for the infant ESDP'. Its regional crisis management mechanisms (including a Rapid Reaction Force, an international civilian police contingent, and a deployable group of judicial officials oriented to Balkans-type circumstances) were still new. Hence, '[i]t was not surprising that the EU, while making largely declaratory policy on counter-terrorism, should predominantly continue to develop its existing projects' – one of which is to provide the EU with a capability to undertake non-coercive peace operations in Europe. With this policy of basic continuity, the EU initially postponed making crucial decisions raised by the events of 11 September. As noted earlier, these were decisions about its perceptions of threats, its responses to threats, and its relations with others in Europe and beyond, including with the United States. In short, the EU is an organization that has yet to resolve issues that could lead to significant change.

The United States is the only national actor receiving extensive attention is this volume – a position that flows from its being both the target on 11 September and the unipolar hegemon of the international system (administering a 'Pax Americana', to use Nicholas Stockton's phrase). Eric Schwartz's analysis began and ended with the argument that, regardless of which president or party is in power, American policy-makers are deeply reluctant to finance peace operations and to deploy US military forces to them. The Congress opposes financing endeavours whose costs are not under its control, and the Executive Branch, wary of compromising the freedom of action of American troops, sees peace operations as potential entanglements. Notwithstanding a self-imposed electoral mandate to reduce involvement in peace missions, the Bush Administration did soften its position after 11 September, pushing the Congress for full payment of US dues to the UN, advocating approval of UNAMA and ISAF, and pledging to support them. Yet this softening, in Schwartz's view, did not alter fundamentally the Administration's general resistance to employing US soldiers in international peace operations. In fact, resistance solidified, driven by a determination to maximize the availability of US military forces for counter-terrorism combat operations.

One last 'continuity' deals with the conduct of operations, and is derived from Kühne's analysis. He asked: 'Has 11 September, often labeled as … beginning … a new era of international policing for peace and security, improved the likelihood that past errors regarding peace operations will not be repeated?'[1] The historical record demonstrates that, to succeed in complex and hazardous missions, the participants must have a proper mandate and commit considerable resources, including well-led, trained and robust military forces. While acknowledging several operational successes in the 1990s, Kühne dwells on a recurring tendency of national governments to support operations in the field inadequately, thereby causing them to fail or to become more costly in the long run. From that perspective and with ISAF and UNAMA as his test cases, he concludes that 11 September has not improved the likelihood of avoiding past errors. Among his reasons are that ISAF is not robust enough, its mandate is too narrow in responsibility and geographic scope, and the command and communications structure binding the military and civilian elements throughout Afghanistan is too 'fragmented'.

In sum, the crisis both solidified some continuities or simply did not produce changes that some observers might have expected or hoped for. The changes to which we now turn are probably more consequential if we can assume that they will persist.

MORE CHANGE THAN CONTINUITY

The heightened sense of insecurity triggered by the attacks in the United States led to several policy changes in the United States and Europe. One was a new scheme of prioritization for peace operations. With few exceptions, the Americans and their partners will assign high priority only to operations they see as contributing to anti-terrorism. Both directly and through international institutions, they will incorporate them into their national security strategies. Conversely, they will give less attention and resources to lower priority humanitarian and nation-building missions, perhaps thereby jeopardizing their prospects for approval or success. Though addressing only law enforcement, Jacques Klein details the complexity of these operations. Even before 11 September, such missions severely strained the attention of governments that struggled to allocate resources to start and sustain them. Now, as Nicholas Stockton ruefully notes, the 'DRCs of the world' paradoxically might wish to qualify as terrorist breeding grounds so as to raise their profile with the Security Council and mission donors.

A second change, flowing directly from that above, is NATO's re-emphasis of its original *raison d'être*, though there may be less here than meets the eye. Compared to the EU, NATO reacted quickly to the events of 11 September. It made history when, for the first time since its inception in 1949, it invoked Article 5's dictum that an attack against one would be considered as an attack against all. It set in hand a process to reassert, as Leurdijk tells us, 'its core business: collective defence' after having shifted away from it in the 1990s in favour of 'collective security (through peace operations)'. Leurdijk predicts that NATO's longer-term agenda probably 'will be dominated by preoccupation with counter-terrorism measures' and that the organization will reduce its participation in south-east Europe (perhaps to be replaced by the EU) and peace support operations elsewhere.

That said, one should probably distinguish between what NATO does institutionally and what nations that also happen to be members of NATO do since ultimately the latter is probably more significant. NATO, for instance, provides ISAF with planning and material support, and its members constitute ISAF's core. But, ISAF is not a NATO operation. It encompasses a coalition of willing states that are not there in a NATO capacity. Except possibly for peace operations in Europe's periphery or near-abroad, this model may well dominate missions that have anti-terrorist dimensions and thus tie down potential NATO resources to such missions.[2]

A third change concerns the politicization of peace operations. Both Nicholas Stockton and John Mackinlay highlight this issue but from very different perspectives. Stockton focuses on non-governmental organizations (NGOs). Operational NGOs are a key to the performance of civilian tasks in complex peace missions, and they cherish their reputations for providing aid with no political strings attached. They also cherish their independence, being far more willing to cooperate with others than to accept direction from others. In the course of the 1990s some larger NGOs offset declines in income by providing governments with the means to channel their official aid. They were able to do so without ceding much autonomy in how they conducted business. Over time, however, some European governments wanted more from aid than simply setting things right in failed states. Specifically, they sought greater coherence between their assistance efforts and their domestic and foreign policy priorities. After 11 September, the United States reversed its own relative disinterest in needy states, and 'the emerging agenda, especially for US funded aid programmes, does represent a radical extension of this logic' of evaluating aid projects for their 'effects in the domestic domain of the donor nation'. In Afghanistan this radical extension manifested itself 'in the incorporation of the entire assistance effort into the US-led pacification strategy'.

Stockton is sceptical of the wisdom of this emerging trend. Particularly for peace operations in countries linked to counter-terrorism, he foresees several probabilities. One is that independent-minded NGOs will suffer a reduction in official funding; a second is that other service providers will be turned to instead; and a third is that NGOs too closely associated with the sponsors of counter-terrorism will lose their reputation for impartiality and thus place their personnel at greater risk of attack.

Offering a different focus, Mackinlay is more positive. Analyzing the requirements for countering a global terrorist 'insurgency', he characterizes the international response to complex emergencies prior to 11 September as 'inherently unmanageable' because of 'too many independently moving parts'. In contrast, the peace and combat operations in Afghanistan are 'in the hands of a single nation, or a small group of nations', making for a level of efficiency and political coherence he thinks necessary. Among his recommendations is a call to appoint formally one individual to control all military and civilian elements operating in a country or region where terrorists find succour.

In short, Mackinlay's perspective differs in some respects from Stockton's, but both highlight the politicization of peace operations associated with anti-terrorism. To any student of peace missions, politicization is less a novel development than business as usual.[3] The last decade alone is replete with examples – the western Europeans and later the Americans undertaking missions in south-east Europe, the Americans in Haiti, the Australians in East Timor, the Nigerians in Liberia and Sierra Leone, and others – where self-serving national political agendas drove decisions to call for and underwrite missions. But the analyses by Stockton and Mackinlay indicate that counter-terrorism has accelerated this trend to a qualitatively new and unprecedented level.[4]

Passing reference has already been made to a fourth change: the adjustment of agendas and procedures in operations linked to counter-terrorism. Leurdijk relates how NATO forces in south-east Europe undertook measures both to increase force protection and to apprehend suspected terrorists. Klein notes that the UNMIBH mission fostered joint programmes to combat terrorism within the political entities in Bosnia and Herzegovina. Neither ISAF nor UNAMA are mandated to root out Al Qaeda or the Taliban, but to both outlawed groups, ISAF and UNAMA are instruments of the United States and thus fair targets. The coalition forces must protect the personnel and assets of these missions, and all concerned must pre-plan and coordinate how this is to be done. As noted earlier, Mackinlay and Stockton provide food for thought, with Mackinlay advocating close coordination under the aegis of one director and Stockton emphasizing the disadvantages of too close a connection between NGOs and military forces hunting down terrorists.

In sum, 11 September generated several changes, four of which are a new prioritization scheme for peace operations, a reorientation of NATO's own priorities away from such operations, a qualitative jump in politicization, and an adjustment of agendas and procedures for operations. If these changes persist, they may have profound consequences, as yet unpredictable.

MORE CHANGE YET?

Both NATO and the EU face similar challenges: what to do after having taken relatively easy steps in response to 11 September. Now that NATO has reaffirmed that it is a collective defence organization, what exactly is its role when the member driving the anti-terror agenda possesses more military capability than its allies combined, and makes clear it will not brook limitations on its autonomy? Will European members (and Canada) narrow the military gap in an effort to ensure that NATO and themselves are significant players in decision-making and in operations? Does it make more sense for NATO minus the United States to specialize in conducting hazardous complex peace operations after all? Is that where its comparative advantages lie? On the other hand, if NATO takes that direction, will it lose leverage to influence the United States especially when the hegemon may be driving the Alliance in a direction, such as war with Iraq, that is extremely uncomfortable for some members? If the rest of the NATO membership follows the US lead but is unsuccessful in exerting influence, will it merely be legitimizing a new doctrine – 'preemption' – that many of them profoundly disagree with? What are the implications of Leurdijk's observation that the pressures now being exerted on the Alliance are 'provoking a return to the same kind of "bitter disputes" on NATO's future as in the months preceding [its] establishment'?

To talk of NATO minus the United States automatically draws attention to the EU. Howorth tells us that its 'post-11 September threat assessment must ... lead to a lucid analysis of the extent to which the interests of the US and ... of the EU are – and are not – compatible'. The EU is presumably the vehicle by which a united Europe could parley as an equal with the United States and play a major role independent of it. But should it seek such independence? What will it take to achieve it? How should it coordinate with NATO? With regard to peace support operations, should it concentrate on non-coercive missions only? Is this too restrictive if it wishes to be independent? Should it broaden its potential operational horizons beyond Europe? In order to work with and influence the United States, what should the EU (as opposed to NATO) do about the military gap? What comparative advantages should it offer?

In a different context, the UN may also be faced with new challenges if the 'indirect link' between peace operations and terrorism described by Tardy has any credit. Because they are deployed in 'environments that may be favourable grounds for the development of terrorist groups', peace operations could be seen differently and, therefore, acquire an 'anti-terrorism dimension'. The two fields of conflict prevention and peacebuilding would be particularly concerned. In any case, the consequences – for the nature of the operations and for states' policies – of such an evolution are still to be identified. The ability of the UN to deliver security in this new environment is also at stake, especially as the organization has not benefited from a renewed support since 11 September.

While the UN, NATO and the EU confront numerous choices, NGOs seem to have one overarching question with which to contend: should they resist governmental attempts at politicizing peace operations even if it means losing official funding? From Stockton's point of view, NGOs that channel official funding may have to resolve a conflict of interests between their commitment to 'the independent and impartial pursuit of justice and equity' and allowing themselves to be used to further 'donor strategies designed first and foremost to enhance Western domestic security'.

The answers to these questions could be far more significant for the future of peace operations than what has transpired so far since 11 September 2001. The answers will revolve largely around what the United States does and how the Europeans react. Howorth's sobering statement that 'the two sides of the Atlantic do not view the world through the same strategic lens' really describes more a process than a point in time. The attacks of 11 September initially caused governments on both sides of the Atlantic to affirm a common interest in confronting a common threat, but that solidarity has fissured, exposing differences over how to confront terrorism. These differences may well spill over in peace operations. One impact may be to reinforce even more the United States' determination not to participate in or involve itself closely with any international endeavours, including peace operations, that would limit its freedom to employ its military forces. A second impact may be to put in starker relief Europe's military inadequacies to take on both anti-terror and peace operation burdens. What is done for the former will come almost certainly at the expense of the latter and vice-versa.

That said, however, it remains the case that American and European differences occur within the context of a framework of broadly common agreement among them that in turn puts them at odds with many others in the rest of the world. During the cold war, Myres McDougal and Harold Lasswell argued that there existed competing conceptions of world public order with the 'Western' and 'Communist' conceptions vying for domi-nance.[5] These conceptions reflected divergent views about the political and economic relations that should exist between peoples and between states. Notwithstanding Francis Fukuyama's claim, the triumph of western values – labelled the 'liberal peace' by one scholarly critic[6] – marked only a new stage of history, not its end. The fading attraction of communist ideology and disenchantment in many countries with globalization have allowed greater scope to previously less prominent conceptions of public order. To speak of the 'West and the rest' oversimplifies, but this term, coined by a Singaporean diplomat,[7] captures the frustration of many 'resterners' with the controlling role that the Americans and Europeans play in arenas such as the UN Security Council, the World Trade Organization, the International Monetary Fund and the World Bank. This frustration was palpably evident, for instance, at a 2001 international meeting on peace operations that 'heralded worsening tension between the Five Permanent ("P5") Members of the Security Council (with the United States viewed as the first among equals) and the newly industrialized and developing [NID] … states'.[8] Represen-tatives from the latter roundly accused the P5 of inflating or suppressing demand for operations based on their national interests. They wanted more say about which operations would be approved and how they should be conducted. To their mind the western conception of world order did not live up to its own ideals and served instead to maintain western political and economic dominance at the expense of everyone else.

In short, views about peace operations in global governance are not necessarily neutral, but can be interpreted, as many NID spokesmen did, as advancing an existing system of world order, or more accurately a design for world order. Within the liberal peace framework, one can debate how to improve peace operations performance, how to coordinate NGOs, how to keep the western alliance together, or how to legitimize anti-terrorism. The analysis can yield important practical lessons on divisions of labour between enforcement and peacebuilding as well as on other critical issues. But the prevailing wisdom among Europeans and Americans does not interrogate the order itself. By accepting it as the totality of the 'real world', it reinforces values and structures that appear to serve an existing hierarchy of power, but also breed deep-seated resentments that ultimately harm the interests of those who dominate the hierarchy.

To step outside the framework (as Stockton did relative to NGOs) and take a more Olympian view makes it possible to devise three perspectives on the relation between peace operations and counter-terrorism. First, at an epistemological level, one can consider them as completely separate with nothing in common at all. In spite of the reinvention of the 1960s Congo operation (MONUC) to tackle modern intra-state conflicts through multi-dimensional and 'robust peacekeeping', peace operations are minimalist expressions of force designed to resolve or freeze conflicts rather than to combat identified enemies. They genuinely reflect the Clausewitzian ideal of force as a continuation of politics and diplomacy. By contrast, anti-terrorism directed against groups like Al Qaeda denies the relevance of diplomacy. Nothing is negotiable.

Second, at a representational level, to link peace operations and anti-terrorism is to conflate them, perhaps unwisely, as different dimensions of the same goal of maintaining peace and security. Thus 'peace support' and 'anti-terrorism' are positive signifiers, suggesting a moral concern for order and security in the international system. Above all, these terms convey the sense that external actors are not only intent upon, but actually engaged in, maintaining or creating peace, even though in their unforseen and unplanned consequences, as Stockton points out, the reverse may also be true.

A third Olympian perspective goes beyond and to some degree may contradict the second. It contends that the vision of liberal peace has indeed moulded peacekeeping, peacebuilding and peace operations into a purpose which differs little from anti-terrorism. Following Robert Cox's concerns with the limitations of the vision, modern versions of peacekeeping can be considered as forms of riot control directed against the unruly parts of the world.[9] Preoccupations with meeting threats to that vision, whether expressed in terms of support for human rights, for humanitarian activities, for engineering societies to conform to a 'global model' or for proactive anti-terrorist operations, detract us from contemplating flaws in the vision itself. As Paul Rogers has eloquently argued, 'longer-term action requires some fundamental changes in Western policies aimed at reversing socio-economic divisions and engaging in effective environmental management linked to sustainable economies'.[10]

In this respect, this book can be regarded as the beginning of a new dialogue that could bring very considerable change indeed. From these important contributions to the debate about the impact of the crusade against terrorism on peace operations, a path has been cleared to open up broader enquiries about the relationship between peace operations and the representations and constructions of international politics. For, as Thierry Tardy remarked in his introductory chapter, whether or not the crisis will exhibit more continuity than change, peace operations cannot be treated as somehow insulated from perceptions of the international system that gave birth to them.

NOTES

* The views expressed by this author are his only and should not be attributed to his present or previous employers.

1. It was especially difficult to decide whether to place discussion of Kühne here or in the next section, but the way his question was phrased and answered seemed more in line with continuity than change.
2. Another issue that may become important for NATO, the EU and the UN is double and triple counting, that is, member nations earmarking the same units for duty in NATO, EU or UN contingencies.
3. This is another example of a judgement about continuity versus change. The way in which Stockton and Mackinlay dealt with the politicization issue determined placing discussion of their analyses in this section.
4. Mackinlay's analysis contrasts with Kühne's. As highlighted above in the text, the latter emphasizes the shortcomings of ISAF and UNAMA, including their 'fragmented' structure for command and communications. The two analyses, however, are not necessarily at odds. The authors have different objectives for their chapters. Also Kühne simply may have focused more on the degree to which change did not occur than did Mackinlay.
5. See Myres S. McDougall et al., *Studies in World Public Order*, New Haven: Yale University Press, 1960.
6. Mark Duffield, *Global Governance and the New Wars: The Merging of Development and Security*, London: Zed Books, 2001.
7. See Kishore Mahbubani, 'The Dangers of Decadence,' *Foreign Affairs*, Vol. 72, No. 4, Autumn 1993, pp. 11–14.
8. National Intelligence Council, *'The Future of Peace Operations: Findings from a Workshop'*, NIC report 3792-01, 18 Sept. 2001, p. 3. This is a report of a meeting sponsored by the US Institute of Peace, the United Nations Association of the USA and the National Intelligence Council that was held on 9 and 10 July, 2001, and brought together from around the globe 40 diplomats and practitioners with experience of peace operations.
9. Robert W. Cox, with M. G. Schechter, *The Political Economy of a Plural World: Critical Reflections on Power, Morals and Civilization*, London: Routledge (RIPE series), 2002.
10. Paul Rogers, 'Political Violence and Global Order', in Ken Booth and Time Dunne (eds), *Worlds in Collision: Terror and the Future of Global Order*, Basingstoke: Palgrave, 2002, p. 223.

Select Bibliography

Adebajo, Adekeye and Chandra Lekha Sriram (eds), *Managing Armed Conflicts in the 21st Century*, London: Frank Cass, 2001.

'After September 11: A Conversation', *The National Interest*, No. 65-S, 2001.

Alger, Chadwick (ed.), *The Future of the United Nations System: Potential for the Twenty-First Century*, Tokyo: United Nations University Press, 1998.

Alger, Chadwick, 'The Emerging Role of NGOs in the UN System: From Article 71 to a People's Millennium Assembly', *Global Governance*, Vol. 8, No. 1, Jan.–Mar. 2002.

Altenburg, Günther, 'NATO in Crisis?', *Internationale Politik (Transatlantic Edition)*, Vol. 3, Autumn 2002.

Al Sayyid, Mustapha, 'Mixed Message: The Arab and Muslim Response to "Terrorism"', *The Washington Quarterly*, Vol. 25, No. 2, Spring 2002.

Anderson, Mary, *Do No Harm: Supporting Local Capacities for Peace Through Aid*, Cambridge, MA: Collaborative for Development Action, Local Capacities for Peace Project, 1996.

Bannerman, Edward et al., *Europe after September 11th*, London: Centre for European Reform, 2001.

Berdal, Mats and David Malone (eds), *Greed and Grievance: Economic Agendas in Civil Wars*, Boulder, CO: Lynne Rienner, 2000.

Berdal, Mats and Monica Serrano (eds), *Transnational Organized Crime and International Security: Business as Usual?*, Boulder, CO: Lynne Rienner, 2002.

Bergen, Peter, *Inside the Secret World of Osama Bin Laden*, London: Weidenfeld & Nicholson, 2001.

Biermann, Wolfgang and Martin Vadset (eds), *UN Peacekeeping in Trouble: Lessons Learned from the Former Yugoslavia*, Aldershot: Ashgate, 1998.

Booth, Ken and Time Dunne (eds), *Worlds in Collision: Terror and the Future of Global Order*, Basingstoke: Palgrave, 2002.

Bremer, Paul, 'A New Strategy for the New Face of Terrorism', *The National Interest*, No. 65-S, 2001.

Bryans, Michael, Bruce Jones and Janice Stein, *Mean Times: Humanitarian Action in Complex Political Emergencies – Stark Choices, Cruel Dilemmas*, Toronto: Center for International Studies, University of Toronto, 1999.

Byford, Grenville, 'The Wrong War', *Foreign Affairs*, Vol. 81, No. 4, July–Aug. 2002.

Campbell, Kurt M. and Michèle A. Flournoy, *To Prevail: An American Strategy for the Campaign Against Terrorism*, Washington DC: CSIS Press, 2001.

Campbell, Kurt, 'Globalization's First War?', *The Washington Quarterly*, Vol. 25, No. 1, Winter 2002.

The Challenges Project, *Challenges of Peace Operations: Into the 21st Century – Concluding Report 1997–2002*, Stockholm: Elanders Gotab, 2002.

Chesterman, Simon, *Just War or Just Peace?: Humanitarian Intervention and International Law*, Oxford: Oxford University Press, 2001.

Chopra, Jarat, Jim McCallum and Alexander Thier, 'Planning Considerations for International Involvement in Post-Taliban Afghanistan', *The Brown Journal of World Affairs*, Vol. VIII, Issue 2, Winter 2002.

Command from the Saddle: Managing United Nations Peacebuilding Missions, Fafo, Peace Implementation Network, 1999.

Cousens, Elizabeth M. and Chetan Kumar with Karin Wermester (eds), *Peacebuilding as Politics: Cultivating Peace in Fragile Societies*, Boulder, CO: Lynne Rienner, 2001.

Daniel, Donald and Bradd Hayes with Chantal de Jonge Oudraat, *Coercive Inducement and the Containment of International Crises*, Washington DC: US Institute of Peace Press, 1999.

Daniel, Donald, Jean Krasno and Bradd Hayes (eds), *Leveraging for Success in United Nations Peace Operations*, Westport, CT: Greenwood Press, 2003.

David, Dominique, *Sécurité: l'Après-New York*, Paris: Presses de Sciences Po, 2002.

Delpech, Thérèse, *Politique du chaos: L'autre face de la mondialisation*, Paris: Seuil, 2002.

Dover, Robert, 'Reflections on the Role of the EU and the War against Terrorism', *Foreign Policy Network Newsletter*, Nov. 2001.

Duffield, Mark, *Global Governance and the New Wars: The Merging of Development and Security*, London: Zed Books, 2001.

Durch, William (ed.), *UN Peacekeeping, American Politics, and the Uncivil Wars of the 1990s*, New York: St. Martin's Press, 1996.

European Council, *Conclusions and Plan of Action*, Brussels Extraordinary European Council, 21 September 2001.

European Council, 'Draft Declaration on the Contribution of CFSP, including ESDP, in the Fight against Terrorism', annex to the *Presidency Conclusions*, Seville Council, 21–22 June 2002.

Everts, Steven, *Shaping a Credible EU Foreign Policy*, London: CER, 2002.

Fishel, John (ed.), *The Savage Wars of Peace: Toward a New Paradigm of Peace Operations*, Boulder, CO: Westview Press, 1998.

A Force for Peace and Security. US and Allied Commanders' Views of the Military's Role in Peace Operations and the Impact on Terrorism of States in Conflict, Washington DC: Peace Through Law Education Fund, 2002.

Forster, Anthony and William Wallace, 'What is NATO for?', *Survival*, Vol. 43, No. 4, 2002.

Freedman, Lawrence (ed.), *Superterrorism: Policy Responses*, Oxford: Blackwell, 2002.

Frye, Alton (ed.), *Humanitarian Intervention. Crafting a Workable Doctrine*, Council on Foreign Relations, 2000.

Gordenker, Leon and Thomas Weiss (eds), *NGOs, the UN and Global Governance*, Boulder, CO: Lynne Rienner, 1996.

Gordon, Philip, 'NATO after 11 September', *Survival*, Vol. 43, No. 4, Winter 2001–02.

Gordon, Philip, 'Reforging the Atlantic Alliance', *The National Interest*, Vol. 69, Autumn 2002.

Gordon, Stuart and Francis Toase (eds), *Aspects of Peacekeeping*, London: Frank Cass, 2001.

Gunaratna, Rohan, *Inside Al Qaeda, Global Network of Terror*, London: Hurst, 2002.

Hampson, Fen Osler and David Malone (eds), *From Reaction to Conflict Prevention: Opportunities for the UN System*, London: Lynne Rienner Publishers, 2002.

Heisbourg, François (ed.), *Hyperterrorisme: la nouvelle guerre*, Paris: Odile Jacob, 2001.

Held, David, Anthony McGrew, with David Goldblatt and Jonathan Perraton, 'Globalization', *Global Governance*, Vol. 5, No. 4, 1999.

Heymann, Philip, *Terrorism and America: A Commonsense Strategy for a Democratic Society*, Cambridge: MIT Press, 2nd edn, 2001.

Hoge, James F. and Gideon Rose (eds), *How did this Happen?: Terrorism and the New War*, New York: Public Affairs, 2001.

Howorth, Jolyon, 'European Integration and Defence: the Ultimate Challenge?', *Chaillot Paper* 43, Paris: WEU-ISS, 2000.

Howorth, Jolyon and John Keeler (eds), *Defending Europe: NATO and the Quest for European Autonomy*, London: Palgrave, 2003.

Hunter, Robert, *The European Security and Defence Policy: NATO's Companion – or Competitor?*, Santa Monica: RAND, 2002.

Jakobsen, Peter Viggo, 'Overload, Not Marginalization, Threatens UN Peacekeeping', *Security Dialogue*, Vol. 31, No. 2, 2000.

Kagan, Robert, Christoph Bertram and François Heisbourg (exchange), 'One Year After: A Grand Strategy for the West?', *Survival*, Vol. 44, No. 4, Winter 2002–03.

Kühne, Winrich, *The Brahimi Report. Overcoming the North-South Divide*, Berlin: 6th International Workshop, 29–30 June 2001.

Laurenti, Jeffrey (ed.), *Combating Terrorism: Does the UN Matter ... and How*, A Policy Report of the UN Association of the USA, New York, 2002.

Leonard, Mark, *Re-ordering the World: The long-term Implications of September 11*, London: Foreign Policy Centre, 2002.

Leurdijk, Dick, 'The Fight Against International Terrorism: the Right to Self-Defence, and the involvement of the UN and NATO', in *Terrorism and Counter-terrorism: Insights and Perspectives after September 11*, The Hague: Netherlands Institute of International Affairs ('Clingendael'), December 2001.

Leurdijk, Dick and Dick Zandee, *Kosovo: From Crisis to Crisis*, Aldershot: Ashgate, 2001.

Lindley-French, Julian, 'Empty Threats? America, Europe, NATO and the Threat Environment', Rome: CeMISS and Istituto Affari Internazionale, 2001.

Lindley-French, Julian, 'Terms of Engagement: The Paradox of American Power and the Transatlantic Dilemma post-11 September', *Chaillot Paper* 52, Paris: EU-ISS, 2002.

Macfarlane, S. Neil, *Politics and Humanitarian Action*, Providence: Thomas J. Watson Jr. Institute for International Studies, Occasional paper No. 41, 2000.

MacFarlane, S. Neil, 'Interventions in Contemporary World Politics', *Adelphi Paper*, No. 350, 2002.

Mackinlay, John, 'Globalisation and Insurgency', *Adelphi Paper*, No. 352, 2002.

Macrae, Joanna and Nicholas Leader, *Shifting Sands: The Search for 'Coherence' between Political and Humanitarian Responses to Complex Emergencies*, London: ODI, HPG Report 8, 2000.

Macrae, Joanna (ed.), *The New Humanitarianisms: a Review of Trends in Global Humanitarian Action*, London: ODI, HPG Report 11, April 2002.

Mani, Rama, *Beyond Retribution: Seeking Justice in the Shadows of War*, Cambridge: Polity Press, 2002.

Meiers, Franz-Joseph, *NATO's Peacekeeping Dilemma*, Bonn: Forschungs-institut der Deutschen Gesellschaft für Auswärtige Politik, 1996.

Miall, Hugh, Oliver Ramsbotham and Tom Woodhouse, *Contemporary Conflict Resolution*, Cambridge: Polity Press, 1999.

Miller, Steven, 'The End of Unilateralism or Unilateralism Redux?', *The Washington Quarterly*, Vol. 25, No. 1, Winter 2002.

Mingst, Karen and Margaret P. Karns, *The United Nations in the Post-Cold War Era*, Boulder, CO: Westview Press, 2000.

Missiroli, Antonio, 'EU–NATO Cooperation in Crisis Management: No Turkish Delight for ESDP', *Security Dialogue*, Vol. 33, No. 1, March 2002.

Nye, Joseph, *The Paradox of American Power. Why the World's only Super-power can't go it Alone*, Oxford: Oxford University Press, 2002.

Ojanen, Hanna, *Theories at a Loss. EU–NATO Fusion and the 'Low Politicisation' of Security and Defence in European Integration*, Helsinki: Finnish Institute of International Affairs, UPI Working Papers 35, 2002.

O'Neill, William, *Kosovo: An Unfinished Peace*, Boulder, CO: Lynne Rienner, 2002.

Pillar, Paul, *Terrorism and US Foreign Policy*, Washington DC: Brookings, 2001.

Pugh, Michael and Waheguru Pal Singh Sidhu (eds), *The UN, NATO and Regional Security Actors: Partners in Peace?*, Boulder, CO: Lynne Rienner, 2002.

Ramsbotham, Oliver and Tom Woodhouse, *Humanitarian Intervention in Contemporary Conflict*, Cambridge: Polity Press, 1996.

Reinares, Fernando (ed.), *European Democracies Against Terrorism. Governmental Policies and Intergovernmental Cooperation*, Darmouth: Ashgate, 2000.

Roberts, Adam, 'Counter-terrorism, Armed Force and the Law of War', *Survival*, Vol. 44, No. 1, Spring 2002.

Ronfeldt, David and John Arquilla (eds), *Networks and Netwars: The Future of Terror, Crime and Militancy*, Santa Monica: RAND, 2001.

Roy, Olivier, *L'Islam Mondialisé*, Paris: Seuil, 2002.

Sarooshi, Danesh, *The United Nations and the Development of Collective Security: The Delegation by the UN Security Council of its Chapter VII Powers*, Oxford: Oxford University Press, 1999.

Schnabel, Albrecht and Ramesh Thakur (eds), *Kosovo and the Challenge of Humanitarian Intervention: Selective Indignation, Collective Action, and International Citizenship*, Tokyo: United Nations University Press, 2000.

Schrijver, Nico, 'Responding to International Terrorism: Moving the Frontiers of International Law for "Enduring Freedom"?', *Netherlands International Law Review*, Vol. XLVIII, No. 3, 2001.

Shaping the UN's Role in Peace Implementation, Recommendation Report of the Forum on the Role of the Special Representative of the Secretary-

General, Fafo, Programme for International Cooperation and Conflict Reduction, New York, 1998.

Shawcross, William, *Deliver us from Evil: Peacekeepers, Warlords and a World of Endless Conflict*, Simon and Schuster, 2000.

Sloan, Stanley, *NATO, the European Union, and the Atlantic Community: The Transatlantic Bargain Reconsidered*, Rowman & Littlefield, 2003.

Sorbo, Gunnar, Joanna Macrae and Lennart Wohlegemuth, *NGOs in Conflict – An Evaluation of International Alert*, Bergen: Chr. Michelsen Institute, 1997.

Spillmann, Kurt, Thomas Bernauer, Gabriel Jürg and Andreas Wenger (eds), *Peace Support Operations: Lessons Learned and Future Perspectives*, Bern: Peter Lang, 2001.

Stedman, Stephen John, Donald Rothchild and Elizabeth Cousens, *Ending Civil Wars: The Implementation of Peace Agreements*, Boulder, CO: Lynne Rienner, 2002.

Stockton, Nicholas, 'The Failure of International Humanitarian Action in Afghanistan', *Global Governance*, Vol. 8, No. 3, 2002.

Stockton, Nicholas, *Strategic Coordination in Afghanistan*, Kabul: Afghanistan Research and Evaluation Unit, Issues Paper Series, 2002.

Talbott, Strobe and Nayan Chanda (eds), *The Age of Terror: America and the World After September 11*, New York: Basic Books and Yale Center for the Study of Globalization, 2001.

Tardy, Thierry, *La France et la gestion des conflits yougoslaves (1991–1995). Enjeux et leçons d'une opération de maintien de la paix de l'ONU*, Brussels: Bruylant, 1999.

Tardy, Thierry, *The UN in Europe: Towards a Subsidiary Role*, Research Document No. 17, Paris: Fondation pour la recherche stratégique, Oct. 2000.

Terrorism and Counter-terrorism: Insights and Perspectives after September 11, Netherlands Institute of International Relations ('Clingendael'), Dec. 2001.

Thakur, Ramesh and Albrecht Schnabel (eds), *United Nations Peacekeeping Operations. Ad hoc Missions, Permanent Engagement*, Tokyo: United Nations University Press, 2001.

United Nations, 'The Fall of Srebrenica', Report of the Secretary-General in application of Resolution 53/35 of the General Assembly, A/54/549, 15 Nov. 1999.

United Nations, 'Report of the Panel on UN Peace Operations' ('Brahimi Report'), A/55/305, 21 Aug. 2000.

United Nations, 'Prevention of armed conflict', Report of the Secretary-General, A/55/985, 7 June 2001.

United Nations, 'Report of the Policy Working Group on the UN and Terrorism', S/2002/875, 6 August 2002.

Van Tongeren, Paul, Hans Van der Veen and Juliette Verhoeven (eds), *Searching for Peace in Europe and Eurasia: An Overview of Conflict Prevention and Peacebuilding Activities*, London: Lynne Rienner, 2002.

Waal, Alex de, *Famine Crimes: Politics and the Disaster Relief Industry in Africa*, Indiana University Press, 1998.

Walt, Stephen, 'Beyond bin Laden. Reshaping US Foreign Policy', *International Security*, Vol. 26, No. 3, Winter 2001/02.

Weiss, Thomas (ed.), *Beyond UN Subcontracting: Task-sharing with Regional Security Arrangements and Service-providing NGOs*, London: Macmillan, 1998.

Weiss, Thomas, *Military–Civilian Interactions: Intervening in Humanitarian Crises*, Lanham: Rowman and Littlefield, 1999.

Weiss, Thomas and Jane Boulden (eds), *The UN and Terrorism: Before and After September 11th*, Bloomington, IN: Indiana University Press, 2004.

Wilkinson, Paul, (ed.), *Terrorism Versus Democracy. The Liberal State Response*, London: Frank Cass, 2000.

Woodhouse, Tom and Oliver Ramsbotham (eds), *Peacekeeping and Conflict Resolution*, London: Frank Cass, 2000.

Yost, David, *NATO Transformed. The Alliance's New Roles in International Security*, Washington DC: United States Institute of Peace Press, 1998.

Abstracts

UN Peace Operations in Light of the Events of 11 September 2001
by Thierry Tardy

United Nations (UN) peace operations have always integrated, and to a certain extent reflected, the evolutions of the international system, particularly in the post–cold war era. Insofar as they constitute a defining moment of international life, the events of 11 September 2001 may therefore have some impact on peace operations at a time when the whole field of peace operations is being reconsidered. This essay presents and analyzes the possible consequences of the events of 11 September on the way UN peace operations are created and conducted, and on the way states see the role of the UN in this field. It is argued that the events of 11 September have had no fundamental consequences on the UN role in peace operations. The 'fight against terrorism' might imply some modifications in the mandates and practices of peace operations, in the two fields of conflict prevention and peacebuilding in particular, but the overall approach should not be dramatically altered.

US Policy Toward Peace Operations *by Eric P. Schwartz*

When it assumed office, the Bush Administration expressed profound scepticism about the value of US military deployments in support of peace operations. Moreover, its commitment to the non-military dimensions of peacebuilding was uncertain. After the events of 11 September, the Administration more clearly recognized that US support for peace stabilization and development could have implications for international stability and US national security interests. Nonetheless, as of spring 2002, the Administration continued to resist a significant role for US troops in peacekeeping operations and was not aggressive in developing US capacity to support the non-military dimensions of peace stabilization. However, it was unclear whether the Administration's approach was sustainable over time, given the requirements for success in Afghanistan, and in other states that have experienced political turmoil.

NATO's Shifting Priorities: From Peace Support Operations to Counter-Terrorism *by Dick A. Leurdijk*

The essay identifies the relevance of international terrorism as a 'new threat' for the North Atlantic Treaty Organization (NATO). The historic decision to invoke Article 5 of the NATO Treaty underlined its original character as a collective defence organization – after a decade in which NATO, following a 'dual-track' policy, presented itself mainly as an instrument of collective security, largely involved in peace operations. After the 'wake-up call' of 11 September, NATO recognized the need for an 'adaptation' to the new security environment, aimed at formulating a new conceptual and operational 'job description' in its capacity as a collective defence organization with a new face.

The European Union, Peace Operations and Terrorism *by Jolyon Howorth*

The terrorist attacks of 11 September 2001 obliged the European Union (EU) to re-assess its security and defence policy requirements and its approach to peace operations in light of the new context. Yet, despite a declaratory policy which has insisted that the fight against terrorism is 'a priority objective', little has yet been done to instrumentalize that objective. This essay analyzes the EU's performance in terms of threat assessment, of military force planning, and of its institutional capacity to deliver civil and military coordination under the European Security and Defence Policy (ESDP). It also assesses the likely direction of EU–US and EU–NATO relations in coming years, concluding that the EU is at a turning point. Over the next few years, ESDP will either move resolutely towards autonomy, or re-insert itself fully into NATO.

Peace Operations and Governance: Lessons Learned and Perspectives *by Winrich Kühne*

After 11 September 2001, there is wide agreement that taking better care of war-torn, failed states is an important element of successfully fighting terrorism and improving global governance. This essay addresses one of the key instruments the international community has developed over the last decades to handle violent conflict: peace operations, including peace-building. It elaborates on the evolution of peace operations from first to fourth generation, as well as important lessons learned, such as the need for a functioning military-police-civilian cooperation, integrated organization and command, establishing basic public security and rule of law, as well as fighting organized crime.

UNMIBH: Combating Organized Crime and Terrorism Through Law Enforcement Capacity Building *by Jacques Paul Klein*

The terrorist attacks of 11 September 2001 exerted immediate and wide-ranging impact in the Balkans. In Bosnia and Herzegovina, the events served as a catalyst to further the United Nations mandate of police reform and restructuring. In the weeks that followed, domestic, regional and international security arrangements quickly fell into place. Existing state institutions were strengthened, as was evident in the progress made towards fortifying borders not covered by the BiH State Border Service (SBS); a more systematic analysis of people entering and exiting the country was instituted; and a State Information and Protection Agency (SIPA) was established. UNMIBH also facilitated improved inter-entity and regional information sharing; training and equipping of anti-terrorist units; and better cooperation with INTERPOL and regional law enforcement agencies.

NGOs and Peace Operations in the post-11 September Context *by Nicholas Stockton*

The events of 11 September 2001 have triggered a vigorous and multi-dimensional re-engagement of the United States in international affairs which will provoke reaction and excite demands for retribution and revenge. For NGOs involved in peace operations, the litmus-test will be their ability to defend their independence and impartiality at a time when powerful forces of instrumentalization will be at work. In theatres where the 'war against terrorism' is carried forward, NGOs will be expected to contribute to the political utility of the operation through providing assistance to particular ethnic or political constituencies. The conventional humanitarian principles of neutrality and impartiality will be placed under increased pressure. In 'terrorist-free' contexts, major power engagement is likely to weaken still further, leaving NGOs to shoulder a greater burden of political and humanitarian tasks, with a smaller proportion of official aid funds available.

Opposing Insurgents, during and beyond Peace Operations
by John Mackinlay

Through the 1990s, international leaders, military forces and humanitarian agencies were beset with the baggage of the cold war for too long. However, as military doctrine writers began to sharpen their pens to formalize the institutional lessons of the Kosovo campaign, Usama Bin Laden's attacks on the United States pushed them across the page to a new chapter of events which superseded containment as an acceptable response. The events of 11 September compelled us to notice and react to developments which had been gradually altering our security for some time. Global change had expanded the definition of insurgency, enabling the more commercially adroit and internationally structured insurgent organizations to challenge powerful states with relative impunity. The 2001/2 operations in Afghanistan heralded a new relationship between the leading civil agencies in the conflict area and the western governments, a relationship that was increasingly underwritten and controlled by donor-government funding.

Index

ABC News, 45
Afghanistan, 4, 7, 19–21, 32, 39, 45–9, 52–3, 70, 84–5, 89, 101–2, 113–14, 118–22, 142–3, 145–8, 152–4, 156, 160, 167–72, 184
Albright, Madeleine, 43
Al Qaeda, 22, 30, 39, 61, 65–6, 75, 80, 83–6, 101, 118–20, 122, 148, 152, 161, 164, 169–72, 185, 188
Amnesty International, 151–2
An Agenda for Peace, 14, 103
Anderson, Mary, 142
Annan, Kofi, 15, 23, 102, 104, 108, 117, 121
Armitage, Richard, 69
Army's Peacekeeping Institute, 53
Article 5 (Washington Treaty), 4, 18, 58–61, 64–5, 67, 70, 183

Best Practices Unit (DPKO), 105
Biden, Joseph, 49
Bin Laden, Usama, 22, 101, 118, 160, 162, 170–1
Blair, Tony, 86, 145
Bosnia and Herzegovina, 7–8, 14–15, 30, 39, 44–5, 49–50, 63, 70, 87, 102, 104, 106, 109–10, 113–14, 117, 126–37, 185
Brahimi, Lakhdar, 19–20, 23, 105, 121
Brahimi Report, 2, 15–16, 20–4, 26, 106–8, 110, 142, 146, 168–9
Burns, Nicholas, 75

Bush, Georges, 18, 21, 31, 44–9, 61, 66, 68, 84, 101–2, 118, 144, 148–9
Bush Administration, 18, 43–4, 46, 47–53, 64, 67, 70, 75, 121–3, 182

CARE, 151
Chapter VII (UN Charter), 20, 104, 109, 118, 181
China, 17, 84–5
Clinton Administration, 41, 43–4, 46, 50
Common Foreign and Security Policy (CFSP), 81–2, 84, 91–2
Commonwealth of Independent States (CIS), 2
Conflict Prevention, 2, 7, 14–15, 26–7, 29–32, 72, 82, 91, 186
Counter-Terrorism Committee, 4, 18–19, 22, 24, 29
Cox, Robert, 188

Dayton (Peace Agreement), 14–15, 167
Democratic Republic of Congo, 26, 39, 41, 87, 113, 142–3, 148, 154–6, 183
DFID, 142, 146
Disarmament, Demobilization and Reintegration (DDR), 103, 115–16
DPA, 29, 30
DPKO, 16, 29, 104, 108, 116, 169

East Timor, 2, 21, 26, 41–2, 50–1, 54, 102, 105–6, 112–14, 117–19, 184

Eritrea, 26, 105
Ethiopia, 26, 105
EU Police Mission, 87
European Rapid Reaction Force, 87–9, 181
European Security and Defense Policy (ESDP), 7, 81–4, 86–7, 90–3, 180–1
European Union, 1, 4–5, 7–8, 14, 33, 72, 76, 80–93, 112, 115, 179, 181, 183, 185–6
Executive Committee on Peace and Security (ECPS), 24

France, 91–2
Fukuyama, Francis, 187

General Framework Agreement for Peace in Bosnia and Herzegovina (GFAP), 126
Georgia, 2
Germany, 91, 119
Gordon, Philip, 64
Greenpeace, 151–2
Greenstock, Jeremy, 18
Guantanamo Bay, 17
Guéhenno, Jean-Marie, 28

Haiti, 44, 184
Headline Goal, 88–9
Howorth, Jolyon, 179–81, 186
Human Rights Watch, 152
Hussein, Saddam, 70, 122–3
Hutton, Will, 86
Hyde Henri, 49

ICC, 51, 75, 87
ICRC, 151
IFOR, 104
IFRC, 151
India, 23, 85
Information and Strategic Analysis Secretariat (ISAS), 105
Integrated Mission Task Force (IMTF), 24

Inter-American Development Bank, 47
INTERFET, 21, 50
IPTF, 126–7
Iran, 66
Iraq, 66, 70, 76, 87, 123, 148
ISAF, 21–2, 48–9, 67, 76, 85, 118–19, 121, 123, 145, 170, 181–3, 185

Justice and Home Affairs (EU), 4, 83, 87

Karzai, Hamid, 48, 120–1
KFOR, 71, 73–5, 105–7, 110
Klein, Jacques, 183, 185
Kosovo, 7, 17, 21, 26, 39, 44, 49, 63, 70, 72, 74, 80, 102, 105–6, 112–14, 117–19, 145, 160, 165, 168–70
Kühne, Winrich, 180, 182

Lantos, Tom, 49
Lessons Learned Unit (DPKO), 108, 116
Leurdijk, Dick, 180, 183–5

Macedonia, 63, 70, 72, 76, 87, 90
Macfarlane, Neil, 150–1, 153
Mackinlay, John, 183–5
Macrae, Joanna and Nicholas Leader, 142, 149–50
McDougal, Myres, and Harold Lasswell, 187
Médecins sans Frontières, 150–2
MONUC, 148, 188

Nation-building (State-building), xi–xii, 19, 21, 39, 44–7, 84–5, 90, 103, 121–2, 166, 181, 183
NATO, 1, 4, 7, 8, 14, 15, 21, 28, 33, 50, 58–76, 81, 83, 86–7, 89–90, 93, 108, 115, 127, 145, 160–1, 180, 183–6
NATO Response Force, 87, 89
Negroponte, John, 24, 27
NGOs, xi, 6, 8, 91, 110–12, 139–56, 174, 183–8
North Korea, 66

OECD, 141, 146
Operation Allied Force, 17, 21, 74
OSCE, 1, 4, 14, 15, 72, 112
OXFAM, 150–1

Pakistan, 23, 85, 143, 148, 170
'Pax Americana', 143, 150, 181
Peacebuilding, 7, 14–15, 21, 26–7,
    29–30, 32, 39, 46, 102–4, 107, 109,
    111–12, 114–15, 117, 119–20, 122,
    139, 142–3, 145, 153, 155, 162, 166,
    186, 188
Peace Support Operations, 2, 58, 62,
    70–1, 73, 75–6, 160
Peace Through Law Education Fund
    Report, 27, 31, 54
Petersberg Tasks, 2, 80–2, 88–90
Policy Working Group on the UN and
    Terrorism, 27, 29, 31
Political and Security Committee
    (PSC), 92
Powell, Colin, 46, 61, 69
Presidential Decision Directive 25
    (PDD 25), 43–4
Presidential Decision Directive 71
    (PDD 71), 46, 53

Resolution 1368 (Security Council),
    17, 22, 59, 84
Resolution 1373 (Security Council),
    17–18, 22, 143
Rice, Condoleeza, 121–2
Robertson, Georges, 61, 66–8, 70,
    72–3, 75
Rogers, Paul, 188
Rumsfeld, Donald, 45, 48–50, 67,
    121–2
Rushdie, Salman, 149
Russia, 17, 69, 75, 84–5, 87
Rwanda, 15, 43, 104, 110, 118

Save the Children, 150–1
Save the Children Fund, 140
Schwartz, Eric, 181–2

SFOR, 70–1, 73–5, 104, 110, 112, 127
Sierra Leone, 26, 39, 41, 102, 110,
    112–13, 116, 184
Solana, Javier, 91
Somalia, 14, 30, 41, 43, 103–4, 108–9,
    115, 118–19, 141–3, 154, 167, 172
Special Committee on Peacekeeping
    Operations, 24, 105
Srebrenica, 15, 110, 118
Stimson Centre, 39, 52
Stockton, Nicholas, 181, 183–6, 188
Sudan, 101, 142–3, 153, 159, 172

Taliban, xi, 20–2, 47, 61, 66–7, 84,
    101–2, 119, 143, 153, 169–70, 185
Tardy, Thierry, xii, 180, 186, 189
Turkey, 48, 67, 76

UNAMA, 22, 118–19, 123, 181–2, 185
UNAMSIL, 15, 112
UNDP, 111
UNFICYP, 102–3
UN General Assembly, 17–18, 26, 32,
    52, 169
UNHCR, 67, 111–12
United Kingdom, 91–2, 141–2, 145,
    149, 155, 162, 170
United States, xii, 2–6, 8, 17–19, 21,
    23–5, 30–1, 39–59, 64–6, 69–70,
    74–6, 84–7, 90, 92–3, 101, 113,
    119–23, 143–9, 155, 160, 169–70,
    172, 180–2, 184–6
UNMEE, 105
UNMIBH, 112, 125–8, 130–7, 185
UNMIK, 15, 105–7
UNMISET, 117
UNOSOM, 43, 104, 108
UNPROFOR, 104, 110
UN Secretary-General, 5, 15, 20, 24,
    26, 29, 46, 62, 102–4, 105, 148
UN Security Council, 5, 14, 17, 18,
    20–1, 26, 49, 51, 59, 62, 84, 105,
    109, 112, 117, 122, 126, 143, 145,
    169, 181, 183, 187

UNTAET, 15, 105–7, 112, 117, 119
USAID, 147

Welch, David, 46
Western European Union (WEU), 14, 89
Wijk, Rob de, 88

Wider Peacekeeping, 161
Wilkinson, Paul, 5
WMD, 66, 69
Wolfowitz, Paul, 66–7, 121–2
World Bank, 111, 187
World Vision, 151

Printed in the United States
by Baker & Taylor Publisher Services